New Political Religions, or
An Analysis of Modern Terrorism

Eric Voegelin Institute Series in Political Philosophy

Other Books in the Series

New Political Religions,
or
An Analysis of Modern Terrorism

BARRY COOPER

University of Missouri Press
Columbia and London

5   4   3   2   1   08   07   06   05   04

Library of Congress Cataloging-in-Publication Data

Cooper, Barry, 1943–
    New political religions, or, An analysis of modern terrorism /
Barry Cooper.
        p. cm. — (Eric Voegelin Institute series in political philosophy)
    Includes bibliographical references and index.
    ISBN 0-8262-1531-9 (alk. paper)
    1. Terrorism.   2. Terrorism—Religious aspects.   3. Islam
and terrorism.   4. Jihad.   5. Anti-Americanism.   I. Title:
New political religions.   II. Title: Analysis of modern terrorism.
III. Title.   IV. Series.
    HV6431.C656   2004
    303.6'25—dc22   2004001828

♾™ This paper meets the requirements of the American National
Standard for Permanence of Paper for Printed Library Materials,
Z39.48, 1984.

Designer: Kristie Lee
Typesetter: Phoenix Type, Inc.
Printer and binder: The Maple-Vail Book Manufacturing Group
Typeface: Minion

Publication of this book has been assisted by generous
contributions from Eugene Davidson and the Eric Voegelin
Institute.

To the memory of Yusuf K. Umar 1948–1991

They won't believe the world they haven't noticed is like that.
—Graham Greene, *Ways of Escape*

Purifying the world through holy war is addictive.
—Jessica Stern, *Terror in the Name of God*

Contents

ix

Preface

The origin of this study lies in an invitation I received to address the Philadelphia Society in the spring of 2001 on the spiritual dimension of contemporary terrorism. The two other speakers on that occasion were connected to the U.S. Navy: one taught strategy at the Naval War College, the other, a retired admiral, had recently been chief of intelligence for Pacific Command. Those two people had been following the development of modern terrorism as part of their professional duties for many years. In contrast I have spent most of my research life in the area of political philosophy. Notwithstanding the distinct perspectives that political philosophy, naval intelligence, and military strategy brought to the analysis of the phenomenon of contemporary terrorism, the three of us as well as our audience understood that our differences were also complementary.

Accordingly, this study is not primarily about the objectives of terrorists nor their personnel, techniques, strategies, or weapons of choice. Nor is the focus on the aftermath of the disintegration of the Soviet Union, international politics, the defeat of the Taliban, the war in Iraq and anti-terrorist activities elsewhere, the complexities of the Israeli-Palestinian conflict, globalization, the ecumenic resurgence of ethno-religious fundamentalism, the proliferation of the Internet or of small arms and anti-personnel mines. Finally, we are not directly interested in the "clash of civilizations" made famous by Sam Huntington.

The focus of this study is on the motives of terrorists chiefly as expressed in texts they have written to account for their activities. To that extent it makes no great claim to originality. Of necessity we will deal with the evolution or development of terrorist practice, but the focus is on the varieties of a spiritual disorder, what we describe more technically in the chapters that follow as a pneumopathology. Some of the information is well known, given the media saturation on this topic since

September 11, 2001. Some of it is known to specialists in the study of terrorism. Some of it is known perhaps only to political scientists. Whatever insights can be found here have probably come from bringing together what otherwise would be widely separated materials.

The *New York Times Magazine* of March 23, 2003, carried an article on the Islamist ideologue, Sayyid Qutb, whom we discuss in some detail in chapter 4 below. The author, Paul Berman, closed his account by expressing his "worries." Specifically, he said, "it would be nice to think that, in the war against terror, our side, too, speaks of deep philosophical ideas.... The Terrorists speak insanely of deep things. The antiterrorists had better speak sanely of equally deep things." It seems to me there is nothing deep or philosophical about Sayyid Qutb or any of the other terrorists who have committed their reflections to print. For the most part they express a dogmatic certainty that comes from being philosophical and religious ignoramuses. Moreover, as we argue in chapter 2, the terrorists are not clinically insane or, to be more cautious, do not seem to be disproportionately insane compared to the general population. Even if Berman thinks they are insane, he does not name their affliction.

The assumption we make in this study is rather that their disorder is spiritual and that there is accordingly a spiritual dimension to the conflict with terrorists. Of course there is a material dimension as well, as there always will be in politics, but it is peripheral. Whatever the genuine grievances terrorists exploit, they are secondary to their self-destructive, self-defeating spiritual perversity. The argument we make is analytic, which is to say allied in principle at least with reason; and reason is common to all humans, unlike doctrinal formulations and ideological fantasies.

I would like to thank Ellis Sandoz, who first invited me to consider the problem of terrorism. I must also thank the Social Science and Humanities Research Council of Canada and through them the hard-pressed taxpayers of my country for supporting this research. More immediately, Mirja van Herk has processed countless words; the Fraser Institute has provided me with a forum to develop my thoughts on terrorism and an appreciative audience; Peter von Sivers has ensured I did not make too many blunders in my analysis of Muslim thinkers and introduced me to the scholarship dealing with the Islamic dimension of a common human problem, which is raised in the appendix. Again I have tried the patience of my wife, Denise Guichon, and I am very mindful of her forbearance. I would also like to thank Julie Schorfheide for her accurate and helpful editing, and Bev Jarrett for her support in seeing the manuscript through the University of Missouri Press. Special mention must be made of Jane Hungerford and Art Rennison.

In dedicating this study to the memory of Yusuf Umar, I am also recalling a Palestinian exile to the New World, an inquiring mind, a political philosopher who felt a kinship to the exile of Leo Strauss a generation or so earlier, and to Strauss's reflections on Farabi. Yusuf Umar first told me of the many voices of Islam. He was a man with whom it was possible to converse about all things, even the darkest.

New Political Religions, or
An Analysis of Modern Terrorism

1 Context

In a report issued some sixteen weeks prior to the attacks on the World Trade Center and the Pentagon, Colin Powell, the U.S. secretary of state, noted there had been an 8 percent increase in international terrorist attacks during the previous year.[1] Of the 423 attacks recorded in the State Department inventory, 200 were directed against the United States or its citizens. Other summary accounts of international terrorism, including the Rand–St. Andrews Chronology of Terrorism, show similar trends. Only once since 1968, which is usually seen as the start of the age of modern terrorism, has the United States not led the list of countries whose citizens and property were most often attacked.[2]

Over the course of the twentieth century, the greatest period of terrorist group formation was during the 1970s and 1980s; most of these groups were European and left-wing revolutionaries. The first South American terrorist groups were formed during the 1950s, but since about 1970 their numbers have generally been in decline. Terrorist groups in North America have tended to be sporadic in their rate of formation and in their activities. The first Middle Eastern terrorist groups, excluding Irgun and Hagana actions prior to the creation of Israel, were founded in the 1960s and 1970s. Moreover, the causes espoused by terrorists have changed. The social revolutionaries, secular nationalists, and radical right of an earlier day have been largely replaced by terrorists promoting "religiously inspired agendas," or, to be more precise, "militant Islamic"

---

1. Quoted by Lacey, "Attacks Were Up Last Year."
2. In 1995, the PKK (Kurdistan Workers' Party) greatly expanded its terrorist activity in Turkey and Germany (see U.S. State Department, *Patterns of Global Terrorism, 1995*, 1). A vigorous response by the French, German, and Turkish governments had the effect of discouraging acts of international terrorism by the PKK. See Hoffman, *Inside Terrorism*, 79.

ones, that exist often without direct state support.[3] Indeed, one of the most shocking aspects of the attack of September 11 was that this "fury of killing" was "meant to please a deity."[4] This raises an obvious question: what sort of deity would, in the minds of the terrorists, be pleased by the attacks of September 11, 2001?

There is a genuine issue of interpretation here. It has become a commonplace among analysts of Al Qaeda and of other Middle Eastern terrorist groups to distinguish between what was identified above as "militant Islam" or "Islamism" and the religion practiced by Muslims. This distinction is based not on political correctness but on empirical evidence. It is a problem to which we must return below, in chapters 3 and 4. Most Muslims, of course, are neither Islamist fundamentalists nor terrorists; many terrorists, however, proclaim they are Muslims—indeed, many proclaim they are the only true Muslims. It is certainly legitimate for Muslims to object to the term *Islamic terrorists* when no one calls the IRA "Christian terrorists" or "Catholic terrorists." It is also unquestionably true that the complaints should be directed less at analysts or journalists who merely report the self-interpretation of others than at the terrorists themselves for their abuse of Islam.[5] So far as most Westerners were concerned, the killing on the morning of September 11 had nothing to do with God; the killers flew out of nowhere and acted in a manner that was utterly irrational, not to say unintelligible. This is why there were so many simplified attempts, in the fall of 2001, to answer a simple question: Why do they hate us?

During the twentieth century, only fourteen terrorist attacks killed more than one hundred people and none killed more than five hundred. Prior to September 11, 2001, about a thousand Americans had been killed by terrorists.[6] The sheer magnitude of the killing on that day, when in the course of an hour and a half over three times as many people were murdered, was itself extraordinary. Estimates of property and collateral economic damage are likewise enormous. Including market-based estimates of lowered profits and higher discounts for economic volatility,

3. See Pedahzur, Eubank, and Weinberg, "The War on Terrorism and the Decline of Terrorist Group Formation," 141–47.

4. Benjamin and Simon, *Age of Sacred Terror*, 384.

5. This does, of course, happen. See, for example, Murad, "Bin Laden's Violence." See also Lewis, *Crisis of Islam*, 137.

6. Hoffman, "Re-Thinking Terrorism in Light of a War on Terrorism."

one source has calculated a price on the order of $2 trillion.[7] However measured, the attacks were unparalleled, and reason enough to understand why the United States has taken steps to reconfigure the architecture of its national security.

It is easy to be overwhelmed by the sheer quantitative size indicated by such data and to limit one's understanding to the entirely intelligible and initial response by military force in Afghanistan and in other places. Moreover, if one does not begin from the experience of shock at the terrorist attacks of September 11, 2001, and anger at the killing of so many otherwise innocent individuals, then an initial and immediate understanding of the obvious meaning and significance of those events will have been lost. That is, the spectacular nature of the attacks and the outrage the spectacle was designed to evoke is the proper starting point for a more systematic enquiry into the genesis and meaning of those events. For most ordinary Americans and, indeed, for most ordinary human beings, the attacks of September 11 were a reminder of the difference between good and evil. Indeed, in the context of postmodern liberalism, they were a forceful reminder that there is such a difference. The events of that day were and are not completely open to interpretation and judgments were and are not completely relative or simply matters of opinion. When President Bush referred to the terrorists of September 11 he called them "evil-doers." This was not intended to be rhetorical overkill but an accurate description that can be translated directly into Arabic as *mufsidoon.*

At the same time, however, it is insufficient for political science to register only shock and anger. The indignation of a citizen and the demand for justice or retribution is intelligible enough: most people know who the bad guys are and why they are bad. It is as close to self-evident as a thing can be that the terrorists were and remain religious fanatics and murderers. That is where everyone, both citizens and political scientists, must begin.

There are other problems as well. Some aspects of September 11 were merely technical: simultaneous terrorist attacks, even using old-fashioned car bombs, are rare. The bombings of the American embassies in Nairobi and Dar-es-Salaam on August 7, 1998, the eighth anniversary

7. Navarro and Spencer, "September 11, 2001: Assessing the Costs of Terrorism." See also Rhoads, "Long-Term Economic Effects of Sept.11."

of the arrival of U.S. troops in Saudi Arabia, showed the same skill at synchronizing the attacks, as did the ten-car bomb attack on Bombay in March 1993. Likewise in October 1983, Hezbollah managed to kill 240 people at the U.S. Marine barracks in Beirut along with 60 French paratroopers in the same morning; in 1981 three Venezuelan passenger planes were hijacked, and in 1970 four airliners were taken over by the Popular Front for the Liberation of Palestine, two of which were later destroyed on the ground. The relatively small number of such spectacles raises the question: How did they do it?[8] This question suggests others: How were other such attacks averted in the past? How can they be averted in the future?[9] More than careful planning and coordination were needed to carry out such a spectacular operation: the hijackers were also willing to die, not by risking their lives but with absolute certainty they would not survive their mission. As Hoffman observed:

> This dimension of terrorist operations, however, arguably remains poorly understood. In no aspect of the September 11 attacks is this clearer than in the debate over whether all 19 of the hijackers knew they were on a suicide mission or whether only the 4 persons actually flying the aircraft into their targets did. It is a debate that underscores the poverty of our understanding of bin Laden, terrorism motivated by a religious imperative in particular, and the concept of martyrdom.[10]

One of the purposes of the present analysis is to provide some clarity on the nature of a suicide mission. That is, in addition to considering such relatively straightforward issues as who did what and how it was accomplished, we are also concerned with interpreting the phenomena of terrorist action as meaningful within the context of sources provided

---

8. See, for example, the early reports by Der Speigel, *Inside 9–11,* Hoge and Rose, *How Did This Happen? Terrorism and the New War,* or Corbin, *The Base: In Search of Al-Qaeda,* pt. 2.

9. In 1985 a plot by Sikh separatists to bring down three Air India planes succeeded in destroying only one, killing 329 people on board the plane and 2 baggage handlers in the Narita airport. The failure was evidently a result of bad planning by the terrorists. In 1982 a Palestinian plot to bomb two PanAm planes was foiled by diligent police work. Perhaps the most ambitious of the failed terrorist plots was Ramzi Ahmed Yousef's 1995 "Bojinka" plan to blow up a dozen U.S. airliners in transit across the Pacific: again good fortune played a part. See Benjamin and Simon, *Age of Sacred Terror,* 20–26.

10. Hoffman, "Rethinking Terrorism," 304.

by the terrorists themselves. One of the oldest insights of political science is that all political action is self-interpretive; terrorism is no exception.

There are, moreover, analogies, if not precedents, from within Western political history that provide some degree of guidance. There is, to be sure, an extensive and systematic treatment by specialists on, for instance, Japanese "new religions," on various kinds of liberation movements, and on Islamist sects or the "Christian Identity" movement. There is no shortage of information, although a certain amount of imaginative interpretation is needed to bring coherence to an otherwise complex and fragmentary narrative.

To cast this information into a theoretical context while not forgetting the essential atrocity of terrorism is more difficult. Some guidance through this emotional, intellectual, conceptual, and experiential thicket can be found in an exchange during the early 1950s between Hannah Arendt and Eric Voegelin regarding the appropriate way to study, to come to terms with, and indeed to resist, the novel political reality of ideologically inspired totalitarianism.[11] Notwithstanding their differences, which can easily be exaggerated, both these political scientists began from the direct experience of totalitarian domination and were fully aware that it presented the face of evil in its day.[12] Voegelin, for example, characterized Nazi and Bolshevik revolutions in terms of the "putrefaction of Western civilization" and the "earthwide expansion of Western foulness." Arendt likened the extermination camps to hell on earth. Neither, however, was content simply to record adverse judgment on two varieties of a murderous regime. The last edition of Arendt's book on totalitarianism had grown to over five hundred pages; and even then, after a thorough treatment of the problem, she had serious doubts concerning the wisdom of publishing her analysis because her work might contribute to the continued existence of a phenomenon she wished to destroy and remove from the face of the earth. One might argue as well that Voegelin's books of the late 1930s, his monumental

11. I have discussed this problem in *Eric Voegelin and the Foundations of Modern Political Science*, 130 ff.

12. The exchange was initially made in the pages of the *Review of Politics* on the occasion of a review essay by Voegelin of the 1951 edition of Arendt's *Origins of Totalitarianism*. It was followed by a response by Arendt and a further remark by Voegelin. See Voegelin, *Review of Politics*, 68–85. The exchange has been reprinted separately as well: see Voegelin, *Published Essays, 1953–1965*, 15 ff., and Arendt, *Essays in Understanding*, 401 ff.

History of Political Ideas, written during the 1940s, and, indeed, his classic *New Science of Politics* (1952), were aimed at understanding the origin and significance of the foulness and putrefaction he so obviously deplored.

In April 1938, for example, a month after the Nazi Reich had absorbed Austria, Voegelin published *The Political Religions.* He indicated that the purpose of the book was to analyze and comprehend the self-interpretation of the Nazi movement. In particular, he wished to understand the Nazi claim that the party (and thus its self-interpretation) was the "truth" of the German *Volk* and of the place in history of the reality symbolized as that *Volk.* At the same time, however, he sought to analyze and to draw the connection to the obvious conflict with commonsense reality posed by Nazi race doctrines, associated ideological symbols such as *Volk,* and their oppressive and murderous practices. In other words, in 1938 Voegelin was interested not simply in denouncing the Nazis as "merely a morally inferior, dumb, barbaric, contemptible matter" but in understanding them as "a force, and a very attractive force at that."[13] To put it bluntly, it was a question of comprehending the attractiveness of evil. Evil is no less attractive today. Perhaps more to the point, its attractiveness cannot fully be understood apart from its evilness.

Many conventional analyses of contemporary terrorist acts, as noted above, have described a "religious" dimension among the motivations of terrorist violence. During the 1970s and 1980s, terrorists operating in Northern Ireland used Protestant and Catholic Christianity as a screen behind which they pursued their own political agendas. More recently, however, larger numbers of terrorist groups "are using religion itself as the primary motivation behind their attacks."[14] The term *religion,* however, is used in many senses, even in political analyses, and opens up a very wide spatial and temporal field for terrorist activity.[15] For example, "ethno-religious" terrorists often direct their violence at "ethno-secular" leaders of the same "religious" group. President Anwar Sadat, for example, was murdered by an Egyptian Islamist and Prime Minister Yitzhak Rabin was murdered by an equivalent type of Israeli. The terrorist group

---

13. Voegelin, *Modernity without Restraint,* 24. See also Burleigh, "National Socialism as a Political Religion," 1–26.

14. Durham, "Trends in Modern Terrorism," 357.

15. See Arendt, *Between Past and Future,* 126 ff.

Hamas is as opposed to PLO leader Yasser Arafat as it is to Israel. On occasion divisions between terrorists have led to grotesque contrasts, as when Arafat, responding to Abu Nidal's attempt to assassinate him, said, "He's a real terrorist!" An appropriate comment on this farce was made by Christopher Harmon: "The new terrorists use the old terrorists' arguments. There may be an international interest in preserving Arafat's life, but others must make the moral argument for him; Arafat has no credibility to make it himself."[16] This kind of ambiguity is not confined to the Middle East but applies equally to the Balkans or to the Tamils of South Asia.[17] Sometimes analysts argue that "religious" terrorists are inherently more unpredictable than secular ones because, unlike those of the latter, the objectives of "religious" terrorists are often unintelligible to those who do not share their religious outlook.[18]

These and other similarly commonsensical observations express the obvious insight that religion is more than the practices carried on by institutional churches, temples, mosques, and so on, just as politics is more than the practices carried on by states. As Roger Scruton noted at the start of his study of terrorism, the etymology of religion indicates, somewhat ambiguously, the sense of binding together by binding back to an originary event or even a divine revelation.[19] In one way or another, all political orders, including those of the West, are integrated and justified by symbolic narratives that connect political practices in the pragmatic and even secular sense to a larger order of meaning. Thus it is impossible to understand contemporary terrorism without paying close attention to the religiosity or spirituality that terrorists experience as central to their own activities. This can hardly be said to be a new approach in modern political science, to say nothing of the approach adopted by the great philosophers of the past.

For example, about a year before Voegelin's book on political religions appeared, the Japanese ministry of education issued a document announcing the news that Japan was a divine nation. The Japanese, it said, were "intrinsically quite different from so-called citizens of Western nations" because the unbroken bloodlines of its people preserved the "pure" and "unclouded" Japanese spirit. A few years later, in the

16. Harmon, *Terrorism Today*, 190–91.
17. Juergensmeyer, "Worldwide Rise of Religious Nationalism," 4–7.
18. Hoffman, *Inside Terrorism*, 129.
19. Scruton, *The West and the Rest*, 1.

spring of 1942, several Japanese philosophers assembled in Kyoto to discuss how Japan might "overcome modern civilization," the great embodiment of which had been attacked a few months earlier at Pearl Harbor.[20]

A second example appeared the same year Voegelin's book was published. A Hungarian refugee, Aurel Kolnai, wrote *The War against the West*, an analysis not just of the Nazis but of the Japanese as well. This "war," he said, in 1938, was against the Western notion of citizenship, the state, and the political community. Underlying what Buruma and Margalit recently called "occidentalism" are aspects of Western culture that its opponents hate: it is urban, bourgeois, prosperous, and egalitarian.[21] Typically these attributes of Western civilization are denounced as decadent, arrogant, weak, and depraved. Such themes and topics were commonplace during the 1930s. They have reemerged in the early twenty-first century in a modified, but recognizably equivalent, symbolic language, though they are sustained by a quite different spiritual milieu.

Hatred of the city, symbolized as Babylon, is considered necessary to ensure the purity and virtue of rural peasant piety. In both the Bible (Gen. 11:4–6) and the Koran (16:23) God takes deep offense at the famous urban monument, the Tower. The contemporary icon of the mythic tower of Babylon is surely the skyline of Manhattan. The anonymity offered by cities and the liberty that such anonymity fosters is seen by the pure as a source of licentiousness and hypocrisy. The separation of public and private, of the word and the heart, is to such individuals the mark of corruption.

Cities are also venues of markets, which the pure detest as being expressions of greed, selfishness, and the cultural decay that comes when human beings, both natives and foreign or immigrant minorities, meet as equals to exchange goods and services. When the Japanese attacked the United States in 1941 they sought, not to take market share away from Americans and Europeans, but to destroy the competitive markets the foreigners created.[22] The Greater East Asia Co-Prosperity Sphere was never intended to be a market. The attack on September 11 was also a reprise of these common themes that reject the city and the market, the settled bourgeois, the petty clerk, or the plump banker, just the sort of

---

20. Holtom, *Modern Japan and Shinto Nationalism*, 10.
21. Kolnai, *The War against the West*; Buruma and Margalit, "Occidentalism," 4–7.
22. Iriye, *Power and Culture*.

person who might have held down a job at the World Trade Center. They are utterly unheroic specimens, the very antithesis of greatness, risk, peril, and sacrifice that so inspires the pure. Moreover, even to traditional Muslims (to say nothing of Islamist terrorists) the modern city is an unwelcome addition to the world. In the words of Abu-Rabi, "The ancient Muslim city, with the mosque, the *madrasah,* and the bazaar at its center, no longer performs a useful function in the eyes of modern capitalism. Far from being sacred and stable, space is subject to continuous change."[23] After Mohammed Atta left Egypt to study urban planning in Germany, it is significant that he wrote a thesis on restoration of Aleppo, an ancient city where the minarets dominated the skyline.

In addition, cities in the West have been the places where laws are drawn up. Courts and jurists, not gods or God, are the sources of modern Western laws. The notion of "man-made law" is not a term of abuse in the contemporary West, in part because of the lessons learned by Westerners following the European religious wars that attended and followed the Reformation of the sixteenth century. The end of Christendom with the settlements at Augsburg (1555) and Westphalia (1698) led to what Westerners now know as freedom of conscience. Moreover, such a liberty requires, in principle, both a secular and a territorially limited government, legitimated not by obedience to God or God's law but by the consent of the governed. Moreover, Westerners have learned from experience that laws made by the spiritually pure in the name of God invariably turn out to be the univocal, undebated decrees of human beings, which Westerners have come to understand to be an attribute of tyranny. Worse, the human beings who rule in the name of God invariably if not inevitably turn out to be males, holy men, with an agenda of oppression, including the oppression of women as women. Among the issues we must consider are the grounds upon which contemporary terrorists justify their attacks on the modern West and, reciprocally, whether the analysis made here of those grounds is merely the application of Western prejudice and unsubstantiated opinion. That is, we aim to provide an analysis that is more than the rationalization of the nevertheless intelligible emotions of an outraged citizen.

We may begin in a summary way by recalling the ambivalence, the division, or the tension in Western political science between the city and its citizens and the political scientist or the philosopher, a tension

---

23. Abu-Rabi, *Intellectual Origins of Islamic Resurgence,* 49.

that finds expression in a number of different ways. It can be found most famously in the opening scene of Plato's *Republic*—indeed in its opening word, *katebēn*. "I went down," said Socrates, to the port of Athens, Piraeus, the center of its prosperous trade, the market basis of its power, and the symbol of its corruption by that same wealth and power. Moreover, Socrates went down "yesterday," and much as he wished to return to the upper city, the old city, the city of yesterday, he was constrained to stay below, at least for a time. There, with his friends, he used his talents to persuade them to follow him upward and forward to the polis of the Idea, built in their souls and built of speech, after a pattern in heaven.

The insights of Socrates did not exempt him as a citizen from suffering the consequences of the foolish policies of the politicians whose measure he so unfailingly took. As with subsequent expressions of the limits to politics, such as in the Stoic distinction between law and justice or between the two cities of Augustine or the two swords of Pope Gelasius, the language of ambivalence heightens rather than abolishes the distance between the aspiration of the philosopher toward justice or beauty and the pragmatic condition of citizens who must also suffer their absence.

Moreover, one finds in the Bible an equivalent expression of this ambivalence. The Ten Commandments, for instance, were no more God's legislation for the Israelites than Plato's *Republic* was some sort of political "utopia" awaiting establishment by some new and almost divine nomothete. A central biblical distinction (Exodus 20–23) is between the words *(debharim)* of God and God's decisions or ordinances *(mishpatim)*. There is, accordingly, a tension between the two, corresponding approximately to the Ciceronian distinction between the law and justice. Thus, for example, the word of God says (Exod. 20:15) "Thou shalt not steal," but the ordinance of God indicates a legal rule (Exod. 22:1): "if a man steal an ox or a sheep, and kill it, or sell it, he shall pay five oxen for an ox, and four sheep for a sheep," which indicates clearly that the word of Exodus 20:15 has been disobeyed. That is, the ordinances are an attempt by human beings to weave the word of God into a concrete social context. Thus, more than the literal obedience to the word of God is required of the Israelites if they are to live as people under a theopolitical covenant.

There are many examples in Western political speculation to document the transition from the tension between the city and the word of

God into a dogmatic literalism that collapses the distinction between law and justice, the word and the ordinance, the heavenly and the earthly city, and so on. As we shall see, there are close analogues in the transition from puritanical and dogmatic Islam to Islamist terrorism.

In this chapter, however, we will indicate only the Western endpoint: the ideological obliteration of these well-understood distinctions under conditions of totalitarian domination enforced by terror. Specifically, Arendt's discussion of the "novel form of government" that combined ideology and terror provides the most complete and accessible account of the external aspects of the phenomenon.[24] Totalitarian domination is not tyranny—a lawless, arbitrary government where power is both concentrated and exercised in the interests of a single individual.

To begin with, and notwithstanding the notorious tendency of totalitarian regimes to disregard their own laws, totalitarians claim to be executing strictly, directly, and unequivocally the laws of History, of Nature, or of God. In nontotalitarian contexts, of course, History, Nature, and God (and especially the last two) have been invoked as the sources or the ground from which positive laws, decrees, and ordinances have sprung. Likewise, totalitarian rule claims to be immediately obedient to those same laws, the defiance of which is understood to be the utmost in arbitrariness. Nor is rule exercised in anyone's interest: on the contrary, obedience to these suprahuman laws is precisely what enables totalitarians to sacrifice everyone's interest in order to execute and enforce the "higher" law directly.

Laws in the sense of legislation or positive law have as their focus the variegated behavior of human beings. Accordingly, they are particular, pragmatic, and historically circumstantial. Standing apart from positive law or "above" it, the tradition of "divine" or "natural" law expresses a general source of authority for right and wrong that is applied in each case, but that no one case embodies. Totalitarian "lawfulness," in contrast, attempts to translate directly the authority of right and wrong into specific cases but at the same time to retain its generality. The direct execution of the laws of History, Nature, or God does not apply to particular individuals or even to particular classes, races, or religions, but to humanity as a whole.

Arendt has summarized this new understanding of law in the following words: "the term 'law' has changed its meaning: from expressing

24. Arendt, *Origins of Totalitarianism*, chap. 13.

the framework of stability within which human actions and motions can take place, it became the expression of the motion itself." The most peculiar consequence that follows from this novel understanding of law is that the movement that the new law expresses is endless. "If," Arendt wrote,

> it is the law of nature to eliminate everything that is harmful and unfit to live, it would mean the end of nature itself if new categories of the harmful and unfit-to-live could not be found; if it is the law of history that in a class struggle certain classes "wither away," it would mean the end of human history itself if rudimentary new classes did not form, so that they in turn could "wither away" under the hands of totalitarian rulers. In other words, the law of killing by which totalitarian movements seize and exercise power would remain a law of the movement even if they ever succeeded in making all of humanity subject to their rule.[25]

In the same way, the executors of the law of God are engaged in an endless search for the enemies of God who then may justly, piously, and directly be put to the sword. As we shall see in detail below, the Islamist or "salafist" understanding of Islamic law, the Sharia, is that it is to be enforced directly, as the law of God, on all humanity. Because in fact this cannot be done, they too are on an endless treadmill of violence and war.

Terror, especially, is a means not to fight opposition but to create it, in order that it may then be righteously extinguished, thereby enabling totalitarians further to actualize the "higher" law. Terror marks out the enemies of humanity whether they are consciously opposed to the totalitarian movement or not. That is, guilt and innocence in the ordinary sense have been eclipsed by the execution of judgments sanctioned by a "higher" source—Nature, History, God.

Finally, there must be an account, a justification, for all the killing, a narrative that creates "objective" enemies whose existence and subsequent extinction keeps the murderous apparatus in motion. This account and justification is called by Arendt "ideology," and she gives this much-overused term a clear but also somewhat idiosyncratic meaning.

In her argument, ideologies are "isms" that "to the satisfaction of their adherents can explain everything and every occurrence by deduc-

25. Ibid., 464.

ing it from a single premise."[26] The apparent claims of ideology, that an "idea" of something can be the subject matter of a logos, a rational or scientific account, were ridiculed by no less a personality than Napoleon shortly after Destutt de Tracy invented the term. An example will illustrate Napoleon's crude and Arendt's philosophical point: biology is not an account of the "idea" of life but of the reality; but there is no reality to which the "idea" contained in the term *ideology* refers. Since a rational or scientific account is an account of something real—such as life—but since this is the one thing absent from ideology, the very real discourse expressed in ideology does not refer to anything real. In Arendt's language, "The 'ideas' of isms—race in racism, God in deism, never form the subject matter of the ideologies and the suffix -*logy* never indicates simply a body of 'scientific' statements." Thus she proposed that the term be understood "quite literally," as "the logic of an idea" that somehow, by an act of imagination, gets applied to the process of history.

Ideologies provide logical explanations for the entire historical process because history is what is calculated, mapped, measured, and accounted for by the "idea," which in turn serves as a premise for the unfolding of the logic. Only one idea is needed to serve as a premise. Moreover, one idea proves to be sufficient to explain everything without reference to any other experience or reality. More to the point, practically any "idea," no matter how peculiar when examined commonsensically, can serve as a premise. Three aspects of ideology in particular lend themselves to totalitarian politics.

First, the claim to provide a total explanation is invariably focused on coming to be and passing away, on explaining all that happens historically: past, present, and future. Second, the claim to explain all history is independent of all concrete historical experience—indeed it is independent of all experience from which anything new might be learned. Ideology thus aims to explain the hidden meaning of events, a meaning that never is available to commonsense. On the contrary, access to this hidden meaning depends on what Arendt called a "sixth sense" and what we referred to above as an act of the imagination. Typically this "sixth sense" is awakened by focused education, or, to be more precise, by focused indoctrination. Accordingly, to the ideologist things can *never* be what they seem. Finally, because in reality ideologies cannot change the experiences of commonsense, ideologues are driven to ignore com-

26. Ibid., 468.

monsense, to abstract from it on the grounds of the "idea," which then serves as an axiomatic premise from which conclusions can be deduced. Neither the conclusions nor the idea that serves as a premise need have any relationship to commonsense reality nor even refer to it; hence the importance of the imagination.

One example Arendt gives is the statement made by Stalin that the Kulaks were a "dying class." If one accepted that there could be such an imaginary thing as a "dying class," the logical conclusion was that its members were condemned to death. The announcement that the Kulaks were a dying class meant, in clear, simple, and commonsense terms, that the Bolsheviks were about to murder every Kulak they could lay their hands on. When all were dead, there would be no "class" of Kulaks, which in turn would verify the ideological premise, namely, that the Kulaks *were* a dying class.

In the chapters that follow, we shall see the elements that came together in the totalitarian regimes of the twentieth century reconstituted in a recognizably similar ideological context that surrounds contemporary terrorism. Moreover, it seems clear that contemporary religious terrorists have followed a pattern remarkably close to that initially made by several spiritual movements of the late medieval and Christian West.[27] The structural similarities between movements that otherwise have nothing in common suggest that contemporary terrorism is but one kind of modern, ideological, and revolutionary sectarianism. The various components of religious terrorism do not, however, fit together as parts of a systematic doctrine transmitted by the literary tradition of a school. Rather, they are associated as expressions of a specific kind of spiritual experience that is in its most significant aspect independent of the religious traditions and symbols by which it is expressed. To put the matter plainly: contemporary Islamists have more in common with members of the Kach Party in Israel or the Christian Identity movement in Idaho than they do with the broad traditions of Islam.

Even so, religious terrorism has a preferential appeal to some kinds of personalities or members of specific social strata more than to others.

27. We do not put the term *religion* or *religious* in quotation marks in order to indicate the existence of an anomaly—because the notion of using terrorism for genuinely religious purposes seems on the surface to be self-contradictory. Rather, we will analyze the anomaly of religious terrorism, terrorism undertaken for ostensibly religious purposes. In this respect the term is akin to the concept *political religion.*

To understand why, we must touch on some conventional aspects of international politics.

There is a near-consensus that the great political confrontations of the twentieth century involved democratic regimes against totalitarian ones.[28] One need simply recall the obvious: the general war of 1939–1945 was followed by a generation-long cold war. Moreover, so far as the United States was concerned, both began with "sneak attacks." The 1941 attack by Japan on Pearl Harbor was recapitulated with the 1950 invasion of South Korea by North Korea. Moreover, Pearl Harbor was followed by one of the largest general mobilizations in history just as the North Korean invasion was followed by a large (257 percent) increase in the defense budget and a high level of military preparedness that lasted until the end of the Cold War. The external similarities to September 11, 2001, are obvious and have been noted often enough.[29] Both the conflicts with the "axis" of revolutionary national socialism and fascism as well as the later struggle with revolutionary international socialism and bolshevism were a combination of a contest of "ideas" or "values" and traditional struggles of geopolitics involving national interests and political and military "balances." The reason metaphors of balance made sense was because the twentieth-century wars and conflicts looked very much like interstate conflicts, the origins of which can be traced to the Treaties of Westphalia.

It seems clear that the conflicts of the early twenty-first century are not exhausted by lining up Western democracies on one side and states that are opposed to democracy on the other. Nor is it simply a matter of traditional conflicts of interest between, for example, petroleum-producing and petroleum-consuming states. An addition to these traditional sources of conflict, nongovernmental organizations (NGOs) are now in a position to undertake very destructive acts "unbridled by the interests, form, and structure of a state. . . . The use of terrorism implies an attempt to de-legitimize the concept of sovereignty, and even the structure of the state system itself."[30] This is new.

In response to this novel strategic situation, many observers have

28. See, for example, the highly conventional account: Institute for National Strategic Studies, "Globalization Study."

29. On the similarity with Pearl Harbor, see Clymer, "A Day of Terror in the Capital"; von Drehle, "World War, Cold War Won." On the Korean War, see Kagan, "The Korean Parallel"; Bacevich, "What It Takes."

30. Cronin, "Rethinking Sovereignty," 119.

argued that the defining issue of the early twenty-first century is whether generally prosperous democracies can control, or even manage, the generally poor, dangerously chaotic, and unquestionably troubled regions beyond their borders. Moreover, as Lindblom observed a generation ago, and as numerous empirical studies have since confirmed, "not all market-oriented systems are democratic, but every democratic system is also a market-oriented system."[31] As a result, those parts of the world that are neither democratic nor market-oriented are not, in the short or medium term, being made peaceful by the growth of global markets or, more simply still, by globalization. The bimodal structure of international affairs that lasted for most of the twentieth century seems, therefore, to have been perpetuated into the twenty-first. There are, however, some significant social and political changes that have taken place in the last generation or so.

In 1991, Thomas Homer-Dixon argued that war and civil violence are likely in the future to result from conflict over scarcities of environmental resources such as water, arable land, forests and fish, not commodity scarcities.[32] The social indices for his prognostication are also well known. Global population over the next half-century has been projected to grow from about five and a half billion to around nine billion, and most of that growth will be in nondemocratic countries that have a low probability of future prosperity. Most do not have "information-age" economies; many are agrarian and are characterized by dysfunctional governments and poorly educated workforces. These places may not be able to provide minimal government services—defense of the realm and the administration of justice, to use Western medieval categories; they are almost certain not to be friendly to democracy or to the West. Internally, these stressed regimes can range from the frankly totalitarian to loose warlord alliances. Many are often referred to as "failed states," and others have avoided or postponed state failure by pursuing a deliberate policy of exporting troublemakers, including terrorists, by turning them into twenty-first century remittance men. In the nineteenth century many younger sons were sent abroad from Britain to the "settlement colonies" and to America; this practice, said James Mill,

31. Lindblom, *Politics and Markets*, 116. As an example indicating the association of markets, prosperity, and liberty, see Gwartney and Lawson, *Economic Freedom of the World*.

32. Homer-Dixon, "On the Threshold," 76–116.

constituted "a vast system of outdoor relief for the upper classes." In the same way, many of the Saudi upper classes have expelled their own younger sons and maintained them financially so long as they remained abroad. Obviously, not all became terrorists; just as obviously, some of them did, and others drifted to the periphery of terrorist organizations.

Speaking of an especially unsettled region, Fareed Zaharia noted that "almost all of the Arab world is governed by political elites that dare not liberalize because to do so would unsettle their own power. To them, globalization is not an opportunity but a threat."[33] The leaders and governments of such countries are not eagerly awaiting the beneficial effects of a global market. Indeed, with or without globalization the existing situation seems pregnant with a future of chaotic turbulence and trouble in many places, not ecumenic tranquillity. Fouad Ajami drew a more sensitive but equally unappetizing picture:

> In the simplified interpretation we have of that civilization, the young had taken to theocratic politics; they had broken with the secular politics of their elders. They had done that, but there was more at stake in that great cultural and political drama. Home and memory, the ways of an inheritance, the confidence in unexamined political and social truths, had been lost. . . . A great unsettling of things had been unleashed on Arab lands, and they had not been ready for it. What Arabs had said about themselves, the history they had written, and the truths they had transmitted to their progeny had led down a blind alley.[34]

Often novelists are better at capturing the kinds of lives that people lead in such countries than are prosaic economic statistics and the narratives of political observers. For example, even though V. S. Naipaul was writing of India, usually seen as a triumph of political development, he subtitled his famous book *A Wounded Civilization*. This is what he said of "modernizing" Indians: "They saw themselves at the beginning of things: unaccommodated men making a claim on their land for the first time, and out of chaos evolving their own philosophy of community and self-help. For them the past was dead; they had left it behind in the villages."[35] The past was dead. For recently urbanized peasants,

---

33. Zaharia, "The Return of History," 311.
34. Ajami, *Dream Palace of the Arabs*, 7.
35. Naipaul, *India*, 143.

the entire world had become new, but unlike the "new world" encountered by the pioneers of the Americas, it was unaccommodating, unleav-
ened by hope and the promise of opportunity. Possibly the least pleas-
ant aspect of this newness is the unstable poverty of urban life, a poverty
spiked with resentment, and much different than the poverty of the
villages. In the villages, poverty was a traditional dispensation, but tradition has died as well.

Imagine life in a pseudo-modern city for one of these new men or
women. You are at the beginning of things; you have no tradition to
guide you into the future. Basic services such as electricity and running
water are scarce, are interrupted, or are simply not available. There is
clear evidence of what Homer-Dixon called human-induced environmental pressure. In plain language, the air stinks and the drinking water
makes you sick. The order, to say nothing of the comfort, of Western
urban life is unknown to immediate experience, but it may be available
as a kind of utopian TV-mediated image. Under such circumstances,
material discomfort can easily be given a historical, even a spiritual
significance. As Ranstorp observed, "Economic change and disruption"
combined with "political repression, economic inequality, and social upheaval common among desperate religious extremist movements, have
all led to an increased sense of fragility, instability, and unpredictability
for the present and the future."[36] A semi-Western or semi-modern new
culture looks like an assault upon a tattered tradition. "In these depressing circumstances," said Lieven,

> adherence to a radical Islamist [or other religious] network provides
> a sense of cultural security, a new community, and some degree of
> social support—modest, but still better than anything the state can
> provide. Poverty is recast as religious simplicity and austerity. Per-
> haps, even more important, belief provides a measure of pride: a rea-
> son to keep a stiff back amid continual humiliations and temptations.
> In the blaring, stinking, violent world of the modern "Third World"
> Muslim city, the architecture and aesthetic mood of the mosque is
> the only oasis, not only of beauty but of an ordered and coherent
> culture and guide to living. Of course this is true ten times over for a
> young male inhabitant of an Afghan, Chechen, or Palestinian refugee
> camp.[37]

36. Ranstorp, "Terrorism in the Name of Religion," 50.
37. Lieven, "The Cold War Is Finally Over," 303–4.

Indeed, as a purely pragmatic contrast, the difference between, for example, the hot, filthy, ugly, and chaotic streets of Cairo or Damascus and the cool, clean, ordered, and beautiful mosque well expresses the tension of ordinary, daily existence for many of the inhabitants of those ancient cities.

The social and political structures of all societies are tightly linked. According to Zaharia, "Radical Islam has risen on the backs of failed states that have not improved the lots of their people. It festers in societies where contact with the West has produced more chaos than growth and more uncertainty than wealth. It is, in a sense, the result of failed and incomplete modernization." But modernization is not a kind of inevitable historical fate. Modern Western liberties, to say nothing of consumer prosperity, are not likely to be welcomed by those who are sheltered by religious prohibitions. As Jonathan Sacks observed, "The emphasis on consumption is seen as trivializing to those with ancient spiritual heritages, and deeply exclusionary to those who are the losers in the race to riches." Indeed, for those yet sensitive to ancient spiritual heritages, Western liberties and prosperity are apt to look like aggressive temptations, for which a typical human response is either to give in to them or to punish those who offer them. As Scruton said,

> In the days when East was East and West was West, it was possible for Muslims to devote their lives to pious observances and to ignore the evil that prevailed in the *dar al-Harb*. But when that evil spreads around the globe, cheerfully offering freedoms and permissions in place of the austere requirements of a religious code, so that the *dar al-Islam* is invaded by it, old antagonisms are awakened, and with them the old need for allies against the infidel.

The individuals who are caught in the uncertainty of incomplete modernization, whether tempted or not, are not poor. Several sociological studies of the background of Islamist terrorists, for example, have shown clearly that they are not "the downtrodden rising up." On the contrary, they tend to be middle class, with a strong sense of entitlement and education, but little opportunity to find useful and modern employment in their own countries. "As a result," wrote Benjamin and Simon, "the region is filled with young men who are too well educated for the lowest kinds of manual labor, but lack the skills that would enable them to join the globalized economy." Even more ominous, their numbers are growing at about 3.4 percent a year. In any event, apart from investment in the energy sector, foreign direct investment in the Muslim Middle East is lower than it is in sub-Saharan Africa: "The Arab world has, in effect, disengaged from the world economy."[38] On economic grounds alone, therefore, it is no surprise that so many of the world's refugees are Muslims—up to 70 percent by some estimates. The trend is comforting neither for the West nor for the Muslim world.

Many of those attracted to Islamist movements are technically rather than religiously educated.[39] As was the leadership of the underground revolutionaries in Central Europe between the two world wars, "the vast majority of Islamists in leadership roles have been drawn from the ranks of applied scientists, notably physicians and engineers."[40] On the one hand, as Ibrahim noted in a study of the jailed members of an Egyptian Islamist group, most "would be considered model young Egyptians."[41] But on the other hand, such people were religiously uneducated, unacquainted with the generations of learning and religious teaching that constitute the substance of Islam. Indeed, as is discussed below, some Islamists see the traditional learning as an impediment to their revolutionary dreams, as indeed it is. They find themselves, therefore, in a multidimensional bind, Foujami's "dead end." Unable to create a political opposition because of repression in their own countries, unable to integrate into Western societies, unwilling to undertake the lengthy studies needed to understand, let alone adapt, their own religious heritage, such young men see themselves as exiles in the world. It is easy enough to imagine that religious violence can both "preserve their religious identity" by harming their enemies and "fundamentally shape their future" by restoring a sense of purpose and meaning to their lives.[42]

Like the Bolsheviks or Nazis who thought "history" would justify them, so too do terrorists typically evoke a future where the oppressed of today emerge radiant and triumphant, the initiators of a new regime,

38. Zaharia, "The Return of History," 316; Sacks, *The Dignity of Difference*, 31; Scruton, *The West and the Rest*, 123; Benjamin and Simon, *Age of Sacred Terror*, 79, 177–78. See also United Nations Conference on Trade and Development, *World Investment Report, 2002*; United Nations Development Program, *Arab Human Development Report, 2002*, 4.

39. Hoffman, "Muslim Fundamentalists," 204.

40. Ruthven, *A Fury for God*, 112.

41. Ibrahim, "Anatomy of Egypt's Militant Islamic Groups," 440; see also Ibrahim and Hopkins, eds., *Arab Society*, 503.

42. Ranstorp, "Terrorism in the Name of Religion," 46.

usually identified with peace and justice. For example, Leila Khaled, a Palestinian terrorist who masterminded successful hijackings during the late 1960s, wrote: "We shall win because we represent the wave of the future... because mankind is on our side, and above all because we are determined to achieve victory."[43] It may be a short step, therefore, from political opposition to resistance to secularization, from a call to "shape" the future to the evocation of a religiously inevitable historical course that leads to victory. When things do not go according to the way a particular individual knows they must, when the political struggle to ensure the existence of the religious community runs into resistance, as political struggles tend to do, then it is easy enough to see another and diabolical religious force as being responsible. Thus does a political struggle become a battle between good and evil or, to use the symbolism often favored by Islamists as well as by Christian and Jewish fundamentalists, resistance to secularization is a struggle against "Satanic forces."[44] As we shall argue below, a specific set of analytic terms is needed to understand the significance of recasting a political problem into religious language. One thing however, seems clear: when religiously motivated individuals seek to leave the exile in which they find themselves by acting violently in the world, they end up harming their fellow beings merely for being human.

More specifically still, the "Afghan Arabs" who make up a disproportionate number of the Al Qaeda network have been cut loose or expelled from their traditional world. Ajami described them as "insurrectionists, caught in no-man's-land, on the run from their homelands but never at home in the West."[45] Yet only in the West could they hide and nurse resentments against the West for the misery of transitional life at home.[46] Moreover, if even the relatively well-educated engineer emigrates to Europe or North America, there is no assurance that his skills will be acknowledged; and if they are, the miseries of exile still may not go away. As Ruthven observed: "Loneliness and uncertain identities, sometimes compounded by the sexual misery of desire and repulsion, create

43. Khaled, *My People Shall Live,* 209.
44. Laqueur, *The New Terrorists,* 81.
45. Ajami, "The Uneasy Imperium," 17.
46. Wright, *Sacred Rage,* 120. Thus Sheikh Omar Bakri, an Islamist cleric in London, lives on the largesse of the British taxpayer (*[London] Daily Mirror,* September 7, 1996); likewise the education of Mohammad Atta was largely paid for by German taxpayers.

dangerous tensions in the hearts and souls of young Muslim men in the West, where they are surrounded by the endless temptations to transgress from the 'straight path' decreed by God."[47] These experiences are not just psychological difficulties associated with adjustment to the dislocations of immigration, but have an important spiritual dimension as well.

In a lengthy interview with Mahmud Abouhalima, one of the team that carried out the first attack on the World Trade Center in 1993, Juergensmeyer brought to light the experience of the Islamists that the West, especially the United States, was spiritually empty:

> "The soul," he said, "the soul of religion, that is what is missing." Without it, Abouhalima said, Western prosecutors, journalists, and scholars like myself "will never understand who I am." He said that he understood the secular West because he had lived like a Westerner in Germany and in the United States. The seventeen years he had lived in the West, Abouhalima told me, "is a fair amount of time to understand what the hell is going on in the United States and in Europe about secularism or people, you know, who have no religion." He went on to say, "I lived their life, but they didn't live my life, so they will never understand the way I live or the way I think."
>
> Abouhalima compared a life without religion to a pen without ink. "An ink pen," he said, "a pen worth two thousand dollars, gold and everything in it, it's useless if there's no ink in it. That's the thing that gives life," Abouhalima said, drawing out the analogy, "the life in this pen . . . the soul." He finished his point by saying, "the soul, the religion, you know, that's the thing that's revived the whole life. Secularism," he said, looking directly at me, "has none, they have none, you have none."
>
> And as for secular people, I asked, who do not know the life of religion? "They're just moving like dead bodies," Abouhalima said.

Abouhalima's indictment must be balanced by the consideration that his own life in Germany was a long round of sex and booze that, Juergensmeyer said, "masked an internal emptiness and despair."[48] Moreover, Abouhalima, like his predecessors and his successors, never made any attempt to experience the spiritual realities of the West. They came to master Western technologies: how to fly airplanes, mix chemicals, or

---

47. Ruthven, *A Fury for God*, 19.
48. Juergensmeyer, *Terror in the Mind of God*, 69, 222.

program computers. Such people knew nothing of the evolution of Western culture beyond their own direct experience of a milieu that was monolithic, hegemonic, and alien.[49] Accordingly, their experience in the West was deeply divided. On the one hand, Islam provided them with a sense of spiritual direction and meaning, and Western technology in particular provided them with a means of succeeding in the world. That these two aspects of their life were at odds is indicated by a common myth from the early days of Islam: the Muslim and Arab conquests were evidence of God's approval; how, then, to bear the later success of the West?[50]

At the center of the spiritual crises of so many technically educated Muslim men living in the West, Hoffman indicates, is sexuality.[51] In part because conventional Islam is orthopractic in its emphasis on external behavior rather than internal moral discipline, the evident availability of young women is seen as a particularly poignant Satanic temptation. Moreover, television shows, whether dramas or sit-coms, are not experienced as ironic diversions or entertainment but as moral celebrations of lust, greed, and pornography, not affirmations of morality because, at the end of the show, transgressions are usually punished.

The commonsense observations of social psychologists can be summarized by the observation that Islamist immigrants plot the fall of the West because the spiritual emptiness of its materialism and hedonism is all they know. Indeed, many of those whose spiritual sensitivity leads them to Islamist violence as a source of meaning lack the cultural and intellectual resources to formulate a more adequate understanding.

It is unlikely that such undoubtedly sound observations will be of avail in coming to terms with terrorists because it is unlikely such individuals will find Western social science persuasive. In this context one can see the categorical limitation of all "root cause" arguments. There are no "root causes" because every grievance, whether political or personal, is specific. Moreover, the use of terrorism to address a grievance is bound to make matters worse, not better, because if it is successful, and a particular grievance is indeed addressed, the result will be to encourage

49. Waltz, "Islamist Appeal in Tunisia," 651–70; Hoffman, "Muslim Fundamentalists," 210.

50. This is a problem to which we shall return in chapter 3. It has been explored in Bernard Lewis's best-selling *What Went Wrong? Western Impact and Middle Eastern Response.*

51. Hoffman, "Muslim Fundamentalists," 218.

someone else, with an entirely different grievance, to use terrorism in a quite different context. Here the image of an up-bound escalator is not misleading. On a personal level, if a wife has a grievance against her husband and kills him in order to deal with it, we do not look for the "root cause" of a bad marriage; we seek to arrest a killer.[52] As Paul Bremmer, former counterterrorism coordinator for the State Department, said: "There's no point in addressing the so-called root causes of bin Laden's despair with us. We are the root causes of his terrorism. He doesn't like America. He doesn't like our society. He doesn't like what we stand for. He doesn't like our values. And short of the United States going out of existence, there's no way to deal with the root cause of his terrorism."[53]

The patriotic response of one such as Bremmer, the psychological profiles of terrorists such as Abouhalima, and the accounts of the "depressing circumstances" of failed or near-failed states may remind readers of chapter 13 of Hobbes's *Leviathan,* which is devoted to "the natural condition of mankind." There one finds his account of a potential for disorder into which common human life may at any time relapse. Hobbes attributed the cause to pride and vanity but saw as well that the absence of "a common power to fear" was needed. In any event, in such a condition, Hobbes said in his most oft-quoted phrase, there is "continual fear and danger of violent death; and the life of man, solitary, poor, nasty, brutish, and short." It is a state of war without law and without justice, filled only with force and fraud, the "two cardinal virtues" of war. At the same time, however, a genuine state of war clarifies all ambiguities: individuals know who they are and who they might become; they know why they have suffered and who is responsible for their humiliation; they know the costs of their own faithfulness and what must be done. And just as war gives men justifications for violence, violence provides them with the illusion of domination.

There is one other feature of Hobbes's account that we should also recall. His analysis of competitions and the race to "out-do" is far more than a vulgar desire for consumer goods. According to him, true joy for a man, which is open to all human beings, "consisteth in comparing himself with other men" and is limited only by a kind of madness where people, believing themselves to have a special grace, begin to compare

---

52. The analogy is borrowed from Dershowitz, *Why Terrorism Works,* 24–25.
53. Bremmer quoted in Ruthven, *A Fury for God,* 30.

themselves to God. When groups of such people come together, their collective madness constitutes, in Hobbes's words, "the seditious roaring of a troubled nation." It is not enough, therefore, to dominate one's opponents; one must do so in the knowledge one is doing God's work.

The "madness" and "roaring" Hobbes had in mind was not so much the clinical disorders listed in the handbooks of psychiatry but a *nosos,* a spiritual disease, as Aeschylus called it (*Prometheus Bound,* 977–78). Or, to use a more recent distinction, to be discussed in the next chapter in more detail, Hobbes was referring to a disease of the spirit. When ordinary human beings see themselves as specially chosen by God or even as gods themselves, they are not necessarily psychopaths. They are not crazy in the commonsense use of the term. They most definitely are, however, spiritually disordered. As we shall argue, the spiritual disorders that are present among contemporary terrorists are expressions of what Arendt indicated by the term *ideology* and are recognizably equivalent to those considered by Hobbes. In any event, otherwise sane and ordinary people have been led to claim divine inspiration or inspiration from other sources, some of them occult, and all of them hidden to the world of common sense, but accessible to something like a sixth sense awakened by indoctrination. It is for this reason that one can compare the spiritually disordered suicide bombers of Al Qaeda to the adherents of modern ideologies in the SS or KGB. The plainly disturbed among all such groups see themselves as political saviors; the mildly disordered may be content to profess the one and only truth. Others may be content simply not to raise questions. All of them, however, can flourish in the context of a past and a tradition that is dead. All can see themselves at the beginning of new but still unaccommodating things, where the temptation of violence has perhaps its greatest appeal.

For spiritually disordered individuals violence is not, as Arendt argued, a pragmatic mode of human activity.[54] It is a magic instrument capable of transfiguring reality. Normal people, living in a shared, commonsensical world, do not believe in magic. Even those who try to use violence as a magic instrument to change reality still live within the real world. There is, after all, nowhere else to live. And yet, spiritually disordered individuals also attempt to live in an imaginary or fantasy-based alternate world, a parallel universe where the magic effects of terrorism are expected to work at the same time as the magician knows

54. Arendt, *On Violence.*

perfectly well that they will not work. As a consequence of this complex double game, characteristic frictions between the world of common reality and the world of imaginary reality typically arise.

As we shall see below with respect to modern terrorism, the most significant conflicts between commonsense and imaginary reality are concerned with the structure of spiritual experiences and their symbolization. We find, for example, the terrorists in Aum Shinrikyo poisoning their fellow citizens and understanding their activity as a means of initiating a worldly apocalypse of history. Because, in fact or in reality, human beings do not have the ability to initiate a worldly apocalypse of history, because, in reality, the language of historical apocalypse is properly part of a speculation of divine rather than human activity, eventually friction between the everyday pragmatic activities of Aum Shinrikyo, namely, murder, attempted murder, kidnapping, and assault, and the Japanese police would arise. At the same time the members of Aum Shinrikyo claimed to be undertaking a salvific activity that they also knew to be impossible. The curious twilight form of existence, where members of a terrorist group both know and refuse to acknowledge what they know perfectly well, is enacted by both leaders and followers. In the example of Aum, it is evident both in the public proclamations of the leader, Shoko Asahara, and in his strenuous efforts to evade capture by the police.

The attractiveness of violence to increasingly large but spiritually deformed populations, both in the West and in the rest of the globe, has conditioned a final aspect of the contemporary context to be noted at the outset of this study: the conduct of war. Again to start with commonsense, war and violence are pragmatic elements of human culture, not inexplicable aberrations or breakdowns. Indeed, the fascinating studies of chimpanzees by Jane Goodall or Michael Ghiglieri have shown that war is part of primate life.[55] As some military historians have argued, what has changed over the past few decades is not war, the attractions of war, or the human proclivity for war, but the forms or formalities of war. What might be termed the orthodox account of modern war was given theoretical precision in the early nineteenth century by Carl von Clausewitz. According to him, war could be waged only by the state, for the state, and against another state; the instrument used in the conduct of war was the army, which was distinguished from the civilian popula-

55. See Goodall, *Through a Window*; Ghiglieri, *Dark Side of Man*.

tion by customs such as the salute, separate laws, and distinct costumes. The third element postulated by Clausewitz is the people, the civilians; their traditional war-related task was to remain quiet and pay their taxes. All of this practice was codified in the second half of the nineteenth century, from about the battle of Solferino in 1859 to the Second Hague Conference in 1907. Some of Clausewitz's contemporary critics have called this account of a *state* using an *army* to fight on behalf of a *people* "trinitarian war."[56]

There is a second "trinity" in Clausewitz's reflections as well, this one being part of actual war. The most basic aspect of war is what he called the "primitive violence of the people" that is expressed in a willingness to kill and to risk death. Such violence may well be part of primate life and is by no means exceptional. What makes it exceptional for Clausewitz is a second attribute of war: primitive violence must be disciplined and directed by military commanders in order to achieve rational military aims *(Ziele)*. The definition of what can serve as a military aim or goal depends, in turn, upon the third aspect, the political purposes *(Zwecke)* of the government that the army and its commander serve. That is, *Ziele* are determined by *Zwecke*, not vice versa.

In the eighteenth century, battles might be decisive because wars were fought in the interests of states. Joseph II, emperor of Austria, famously said: "I have lost a battle; I must pay with a province." When battles are not so understood they can become both more destructive and less likely to settle anything. Battlefield victory requires that the loser agree to his loss. Without a common understanding of the rules of the game the winners of battles can lose wars. A most famous battlefield victory that led to defeat was Napoleon at Moscow. There, however, one may say that the war was won by the second part of the trinity, Russian society. Even though the army had been defeated, it was unlikely that the society would surrender, because surrender for a society, as distinct from an army, means social disintegration. Accordingly, the best battlefield victories are limited ones, victories where both sides can live with the results in a lasting peace. By Clausewitzian accounts, it is always a great mistake to push beyond the culminating point of victory. One must always bear in mind the political *Zweck* for fear of being carried away by the military *Ziel*.

56. von Clausewitz, *On War;* see van Creveld, *Transformation of War*, 35–42, and Keegan, *A History of Warfare*, 18–24, 386–92.

The difficulties of applying the Clausewitzian orthodoxy to a "war on terrorism," a "war on terror," or even a "war on terrorists" are exacerbated by additional changes. First, if only states waged war, the application of violence by peoples or "societies" who knew nothing of the state nor of the divisions between the state, the army, and the people would, by definition, be activities *hors de loi* by collectivities with no legal standing. Historically, the limits of Clausewitzian orthodoxy was a two-edged sword: Europeans operating in uniform outside of Europe were licensed to kill; but the lesson would not be lost upon non-Europeans, who were, after all, as human as the Europeans, notwithstanding their technical and organizational inferiority as warriors in the nineteenth century. When war in the form of headhunting or "counting coup" was made impossible by European armies and by civil and religious administrators, but when such practices of war were central to non-European cultures, an end to war was understood by the non-Europeans as an end to their culture or as what in the twentieth century was called "cultural genocide."

To put it another way, societies that are not organized as states do not *have* armies; rather, they *are* armies. In principle, therefore, where armed force is directed by organizations that are not states, against organizations that are not armies, by people who are not soldiers, modern Clausewitzian categories are, if not eclipsed, then cast into doubt as the only way that conflict can be understood.[57] Likewise, the distinctions between officers and non-coms, military and civilians, combatants and non-combatants, and even the "wounded" as a category of combatant, are called into question because they are all tributary to the modern law of the state. This is one reason for the controversy over the status of Taliban and Al Qaeda fighters captured on the battlefields of Afghanistan and transported to the U.S. Navy base in Guantanamo Bay, Cuba, for incarceration and interrogation. This is also why, to recall an earlier observation, terrorism practiced by NGOs such as Aum Shinrikyo or Al Qaeda aims at destabilizing and delegitimizing the entire state structure by means of which modern politics is conventionally conducted.[58]

The absence of distinctions between armies and peoples or between armies and cultures (or religions) is both what makes the circle of trust among such nonmodern and non-European military organizations so

---

57. See Hoffman, *Inside Terrorism*, 34–35.
58. See van Creveld, *The Rise and Decline of the State.*

restricted, and what makes the circle of their targets so wide. Indeed, it is hard to think of a wider circle of targets than is provided by culture. For example, we were given a preview of the Taliban destruction of 1,500-year-old monumental statues of the Buddha at Bamiyan in Afghanistan when the Serbs obliterated medieval monuments in Croatian Dubrovnik.[59] Tightly based military organizations engaged in cultural conflicts have no use for another aspect of Clausewitzian war, respect for state borders. In addition, at least with respect to modern terrorism, the distinction between war and crime has also grown ambiguous, because that distinction depended on the integrity of the state and its legal monopoly of armed force. Modern terrorists are prepared to contest both armies and the police, and armies and police forces have begun to redefine their mission in terms of "security," which can include both preemptive action and the post-facto investigation of crimes.

The context of this study of terrorism, then, is highly complex. The analogies with the wars against totalitarian domination are bound to be imperfect; the insights drawn from the spiritual conflicts of the Western Middle Ages are bound to be limited. The Second World War no less than the Cold War were unquestionably Nietzschean "wars of the spirit." It is worth remembering, however, that just as the *Blitzkrieg* was a response to the stalemate of trench warfare, it was supplemented and then answered by the destruction of populations and cities, by the original weapon of mass destruction (WMD), the A-bomb.

The question of this and other WMDs in the context of the "war on terrorism" raises further perplexities, at least for a Clausewitzian understanding of war. Even though Clausewitz saw in Napoleon a grave threat to the European state order, he was still convinced that the parties to the conflict had political purposes. The spiritual conflicts emboldened by ideology, however, are much more ambiguous; when, moreover, it is not some fictitious law of History that is to be "proved" by military action but rather the Will of God, it is exponentially more difficult to agree upon the nature of the conflict; but without such agreement it is impossible to claim or agree upon victory and defeat. Indeed, without the order provided by the state it may prove impossible to know who has won, let alone what.

59. Campbell, "Taliban Dismisses Shock over Statues." See also Meddeb, *Malady of Islam*, 134–36.

2 Concepts

Since 1983, the U.S. State Department has, for statistical and analytical purposes, described terrorism as the "premeditated, politically motivated violence perpetrated against noncombatant targets by subnational groups or clandestine agents, usually intended to influence an audience."[1] Excluded, therefore, are terrorist atrocities and war crimes undertaken by soldiers in conventional wars, administrative massacres, killing conducted during siege warfare, campaigns of genocide, or other acts designed to extinguish enemies of a state. Excluded as well, unless their actions are directed against a state, are acts of religious sectarian violence, including such suicidal cults as the People's Temple, the Solar Temple, or the Heaven's Gate cult—all of which show at least a family resemblance to "religious" terrorism.[2] Likewise civil wars, as in Algeria between an Islamist political party and the army, may or may not be considered as terrorist conflicts, notwithstanding the high casualties and gruesome conduct usually associated with them.

There are several other summary descriptions of terrorism available. According to Jessica Stern: "two characteristics are critical for distinguishing terrorism from other forms of violence. First, terrorism is aimed at noncombatants. This is what makes it different from fighting in war. Second, terrorists use violence for a dramatic purpose: usually to instill fear in the targeted population. This deliberate evocation of dread is what sets terrorism apart from simple murder or assault."[3]

---

1. U.S. State Department, *Patterns of Global Terrorism, 2001*, xvi. United States Code, Title 22, Section 2656f (d) uses the identical definition of *terrorism*.

2. Laqueur, *The New Terrorists*, 80–81. See also the Canadian Security and Intelligence Service, *Doomsday Religious Movements*.

3. Stern, *Ultimate Terrorists*, 11.

Christopher Harmon has provided yet another and in some respects more precise definition. "Terrorism," he said, "has always one nature. Capable of different expressions, such as hot rage, cold contempt, and even 'humane' indulgences of certain victims, terrorism never loses its essential nature, which is the abuse of the innocent in the service of political power." It is, he continued, "the deliberate and systematic murder, maiming, and menacing of the innocent to inspire fear for political ends." Bruce Hoffman also defined terrorism

> as the deliberate creation and exploitation of fear through violence or the threat of violence in the pursuit of political change. All terrorist acts involve violence or the threat of violence. Terrorism is specifically designed to have far-reaching psychological effects beyond the immediate victim(s) or object of the terrorist attack. It is meant to instil fear within, and thereby intimidate, a wider "target audience" that might include a rival ethnic or religious group, an entire country, a national government or political party, or public opinion in general. Terrorism is designed to create power where there is none or to consolidate power where there is very little. Through the publicity generated by their violence, terrorists seek to obtain the leverage, influence and power they otherwise lack to effect political change on either a local or an international scale.

Mark Kauppi adds that traditional terrorists, which are our first concern, are "*secular* groups with a *political* agenda requiring *public* support."[4] Taken together, these remarks constitute a reasonable summary of the external attributes of traditional terrorism. As we shall see, however, even with traditional terrorism there is what for simplicity we shall call an "internal dimension" as well that needs to be considered.

All these observations of terrorist behavior indicate that the killing is instrumental and that it is aimed at influencing those other than the victims. That is, while the terrorist murder of "noncombatants" may be brutal and evil, it is not for those reasons also gratuitous and senseless. The purpose identified by the State Department, namely, "to influence an audience," led Brian Jenkins to remark as long ago as 1975 that "terrorists want a lot of people watching and a lot of people listening and not a lot of people dead." In some instances, killing for publicity purposes

---

4. Harmon, *Terrorism Today*, xv, 1; Hoffman, *Inside Terrorism*, 43–44; Kauppi, "Terrorism and National Security," 25.

has become a kind of conventional wisdom. In *The Little Drummer Girl*, for example, John Le Carré has one of his characters declare: "Terror is theatre. We inspire, we frighten, we awaken indignation, anger, love. We enlighten. The theatre also." At about the same time, television personality Ted Koppel remarked: "Let me put forward the proposition that the media, particularly television, and terrorists need one another, that they have what is fundamentally a symbiotic relationship."[5]

At one time there were good reasons to think this way. Indeed, the words of the mid-nineteenth-century Italian terrorist Carlo Pasacane, that terror was "propaganda by deed," were echoed during the 1970s by IRA terrorists such as Maria McGuire. Bombs were preferentially exploded during the evening rush hour; IRA ambushes of the British Army would be accompanied by press releases, thereby ensuring that army accounts would reach the media too late for the six o'clock news. Of sixty IRA bomb explosions in July 1974, nearly fifty were timed to gain maximum television exposure.[6]

The symbiosis of TV and terrorism was of considerable concern to Lord Annan in his report to the British government on the future of broadcasting in the United Kingdom:

> Terrorism feeds off publicity: publicity is its main hope of intimidating government and the public: publicity gives it a further chance for recruitment. The acts terrorists commit are each minor incidents in their general campaign to attract attention to their cause. No democracy can tolerate terrorism because it is a denial of the democratic assumption that injustice can, in time, be put right through discussion, peaceful persuasion and compromise. By killing and destroying, the terrorists are bound to extort publicity—and hence one of their ends—because such news will be reported.[7]

From the perspective of traditional terrorists, making the six o'clock news often achieved just the goals they were aiming for. Before the 1975 train hijackings in the Netherlands, it is safe to say that few people had ever heard of the South Moluccan Islands let alone knew why its inhabi-

5. Jenkins, "International Terrorism: A New Mode of Conflict," 15; Jenkins, "Will Terrorists Go Nuclear?" 511; Jenkins, *Likelihood of Nuclear Terrorism*, 6; Koppel, "Terrorism and the Media," 43.

6. On Pasacane, see Stafford, *From Anarchism to Reformism*, 76–88; McGuire, *To Take Arms*; Clutterbuck, *The Media and Political Violence*, 92.

7. Annan, ed., *Report*, 270.

tants might be sufficiently aggrieved to hijack a train and put its passengers in considerable danger. Likewise the 1980 occupation of the Iranian Embassy in London drew attention to the little known cause of the Arab minority of Iran.

The most obvious danger associated with this symbiosis is that, if the "propaganda by deed" is effective, it provides a long-term incentive for additional acts; if any particular terrorist act is not covered by the media, there is a short-term incentive to escalate the level of violence until it is. As Timothy McVeigh, convicted for bombing the Alfred P. Murrah Federal Building in Oklahoma City in April 1995, said, when asked by his defense lawyer why he could not have aired his grievances without killing anyone: "that would not have gotten the point across. We need a body count to make our point."[8]

On the other hand, live TV coverage can, by itself, prejudice discussions with terrorists, particularly when they have abducted hostages. Moreover, when ongoing terrorist events such as the siege of the Iranian embassy or an airplane hijacking are covered live on television, there is considerable danger that the terrorists will obtain real-time information on the actions of the police or security forces. For example, if pictures of SAS personnel on the Iranian embassy roof or shots of their abseil down to the rear windows had been broadcast live, it is nearly certain that many more hostages would have been murdered. In addition, if television is chiefly, not to say exclusively, a means of entertainment, there is something highly questionable about entertaining a TV audience by showing them terrorism in action.[9]

Apart from the appeal of its evident hard-nosed crudeness, Jenkins's aphorism—that terrorists wanted a lot of people watching or listening and not a lot of people dead—was persuasive because limited terrorist killing appeared to be both effective and instrumental. If this was true, the number of dead from any particular terrorist act had to bear some

8. Brooke, "Newspaper Says McVeigh Described Role in Bombing."

9. Clutterbuck, *The Media and Political Violence*, 138; Postman, *Amusing Ourselves to Death*. Possibly the most unusual illustration of the connection between terrorism and entertainment TV is the story of how, in 1997, Osama bin Laden received a battery for his satellite phone from a sympathizer, Tarik Hamdi, who worked for ABC News, which is owned by the Disney Corporation, in exchange for an interview. Bin Laden later used the phone to order the bombings of the U.S. embassies in east Africa. See Benjamin and Simon, *Age of Sacred Terror*, 451n6. Pipes, *Militant Islam Reaches America*, 149.

intelligible and proportional relationship to political ends. This is why traditional, practical, or conventional terrorists "seemed almost content with their handguns and machine-guns and the slightly higher rates that their bombs achieved. Like most people, terrorists themselves appeared to fear powerful contaminants and toxins they knew little about and were uncertain how to fabricate and safely handle, much less effectively deploy and disperse."[10] Because traditional terrorists were said to be in some degree rational calculators, there were few, if any, realistic demands that could be made by threatening large-scale and indiscriminate killing; looked at the other way around, what such terrorists did want, namely, publicity, could easily enough be gained by limited, though still spectacular, killing and destruction. Until the closing years of the twentieth century, then, weapons of mass destruction (WMDs) were not an appealing option.[11]

Consequently, both the weapons used and the killing and damage achieved tended to be relatively modest. Looking back to the terrorist activities of the nineteenth century, and to attacks carried out for most of the twentieth, one can understand why Walter Laqueur called the phenomenon "nuisance terrorism." Among the variety of quasi-permanent but still lethal nuisance terrorists, apart from various well-known but declining "national liberation" groups, may be included eco-terrorism, agroterrorism, bizarre new-age apocalypticism, and other acts by "single-issue" political obsessives.[12]

Hoffman said that traditional terrorists *seemed* almost content with limited killing and with limited goals. An examination of the history of recent terrorism, as well as the logic of its use, however, indicates that whatever limitations to terrorist violence have been observed have been almost entirely accidental and contingent on, as much as a result of, external limitations and lack of technical competence as of any rational calculation undertaken to gain specific effects. To understand the weight of Hoffman's *seemed* it is necessary to analyze "the rationale and the 'inner logic' that motivates terrorists and animates terrorism. It is easier to dismiss terrorists as irrational homicidal maniacs," he said, "than to

10. Hoffman, *Terrorism and Weapons of Mass Destruction,* 11–12.

11. See Rapoport, "Terrorism and Weapons of the Apocalypse," 55; Stern, "Will Terrorists Turn to Poison?" 208 ff.

12. Laqueur, *The New Terrorists,* 4; Egan, "From Spikes to Bombs," 1–18; Foxell, "Current Trends in Agroterrorism," 107–30; Whitsel, "Catastrophic New Age Groups," 21–36; Monaghan, "Single-Issue Terrorism," 55–65.

comprehend the depth of their frustration, the core of their aims and motivations, and to appreciate how these considerations affect their choice of tactics and targets."[13] To analyze the "inner logic" of terrorism one must examine the structure of terrorist consciousness.

We may begin with the observation that, prior to the nineteenth century, the only acceptable justification for terrorism was religious ritual, in the sense that religion provided both a motive and a limitation to conduct or behavior that today is identified with terrorism. It is significant that the English words *thug, assassin,* and *zealot* are all connected to systematic religiously inspired ritual killing.[14]

The internal inspiration or motive of the conduct of Thugs, for example, was unquestionably religious in a broad and general sense. At the same time, however, their killing was strictly regulated by ritual. The religious task of a Thug was to supply Kali, a god who both sustains and destroys life, with sacrificial blood necessary to keep the cosmos in balance. Over a period of six centuries, the Thugs managed to kill between 500,000 and 1 million victims in service to Kali. Thugs held ordinary murderers and thieves in contempt; and although they confiscated their victims' property, they were required to kill in a prescribed fashion, by strangling (see Herodotus 7.85) a victim chosen by following various omens: then they must ritually inter the corpse before making off with the loot.[15] Given the ritual constraints on Thug murders, their record of killing is astonishing compared to their modern counterparts who have been unable "to achieve anywhere close to the annual average of Thug murders despite more efficacious and increasingly lethal weaponry."[16] Moreover, some people—the blind, lepers, women, and Europeans, among others—were immune to attack. Indeed, the prohibition against killing Europeans is what eventually enabled some thirty to forty British administrators to hunt down and remove from circulation about 10,000 of the Thug Brethren. Likewise the behavior of assassins and zealots was conditioned by strict ritual requirements and limits as well as by an elaborate and complex theology.[17] In contrast to

13. Hoffman, "Rethinking Terrorism," 313.

14. Rapoport, "Fear and Trembling," 658–77.

15. See Pfirrmann, *Religiöser Charakter und Organisation der Thagbrüderschaften* and references for details.

16. Hoffman, "Holy Terror," 272.

17. See Lewis, *The Assassins,* and Hodgson, *The Order of Assassins;* Kingdom, "Who Were the Zealots?" 68–72.

this kind of ritual religious killing, which often has been called a precursor to traditional terrorism, it is far from clear that early modern terrorist activity had any internal limitations at all, notwithstanding the external constraints resulting from the relatively low lethality of their methods.

As with so many other words that constitute the modern political vocabulary—*liberalism* and *conservatism* being the most prominent—the word *terrorism* also came into use during the French Revolution. The *régime de la terreur* of 1793–1794 was ostensibly established to bring stability by consolidating the power of the new revolutionary Jacobin government. In the event, more was involved than an emergency measure made necessary by the fact that France was at war with just about all its neighbors. The outstanding feature of the Reign of Terror is the self-purging of the leaders and then of the Jacobin Party as a whole. Perhaps more important, as Arendt pointed out, is that it was "boundless" because it was undertaken to expose what was hidden, namely, motives, which is an endless task, even for a psychiatrist.[18]

Shortly after the Terror began, Burke denounced the Jacobin government, the "thousands of those Hell hounds called Terrorists . . . let loose on the people."[19] By the mid-nineteenth century, however, terrorism and terrorists had gained the familiar attributes of an anti-state, anti-government conspiracy, though this is not to imply that terror as a mode of governance—as it had been during the French Revolution—ceased to be an option. On the contrary, as was indicated in the preceding chapter, terror is essential to the operation of twentieth-century, ideologically driven totalitarian governments. By the mid-nineteenth century, as well, terrorists conventionally pursued the purposes of publicity and "propaganda by deed." Modern secular terrorists have tended to be intellectuals prepared and committed to using violence to redress what they experience as grave injustices, defects, suffering, and misery, for which they feel great guilt. Typically they provide reasons and arguments to justify their activities as being necessary to ensure political change. Typically as well, terrorists invoke necessities analogous to those of war.

This is not entirely improper. After all, the most obvious attribute of wars is that they are occasions of violence. As we have seen in the previ-

18. Arendt, *On Revolution*, 95.
19. Burke, *Letters on Regicide Peace*, 262.

ous chapter, however, terrorist violence cannot be understood in terms of modern Clausewitzian warfare. It cannot be assimilated to the conventions of ancient war either.

Certainly it is not Greek. The defining aspect of life in a polis is that it was governed by persuasive speech, not violent deeds. That is why Socrates was "persuaded" to drink the cup of hemlock rather than suffer the indignity of execution, which would be a violation of his physical person. On the other hand, beyond the walls of the city, as Thucydides's Melian dialogue demonstrated, "the strong do what they can and the weak suffer what they must." This violent and extramural aspect of war was what, for the Greeks, also made it a nonpolitical enterprise.

Even so, ever since the time of Homer, great wars have inspired great stories, which is to say the strenuous and risk-filled experiences of battle are inherently meaningful. Moreover, the stories told are not simply the songs of victory: Homer sang the praise of Hector and Herodotus told the history of the Persians. Thucydides's opening paragraph explains that the sheer greatness of the crisis, namely, the war between Athens and Sparta, explains why he wrote his book—as if it were self-evident that the great deeds of war needed to be preserved in memory for the sake of posterity. The stories were not a justification of the deeds of warriors before some higher tribunal; even less were they the justification of war. They were, on the contrary, expressions of the meaning of the deeds of warriors, of their heroism and greatness.

The first justifications of war are from Roman antiquity, along with the distinction between just and unjust wars, which was transmitted through the Christian medieval accounts into the present. For the Roman historian Livy, however, "the war that is necessary is just, and hallowed are the arms where no hope exists save in them." That is, necessity, not free choice or the choice of freedom, enabled human beings to call a war just—and for Livy necessity included conquest, expansion of empire, defense of one's own power in the face of threat, and so on. Notably absent as well was any moral or theoretical distinction between offense or aggressive war and defense. And finally, there was the purpose and end of war, namely, peace. For the Romans, peace was found not in victory and defeat but in the concluding alliance of the parties to conflict sanctified by a law that made them henceforth partners. The laws of medieval Christian warfare were equally elaborate, hedged with claims of justice, protection of the innocent, and so on.

The violence of traditional terrorism, however, is surrounded by none of these formalities and, more significant, has given rise to no stories and songs to celebrate the greatness of terrorists' deeds. One reason for this gaping absence of meaning is because, to use a familiar distinction of Hannah Arendt, the violence of terrorists is merely instrumental and purposive. It is not intended to reveal the personality of the agent or the greatness of a deed. Indeed, terrorist violence is a mode of activity belonging to man acting as fabricator, of *homo faber*, and is not, properly speaking, the act of a political being at all.[20]

The following aspects of Arendt's account of *homo faber* have a bearing on the problem of terrorist violence. First, fabrication is inherently violent. Making something consists in working upon material that has already been removed from nature. This removal can be effected only by violence, either literally, as by killing a life in cutting down a tree to provide wood, or metaphorically, as by ripping copper and iron from the womb of the earth.[21] "This element of violation and violence," Arendt argued, "is present in all fabrication, and *homo faber*, the creator of the human artifice, has always been a destroyer of nature." Because it is possible to create a human world only after having destroyed a part of nature created by God, there is always present a Promethean element of revolt.

Second, the work of making something is always guided by a model or pattern that precedes the thing made, the work after which it is constructed. The "idea" is prior to the material thing. Third, "the process of making is itself entirely determined by the categories of means and end." The process ends with the product, and the product, the end, justifies the means. So far as the instrumental use of violence is concerned, the table justifies the violence done to the tree that turns it into material at hand. Paradoxically, however, the end—the table—becomes a means—a means for commodious living, for example.

There are plenty of perplexities that emerge when the experience of making is generalized to the extent that usefulness becomes the ultimate standard. Lessing's query, "what is the use of use?" expresses the paradox that, if usefulness is held to be the criteria of meaning, it is also the source of meaninglessness. That is, the chain of ends and means is

20. See Arendt, *The Human Condition,* 139 ff., 153ff.
21. See Eliade, *The Forge and the Crucible.*

boundless, even though it depends on there being a proximate end to give meaning to a means.

These paradoxes and perplexities are enhanced when the language of fabrication is applied to political activity, that peculiar combination of words and deeds where words disclose the meaning of deeds rather than obscure them, and where deeds are not simply violent, meaningless, and futile but reveal a character about whom a meaningful story can properly be told.[22] The application of the metaphors of fabrication to politics seems to result in little more than a recipe for endless violence. If nation building really were like boat building, except that it employed "the crooked timber of humanity," then attempting to straighten the material out would guarantee that politics would forever be murderous Procrustean trimming. After all, Kant, who first used the image of "crooked timber," ended his aphorism with the cautious qualification that nothing straight ever could be built of it. Political shipwrights nevertheless are willing to try, by bringing violence to bear on the "human material." Moreover, they typically do so with an idea in mind about what the end product will look like.

These remarks regarding fabrication have a bearing on terrorist violence. It was clear from Jenkins's remark that killing civilians is understood by terrorists to be an instrumental spectacle. It is also clear that traditional political terrorism is neither a religious ritual nor Clausewitzian or other war. We took as a clue to the nature of terrorism the absence of stories that glorify the great deeds of terrorists. The closest analogy from ordinary activities that might account for the meaning of terrorist violence and that also pays tribute to the element of rational calculation is that terrorism is a mode of fabrication, the application of violence to human material in order to create a desired product. But because human beings have the capacity to begin, to initiate what never has been before, to act and to reveal in their actions a new meaning and a new story, there is no product. As a result, every so-called product is temporary and, in the context of violent making, nothing more than the pretext for further violence.

Before characterizing the mode of consciousness that makes such a categorical error, there is one additional peculiarity of a typical terrorist that needs to be indicated. We have argued that there is nothing

22. Cooper, *Action into Nature*, chap. 5.

specifically terrorist in the use of violence because violence is inherent in such peaceful activities as carpentry. Aircrews of B-52s are not terrorists because they use bombs and kill civilians, and everyday murderers are not terrorists either, even though they also kill innocent people.

Unlike ordinary military or criminal killing, terrorist killers typically view their own activity as both altruistic and sacrificial. As Hoffman said, "The terrorist is fundamentally an *altruist:* he believes that he is serving a 'good' cause designed to achieve a greater good for a wider constituency—whether real or imagined—which the terrorist and his organization purport to represent." Or in the words of Walter Laqueur, "traditional terrorism rests on the heroic gesture, on the willingness to sacrifice one's own life as proof of one's idealism." Most commonsense individuals reject out of hand the notion that murder ever could be connected to altruism, self-sacrifice, or heroic gestures. Most commonsense individuals, on the contrary, would agree with Harmon that "the essences of terrorism includes immoral kinds of calculations: singling out victims who are innocent; and bloodying that innocence to shock a wider audience." That is, terrorist violence is doubly wrong: first because it is directed at innocent victims, and second, because it kills them instrumentally, to impress somebody else. It is, to use a Victorian term, "moral insanity," which is a phenomenon quite distinct from ordinary insanity, madness, or lunacy.[23]

The reality that terrorists carefully avoid facing is that killing the innocent is inherently illegitimate. Moreover, terrorists are sufficiently aware of this truth or of this ethical reality that they go to great effort to deny it. There is, therefore, an inherent friction between commonsense reality, the common reality of worldly existence, within which the terrorist like everybody else must live, and the occult reality within which the terrorist lives imaginatively, an imaginary reality where killing the innocent to impress others is understood to be heroic, altruistic self-sacrifice. In the previous chapter we characterized as a spiritual disorder what Hobbes identified concretely as "the seditious roaring of a troubled nation," and indicated there that a further elaboration would follow.

Analysts of terrorism have used terms such as *moral insanity* to iden-

23. Hoffman, *Inside Terrorism,* 43; Laqueur, "Postmodern Terrorism," 31; Harmon, *Terrorism Today,* 190; on "moral insanity," see Laqueur, *The New Terrorists,* 231 ff. Ronfeldt has diagnosed a similar phenomenon, which he named the "hubris-nemesis complex." See his *Beware the Hubris-Nemesis Complex: A Concept for Leadership Analysis.*

tify what we have called a spiritual disorder.[24] Specifically, we will use the term *pneumopathology*, as distinct from psychopathology, to describe the disorder in question. The term first appeared in print in 1960, in a short essay by Eric Voegelin. There Voegelin raised the question: why did Thomas More write *Utopia* when he knew his visionary state never could be actualized in the world? Moreover, since More knew that the original sin of pride, *superbia* in the sense used by Augustine, was the reason why the perfect state could not be actualized, why did More indicate that the perfect state would be possible if only pride, "this serpent from hell," were expunged? But More knew as well as anyone, both from his direct experience of the behavior of his king and from long immersion in the great texts of Christian philosophy and theology, that the one thing never to be expunged was, precisely, *superbia*. For Voegelin, More's position raised the question

> of the peculiar psychopathological condition in which a man like More must have found himself when he drew up a model of the perfect society in history, in full consciousness that it could never be realized because of original sin.
>
> And this opens up the problem of the strange, abnormal spiritual condition of gnostic thinkers, for which we have not as yet developed an adequate terminology in our time. In order, therefore, to be able to speak of this phenomenon, it will be advisable to use the term "pneumopathology," which Schelling coined for this purpose. In a case like More's, we may speak, then, of the pneumopathological condition of a thinker who, in his revolt against the world as it has been created by God, arbitrarily omits an element of reality in order to create the fantasy of a new world.[25]

24. Bruce Hoffman, who has spent as much time as anyone analyzing the operations of terrorists, recently looked to T. E. Lawrence's *Seven Pillars of Wisdom* for a suitable vocabulary to describe the new terrorists. He settled upon Lawrence's remarks on the danger of "daytime dreamers." Hoffman, "Rethinking Terrorism," 307. Lawrence wrote: "All men dream: but not equally. Those who dream by night in the dusty recesses of their minds wake in the day to find that it was vanity: but the dreamers of the day are dangerous men, for they may act their dream with open eyes, to make it possible." See Lawrence, *Seven Pillars of Wisdom*, 23. Even Army intelligence officers have come to focus on the "internal discontents" of terrorists. See the UPI report of Ralph Peters's analysis of "apocalyptic terrorists," in Chew, "Kill Apocalyptic Terrorists."

25. More, *Utopia*, 243; Voegelin, *Modernity without Restraint*, 305–6.

It is clear that Voegelin used the term to refer to an intellectual act whereby a thinker arbitrarily denies the reality of one or another aspect of the world in order to fantasize about an imaginary world. It is much less certain, however, that Schelling ever used the word.

In a letter to Theo Broerson, Voegelin said he did not recall precisely where Schelling used the term. "I refer to it only, because I do not want to be accused by some Schelling scholar of having pinched the term without acknowledging its authorship." In his extensive analysis of Schelling and Voegelin, Day noted that Schelling used several closely related terms, *spiritual sickness (Geisteskrankheit), sickness of temperament (Gemüthskrankheit),* and *consumption of the spirit (Verzehung des Geistes),* in the sense of having the substance of the spirit wasted away or used up. Day concluded, quite properly, in my opinion, that "it is likely that 'pneumopathology' is Voegelin's coinage for the host of critical terms used by Schelling."[26]

This philological issue in fact adumbrates a significant problem in modern political science, which it is necessary now to make explicit. Bernard Lonergan has introduced the term *scotosis* to modern philosophy to indicate an intellectual act whereby a thinker prefers to project a kind of daydream than to understand the world. Voegelin has discussed the same issue, initially by using a comparatively imprecise language that referred simply to an "imaginary reality." He then refined the distinction to differentiate between "first" or "common reality" and "second reality" along with the corresponding modes of consciousness. Providing an account of imaginary realities and of the reality of the imagination is a complex undertaking. We might best begin by considering Voegelin's essay "The Eclipse of Reality."[27]

Human beings can imagine themselves to be less than human—to be an ego or a self or a subject—as easily as they can imagine themselves to be more than human—a socialist or positivist or some other sort of superman. At the same time, however, such an act of imagination does not in fact change one's human status nor the relations between human and nonhuman being that constitutes the rest of reality. In the event that someone engages in such an act of imagination and attempts to live as

---

26. Voegelin to Broerson, February 24, 1976, in Voegelin Papers, Hoover Institution Archives, box 8, folder 44; Day, *Voegelin, Schelling, and the Philosophy of Historical Existence,* 24–25, 33–36.

27. Lonergan, *Insight,* 191 ff.; Voegelin, "The Eclipse of Reality," 111 ff.

an infra- or superhuman self, and given the stubborn fact that reality remains as is, whatever the fancy of the imaginator, friction is bound to arise between the imagined reality and the actual surroundings within which human beings, whether they undertake imaginary acts or not, must live.

Typically, the individual who undertakes the initial act of imagination follows it with another and another, as the several frictions appear and need to be met, understood, and dealt with. Thus the act that created the imaginary self is followed by another that creates an imaginary reality that is appropriate to the imaginary life of an imaginary self. This second act of imagination creates a "second reality." The term *second reality* is not original with Voegelin, but as with the term *pneumopathology* it was appropriated by him and used in a precise analytical way that was somewhat different from the way it was originally used. With respect to the term *second reality,* Voegelin relied on two main sources, Robert Musil and Heimito von Doderer, both Austrian novelists of the mid-twentieth century.

Apparently Voegelin first encountered the term in Musil's great work, *Der Mann ohne Eigenschaften,* where it is used synonymously with the term *the other condition,* which is to say a condition of "unreality" created by the character Ulrich, "the man without qualities" of Musil's title.[28] Ulrich lives in an ambiguous relationship with himself because he recognizes his own qualities as belonging, not to him, but rather to a role he adopts according to given but changing circumstances. Complementing the man without qualities are qualities without a human being to whom they may be attributed. In this imaginary world, there is no meditative or erotic center; Ulrich lives as if he were devoid of human spirituality. In this way he can adopt whatever qualities seem at the moment to be desirable and never accept any personal responsibility for his choice. This is possible, according to Musil, because Ulrich cannot summon up any sense or consciousness of reality, even in relation to himself.

A more extensive and explicit discussion of the problem is found in the work of Heimito von Doderer, particularly in his novels *The Demons* and *The Merovingians.* In the latter novel, Doderer establishes the anal-

---

28. Musil, *Der Mann ohne Eigenschaften,* 1129. See also Payne, *Robert Musil's "The Man Without Qualities,"* chap. 6, and Luft, *Robert Musil and the Crisis of European Culture.*

ogy between the spiritual decline of the modern world with that of the late Middle Ages in order to establish continuity between the second reality of witchcraft and that of ideological politics in general and of National Socialism in particular. As Voegelin explained, "The construction of a second reality comes from the desire to have a beyond in this life."[29] The existential story of *The Demons*, very simply, is: if you are incapable or unwilling to experience the divine beyond, then you may as well believe in demons, which are, if nothing else, a "beyond in this life" that exist within the second reality created by the imagination.

Doderer does not, however, leave the matter of demonology and witchcraft as a kind of postmodern option that you can take or leave at will: the choice of trying to live in a second reality, he said, is the consequence of "a refusal to apperceive reality," an *Apperceptions-Verweigerung*. Voegelin said it reflected an "honest dishonesty" precisely because it was not a mistake or an error. In Doderer's political science, "the consolidation of the refusal to apperceive reality, which is thus a second reality," is "the total state." Doderer also indicated that "anger is the catastrophic form of *Apperceptions-Verweigerung*, that finally would sneak about in one of many hundred forms of stupidity." It is an acute form of *Apperceptions-Verweigerung*, "a panic-stricken flight from life, a weird kind of suicide where instead of killing oneself, one wants to kill everyone else. One wills that there be no life."[30] The significance of anger is particularly important for someone such as Hitler, who deliberately chose to whip himself into a state of histrionic anger until he was quite willing to believe what he also knew to be false.[31]

In fact, however, this condition of "honest dishonesty" applies to revolutionaries in general—including terrorists. A revolutionary, said Doderer, is "someone who wants to change the general situation because of the impossibility or untenability of his own position," or rather, "of the fundamentals of life in general." In fact, however, "a person who has been unable to endure himself becomes a revolutionary; then it is others who have to endure him."[32] The development of the precise vocabulary of second reality, of honest dishonesty, of modes of stupidity, and so

29. Doderer, *Die Dämonen* (English version, *The Demons*, trans. Winston and Winston), and Doderer, *Die Merowinger;* Voegelin, *Hitler and the Germans*, 255.

30. Doderer, *Die Wiederkehr des Drachen*, 293; Doderer, *Die Merowinger*, 230–31.

31. Voegelin, *Hitler and the Germans*, 150–51.

32. Doderer, *The Demons*, 491.

on, is not intended to be an idiosyncratic exercise; nor is it a kind of psychological profile. Revolutionaries and others who indulge in the practice do so for a very specific purpose: to screen the "first reality" of common experience from view or to put the common experience of reality into the shadow, to use Lonergan's image. Of course, this second act does not abolish the frictions in response to which it was initially undertaken, but rather enhances them "into a general conflict between the world of his imagination and the real world."[33]

In the essay from which we have been quoting, "The Eclipse of Reality," Voegelin subsequently provided an analysis of the elements that constitute the second reality: first is a discrepancy between the imaginary reality and the reality of common experience; second, the intentional act of projecting an imaginary reality at variance with the reality of common experience; and third, the specific, concrete individual who has deformed his human being into something else and has permitted this deformed, imaginary self to eclipse his human being.

Just as Doderer had to contrast the second reality with the reality of common experience, or "first reality," so too did Voegelin. "But what," Voegelin asked, "is Reality?" In developing his answer, Voegelin, unlike Doderer,[34] did not rely on the technical language of Thomas Aquinas, but rather developed his own by distinguishing several conventional meanings of the term that the analyst is forced to employ. There is, to begin with, the reality projected by the imagination that engenders the deformation of human being. The now-deformed being is still human, however, and is just as real as anyone else; the only difference is that the deformed human being has projected a second reality that is intended to hide first reality, including his status as a human being. Moreover, he may well be successful in the sense that for a longer or shorter period of time and for a larger or smaller number of people, the second reality can, indeed, put first reality into a shadow. "The man with a contracted self," Voegelin concluded, "is as much of a power in society and history as an ordinary man, and sometimes a stronger one. The conflict with reality turns out to be a disturbance within reality." Indeed, unless human beings could, as by magic, change reality rather than merely refuse to apperceive reality, it could hardly be otherwise.

33. Voegelin, "The Eclipse of Reality," 112.
34. See Hesson, *Twentieth-Century Odyssey,* 80–81.

In this context one must pay attention to the vaguely Kantian term *apperception*. It is used by Voegelin and by Doderer instead of the word *perception* because the imaginator, assuming he has a moderate technical competence as a thinker, is never unaware of what he is doing. Indeed most imaginators are perfectly well aware of what they refuse to admit and go to great pains to disguise what they really know. For this reason, as Voegelin observed, those who project a second reality typically accompany their projections with a detailed analysis of the self and by the self who is actually undertaking the projection. The point of the analysis of the projecting self is to justify the self that is doing the projecting. Eclipsing reality is therefore a complex intellectual and practical operation. Any particular example will have to be analyzed with care in order to make the purpose intelligible, along with its structure, the frictions with first reality, the revisions of the second reality that follow from the conflict with first reality, and the reasons why the second reality eventually disintegrates.

Before undertaking such an analysis with respect to specific exemplars of contemporary terrorism, a number of more general observations can be made. First, many terrorists are entirely lucid with respect to their self-analysis, but this clarity is confined to the internal structure of the second reality. It does not extend to clarity with respect to the mode of existence that leads to the projection of a second reality in the first place. Second, since the purpose of the projection is to eclipse first reality or, psychologically considered, to provide a means of dulling the anxieties that exposure to first reality apparently causes to the consciousness of the projector, it will be extremely difficult, not to say impossible, to discuss with the projector the reasons why he (or she) undertakes the projection. Third, because very few projections are simply fantasies, "a project of second reality, if it is effectively to eclipse first reality for any length of time, must have incorporated sufficiently large, important, and emotionally appealing sectors of the reality of common experience to be acceptable by the standards of the audience to whom it is addressed." This pragmatic aspect of a successful projection provides an additional complexity to the analysis and incidentally makes discussion with projectors an even more hopeless enterprise.

In the previous chapter we discussed the appeal of what are conventionally called ideologies. The appeal can now be described in more precise language:

The great projectors of second realities are social forces because they are able to transform rational agreement on an unexceptional point into sweeping existential assent to the deformation of humanity. They are surrounded by the social fields of secondarily deformed humanity in their schools, adherents, admirers, vulgarizers, followers, fellow-travelers, and so forth. Inversely, the imaginator must always be on his guard, because he can never be certain when he enters a discussion that Reason will not suddenly raise its ugly head. His interlocutor may be a man who desires to know and will therefore not abide by the imaginator's rule of the game that a discussion must never touch the question of existence, for if this question were touched, not only would the project have to be abandoned, but the imaginator's existence itself would be in danger of being engulfed by its own nothingness.[35]

This is why when Socrates raises the issue of the truth of existence in the *Gorgias* he is threatened with death (*Gorg.* 511a). The same threat, one hardly need add, is carried out in practice by terrorist killers. Moreover, this issue is central within a part of the intellectual world of contemporary Islam, which poses additional problems. Finally, when the spiritual disturbance of a projector resonates with a large sector of the surrounding society, the projection invariably includes an appeal to the "hard core of first reality," which nevertheless changes with the historical, cultural, and social context. There are always plenty of injustices crying out for redress, so it is no surprise that the production of second realities is often a symptom of a social crisis.[36] At the same time, however, "no list of grievances, however long and formidable, adds up to an ontological denial of the conditions of existence of the world." Or as Berger and Sutphen said, it is important "to distinguish sharply between the purpose [the terrorist] seeks to achieve and the grievances he seeks to exploit."[37] The purposes are almost invariably riddled with pneumopathological elements; the grievances are almost always at hand in the commonsense

---

35. Voegelin, "The Eclipse of Reality," 134.

36. Voegelin, *Hitler and the Germans*, 251.

37. Voegelin, *Israel and Revelation*, 508; Berger and Sutphen, "Commandeering the Palestinian Cause," 123. Jessica Stern has said that terrorism provides a "seductive" solution to a real problem. See her *Terror in the Name of God*, 262. In terms of the approach used in this analysis, the seduction is a kind of self seduction, and the problems are not real in the sense of being addressed by pragmatic political activity.

world. This is why the two constituents of contemporary terrorism must be distinguished. One of the tasks of subsequent chapters in this study will be to distinguish the contingent "hard core" of reality, which is necessary if the projection is to have any appeal whatsoever, and the essentially imaginary project itself.[38]

To summarize the argument of this chapter to this point, recall the observation made earlier that many terrorists understand their own activities as being fundamentally altruistic. In order to do so, they create a second reality where murder can be as sacrificial as martyrdom. In this respect, a suicidal terrorist bears a family resemblance to the final product of totalitarian domination: an individual who is so superfluous, so devoid of conviction or of qualities, that he is indifferent to whether he kills or is killed.[39] A suicidal terrorist today, however, is far from indifferent: he is eager to "sacrifice" himself in order to put his "altruism" into practice. We will see in detail below that the second reality projected by contemporary terrorists is typically derived from a variegated complex of religious symbols; our present concern is to describe why the consciousness doing the projecting—whether it seeks to actualize a second reality derived from the Bible, the Koran, or *The Turner Diaries*—is pneumopathological.

Consider the condition of an active, morally sensitive person living in a social order where the legitimate means of reform are difficult or impossible. Such a person is wracked with guilt at the misery of his fellow human beings and is deeply angered at the appearance of evil in his society. He wishes to make matters better, but he is condemned to impotence: the only escape from the impasse seems to be to sacrifice himself. But as Doderer observed, such individuals, in fact or in first reality, cannot endure *themselves,* which is why they make their fantastic projections and seek to make everyone else endure them. Likewise Voegelin pointed out, with respect to the spiritually disordered terrorist, "The terroristic act offers the opportunity for sacrifice in a double sense:

---

38. Juergensmeyer, *Terror in the Mind of God,* 161–62, makes a similar psychological point: if someone thinks a particular struggle is of ultimate significance and a defense of basic human or cultural identity and dignity, if losing the struggle is "unthinkable," and if it cannot be won in the commonsense world, it is likely that the struggle will be invested with cosmic significance and God or an angel or a prophet will assume the task of fixing things, using human beings as mere instruments.

39. Arendt, *Origins of Totalitarianism,* 457–59.

first, the terrorist risks his life physically, for he will be executed when he is caught, second, and more important, in committing murder the terrorist sacrifices his moral personality." The latter sacrifice is, in fact, the harder one: overcoming the common awareness that killing the innocent is profoundly wrong is understood by the projector to be a supreme sacrifice; at the same time, it is the only proof that he can do something. However, this supreme act also "reveals the pneumopathological state of the person who commits it, for a sacrifice of moral personality can neither be brought into a spirit of love nor is acceptable to other men. It is not an act of love but rather an act of self-assertion by which the man who makes the sacrifice claims for himself an exceptional status in comparison with other men: the men to whom he brings the sacrifice are misused as the audience for his own justification." The pneumopathology of terrorist consciousness or of terrorist existence for common sense lies in the fraudulent claim to be exceptional. Considered psychologically, terrorism is an act of the weak that allows them to attack an ostensibly superior force and proclaim aggressively their own existence: "I bomb, therefore I am."[40]

The philosophical argument is analogous, and its validity is independent of the content projected onto any particular second reality, whether derived from religious symbolism and sentiments or not. By claiming that his act is exceptional, a terrorist killer also makes the accusation that his audience and his victims alike are unexceptional for the simple reason that their refusal to act is evidence they lack a moral personality as great as his. Moreover, the terrorist has placed his audience in the position of appearing to have asked the killer to do murder on their behalf. "It is not surprising," said Harmon, "that terrorist groups' leaders advance arguments to justify the remarkable brutality of their actions.... Many terrorists act as though they believe they are 'beyond good and evil,' as free as Nietzschean supermen of the requirements of normal morality." In reality, they are no more beyond good and evil than anyone else—and the terrorists know it.

> The reality that terrorists and their apologists will not face is that a
> moralizing argument for immoral activity can be a useful lie, but only
> for the short term. Ultimately it is only by way of legitimate political

40. Arquilla, Ronfeldt, and Zanini, "Networks, Netwar, and Information-Age Terrorism," 40.

principles and activity that any group, revolutionary or ruling, can exercise power morally and reasonably. Terrorism, once accepted, is not easily abandoned. It can be as self-destroying for an organization as it is soul-destroying for an individual.[41]

In the short term, however, the terrorist can claim that his own violent act is in fact an act of altruistic sacrifice. Implicitly, therefore, he anticipates its acceptance by those to whom he offers the sacrifice of himself and his victims. But this, too, is illegitimate. In Voegelin's words, the terrorist has no right "to place them [his audience] in a position where his own sacrifice of moral personality would appear as requested by them for their benefit. The terroristic act as a moralistic model is a symptom of the disease in which evil assumes the form of spirituality." As we shall indicate shortly, the language changes when religious experiences, sentiments, and symbols are invoked, but this means only that a pneumopathology identical or at least equivalent to that just described is being expressed through religious language. As Juergensmeyer said, religious terrorism is no less violent than other kinds, though the destructiveness is "sanitized" by virtue of the fact that the violent acts are "religiously symbolic. They are stripped of their horror by being invested with religious meaning."[42] To be more precise, the second reality projected by the pneumopathological consciousness uses religious language to screen the murderous first reality of which they are fully aware. The language, accordingly, needs to be decoded in a different way, and the consequences of religious terrorism may be somewhat different, but the significance is the same: large-scale murder.

The change from what we have loosely called traditional terrorist acts, the propaganda of the deed where the object is to terrify a large number of onlookers by killing a few, to the suicidal mass murderers of September 11, 2001, clearly indicates a change in operational style. But only the style has changed. The substance remains: a pneumopathological consciousness projects a second reality and acts murderously within first reality by killing a lot of otherwise innocent people. For the balance of this chapter we will examine some examples that illustrate the transformation of the style of terrorist acts during the past few decades.

41. Harmon, *Terrorism Today*, 188, 195.
42. Voegelin, *Crisis and the Apocalypse of Man*, 277–78; Juergensmeyer, "Worldwide Rise of Religious Nationalism," 16.

The massive terrorist attacks of the 1990s and early years of the twenty-first century were preceded by a period of transition from traditional terrorism. The beginning of the new era is often identified precisely: July 22, 1968. On that date an El Al commercial airliner was hijacked with the purpose not of diverting the plane to an unscheduled destination but in order to barter the passengers for third parties, imprisoned colleagues of the hijackers—in this instance, Palestinians held by Israel. The novelty introduced by the El Al hijacking was twofold. First, it required coordinated international travel by the hijackers, and second, the target, civilian airline passengers, had nothing to do with the source of the terrorists' grievances.[43] During the 1970s most terrorist acts were what are conventionally called "events of duration," that is, hijackings or hostage-taking completed by nationalist separatists and social revolutionaries, usually Marxists of some sort, using the traditional weapons of bombs and guns. They were violent, but these events were also governed by a cost-benefit rationality, the rationality of political bargaining, and other intelligible negotiations. Even the 1972 murders by the PLO of Israeli athletes at the Munich Olympics were "from the purely propagandistic view-point . . . 100 percent successful."[44] By the 1980s, new methods led to what have been termed "conclusive events," that is, acts that take place too quickly to permit any counterterrorist response—Semtex plastic bombs, remotely detonated car-bombs, bombs that explode in the luggage holds of airliners, and so on. Some of these acts were undertaken by Marxist revolutionaries, but religious and narco-terrorists introduced new motivations as well.[45] These events were supposed to speak for themselves. Negotiations, if conducted at all, were done remotely and through third parties. A car bomb exploding on the streets of Belfast or Paris was assumed to carry the message: "this is what we can do; we will continue to do so until our well-known demands are met."

During the 1980s the first chemical attacks took place, motivated chiefly by economic blackmail: Chilean grapes and Israeli oranges were contaminated by opponents of the governments of those two countries; Mars Bars were contaminated by members of the Animal Liberation

43. Hoffman, *Inside Terrorism,* 67–68.
44. Quoted from *Al-Sayad* (Beirut), September 13, 1972, in Hoffman, *Inside Terrorism,* 74. See also Jonas, *Vengeance.*
45. Medd and Goldstein, "International Terrorism on the Eve of a New Millennium," 282–83.

Front. The 1990s saw the formation of new alliances and networks between and among traditional political terrorists and organized crime:
the Cali cartel joined forces with the Revolutionary Armed Forces of
Colombia (FARC), and other groups established working relationships
with Chinese triads, Russian and Italian mafias, former KGB agents, and
so on. These new organizational alliances, which we discuss in greater
detail in chapter 5, were accompanied by changes in terrorist technology as well as terrorist motivations.

Consider first the simplest change, the introduction of new technology. In its annual public report for 2000, the Canadian Security and
Intelligence Service (CSIS) made the following observation: "Advanced
communications techniques, combined with the ease of international
travel, have broadened terrorism's scope of operations, while greatly
compressing the time frames available to security forces to detect and
neutralize terrorist threats." Moreover, from the perspective of the security forces, matters are likely to get worse in the years ahead. "The use of
advanced explosive materials, in combination with highly sophisticated
timers and detonators, will produce increasingly higher numbers of
casualties. There will likely be terrorist attacks whose sole aim would
be to incite terror itself. . . . Computers, modems, and the Internet are
enhancing the operational capabilities of terrorist organizations. . . . Terrorists also have augmented their security through the use of sophisticated encryption software to protect sensitive communications." According to a Reuters report, Internet bulletin boards carrying pornographic
and sports information are the most popular sites for hiding encrypted
terrorist messages.[46] By "operational capabilities" CSIS referred to such
things as commercially available instruction manuals and guides to
assassination, poison, bomb making, and so on that can be downloaded
from the Internet. In addition, of course, the Internet is by itself a widely
used means of communication.[47] The CSIS appraisal was essentially
the same as that available from open American intelligence sources.
Also during the 1990s the consensus among academic observers of terrorism has been that advanced technology has increased the potential
for damage and so has enhanced *vulnerability*, but the probability of

46. CSIS, *Public Report 2000;* Reuters report in the *Calgary Herald,* January 21,
2002. See also Soo Hoo, Goodman, and Greenberg, "Information Technology and
the Terrorist Threat," 135–55.

47. Thomas, "Al Qaeda and the Internet,'" 112–23.

actual damage, or *threat*, remained considerably lower.[48] Following September 11, the gap between vulnerability and threat has narrowed considerably.

In part, the longstanding divergence between "alarmists" and "minimalists" reflected the difference between physical and social science. Worst-case options seemed possible to the former because they were more aware of the potential of chemical and biological agents and the technical requirements to increase the toxicity and lethality of those agents; their concern was with what *could* happen. Historians and political scientists, however, were more likely to be skeptical "for the simple reason that we know there have always been enormous gaps between the potentiality of a weapon and the abilities and/or will to employ it."[49] The concern of historians and political scientists was not with hypothetical questions of what could happen but what was a reasonable expectation in light of what has happened in the past.[50]

Grim prognostications are always more prudent than optimistic ones because if the grim prognosticators are wrong they are still considered prudent, whereas if they are wrong in underestimating a threat they look irresponsible. And yet, such "prudence" stemming from an overemphasis on vulnerabilities has its own risk because resources are finite and might more effectively be deployed than by addressing vulnerabilities, which are nearly infinite. Besides, historically, there have been good reasons to focus on threats rather than vulnerabilities. Terrorists traditionally had no use for weapons of mass destruction (WMDs) because such weapons were sufficiently lethal to make sense only within the logic of deterrence. Accordingly, states that did have access to WMDs were unlikely to supply weapons to NGOs that might actually want to use them precisely because states possessing them knew their only rational "use" was to deter their actual use.[51] And if a group of unconventional

48. Hoffman, *Inside Terrorism,* 203–4.

49. Rapoport, "Terrorism and Weapons of the Apocalypse," 51.

50. Roberts, *Hype or Reality?;* Dishman, "Understanding Perspectives on WMD," 303–13.

51. In addition there was a conservative symmetry with respect to spheres of influence between the Soviet Union and the United States—tested seriously only with the Cuban missile crisis. The lack of symmetry where "rogue" or nearly "failed" states is concerned is what makes relations between them and the United States less stable and in some respects more dangerous. This was an element, for example, in Kenneth Pollack's argument that Iraq under Saddam Hussein must be forcibly disarmed. See Pollack, *The Threatening Storm: The Case for Invading Iraq.*

terrorists ever were supplied with such weapons, the state that supplied them would also be at risk, either directly from the probably unreliable terrorists, or indirectly through retaliation by other states. Moreover, as was indicated above, mass casualties have not been seen by traditional terrorists as advancing their political, and so limited, objectives. Because politics necessarily imposes limits, even when it is connected to terrorism, there are moral constraints involved as well. Ordinary terrorists kill the innocent, but WMDs kill an excessive number even for ordinary terrorists to stomach. In addition, acquiring WMDs is both risky and expensive, as is using them, and most terrorists prefer simple, cheap, and reliable weapons—guns and explosives.

At the same time as political analysts had good reasons to be skeptical about WMDs ever being successfully employed by terrorists, there was a large piece of statistical evidence that suggested a trend in the opposite direction. Both the State Department data and the data compiled by St. Andrews University and the Rand Corporation indicated that while terrorist attacks declined in terms of sheer numbers of events from the 1970s to the 1990s, the attacks increased in lethality.[52] The 2000 CSIS report alluded to this same issue: "of particular concern," the authors note, "is the emergence of groups . . . whose aim is not to bargain with governments nor to win over public opinion to their point of view, but rather to cause the maximum possible amount of damage and disruption to a people or a system that they consider especially abhorrent."[53] Several terrorist groups that began operations during the 1990s "did not necessarily espouse political causes or aim to take power." Instead, many of them "were intent on harming a maximum number of people."[54] It has been argued that the 1993 attack on the World Trade Center, for example, was mainly an attempt to kill a lot of people, undertaken from a desire for revenge and independent of any "religious" or symbolic sense attributed to bringing down the twin towers.[55] The direction of increasing lethality, however, was by itself ominous, not least of all because the escalator was moving in the direction of WMDs.

---

52. See Stern, *Ultimate Terrorists*, 6–9; Hoffman, "Terrorism and Weapons of Mass Destruction," 21; Kauppi, "Terrorism and National Security," 23–24; Hoffman, *Terrorism and Weapons of Mass Destruction*, 19–21; see also U.S. State Department, *Patterns of Global Terrorism, 2001*, appendixes A, J.

53. CSIS, *Public Report 2000*, 2.

54. Smithson and Levy, *Ataxia*, 15.

55. Parachini, "Combatting Terrorism," 147.

As Kauppi noted, "One reason why terrorism is proclaimed a top national security concern is that in recent years it has been coupled with another national security priority—the proliferation of weapons of mass destruction."[56] States interested in conducting "asymmetric warfare" have sponsored terrorists, with the result that they have become more skilled and technically adept in their operations. At the high-tech end, during the 1990s, there were plenty of munitions such as Stinger anti-aircraft missiles available at reasonable prices;[57] there are also great fears that WMDs may come on the market, sourced from the former Soviet Union. In the medium-tech area, President Vaclav Havel of the Czech Republic noted on the occasion of a state visit to London that the People's Republic of Czechoslovakia during the 1980s manufactured and exported over 40,000 tons of Semtex; it took approximately 200 grams to bring down Pan Am Flight 103, which killed 278 people. Havel calculated that communist Czechoslovakia alone had supplied 150 years' worth of Semtex to state supporters of terrorism.[58] And at the low-tech end of the spectrum, fertilizer, diesel fuel, and icing sugar are available over the counter. The first World Trade Center bomb, for example, did over half a billion dollars damage and cost $400 to build.[59] These considerations bring us to the second theoretical issue, the change in the motivation of terrorists and the language used to express both motives and immediate purposes.

Initially, the chief concern of analysts of terrorism regarding the "new terrorists" was that they did not conform to traditional cost-benefit rationality. Hoffman, for example, explained the increased lethality of terrorist attacks as the result of "the dramatic proliferation of religious terrorism, the increasing 'amateurization' of terrorism, and the growing professionalism of terrorists." The professionalism of the terrorists was purely operational: they became more competent and adept at killing. But they were "amateur" in the sense that they were part-time and religiously motivated. They considered violence to be "a sacramental act or divine duty executed in direct response to some theological demand or imperative." In other words, according to Hoffman, religiously motivated terrorists are not constrained by "the political moral or practical

56. Kauppi, "Terrorism and National Security," 24.
57. The cost in the spring of 1991 was quoted at $80,000. See Ehrlich, "For Sale in Afghanistan: US-Supplied Stingers."
58. Frankel, "Sale of Explosive to Libya Detailed."
59. Highfield, "Explosion Could Have Wrecked City Center."

constraints that seem to affect other terrorists." Such people, Hoffman argues, cannot easily be deterred because they appeal to no common constituency but only to an exclusive and often idiosyncratic divinity.[60] Accordingly, they have no reason to moderate, regulate, or calibrate their violence. The limitless destruction sought by the new terrorists, Hoffman said, is what distinguishes them from the Carloses or Abu Nidals of an earlier era.

An alternative and arguably more adequate way to understand the logic of religious terrorism is to consider it as a second reality. In this context it is intelligible the way that Arendt's analysis of the "logic of an idea" made sense. The continuity with traditional terrorism is indicated by Juergensmeyer's comment that acts of religious terrorism are not tactics linked to a pragmatic political objective but "performance violence" akin to "religious ritual or street theatre, . . . dramas designed to have an impact on the several audiences that they affect."[61] Traditional terrorism is also a performance; the difference is that the performance of the religiously motivated terrorist is conducted on an imaginative "cosmic" stage, a stage with an imaginary world-transcendent dimension, as well as upon the mundane stage of the commonsense world, the real world of first reality.

A number of spiritual consequences follow along with some very practical ones. First, the spiritual. When politics is understood foremost as a spiritual or religious quest, the only audience that counts is divine. Brian Jenkins summed up this first new attribute with characteristic directness: "If God tells you to do it, God knows you did it. So you don't have to issue a communiqué to let God know."[62] The absence of a communiqué increases operational security, but more important, the "transcendent moralism" or the "higher morality," along with a "ritual intensity" provided by the religious imagination, enables religious terrorists to symbolize and so give meaning to their activity in terms of a cosmic drama—or better, as a cosmic war. As Ruthven observed, "Religious violence differs from violence in the 'secular' world by shifting the plane of action from what is mundane, and hence negotiable, to the arena of

60. Hoffman, *Terrorism and Weapons of Mass Destruction*, 21, 26, and see also Gurr and Cole, *New Face of Terrorism*, 251; Hoffman, *Inside Terrorism*, 168–69.

61. Juergensmeyer, *Terror in the Mind of God*, 124.

62. Quoted in Kocieniewski and Bonner, "For Terrorists, the Menace of Silence." See also Hoffman, "Terrorism and Weapons of Mass Destruction," 48.

cosmic struggle, beyond the political realm." Whatever conceptual precision is accorded the notion of a cosmic struggle, it exists beyond the realm of pragmatic problems for which a range of commonsense negotiations based on shared and divergent interests might provide a solution. In addition, of course, the problem of altruism returns, only now in the "sanitized" language of religion.[63]

Ruthven also drew attention to a peculiar aspect of a cosmic struggle that (somehow) involved what he called "the Abrahamic divinity," the God of the Bible and the Koran. "Because," he said, "the Abrahamic divinity has been exempted from evil, the symbolic images of cosmic struggle over which he presides are particularly susceptible to what might be called the 'actualization of eschatology,' in other words the enactment of apocalyptic scenarios on the plane of history, in real time, in the real world." To be more precise, the participants in what they take to be a cosmic struggle are as capable of projecting apocalyptic images onto their own activity as onto that of their adversaries; the spiritual consequence of raising a political conflict imaginatively to the highest height is that, when things go wrong, as invariably they do in first reality, that misfortune can be attributed to an imaginary spiritual adversary. In commonsense terms, the enemy becomes satanic. Juergensmeyer indicated the obvious consequences: "religious concepts of cosmic war, however, are ultimately beyond historical control, even though they are identified with this-worldly struggles. A satanic enemy cannot be transformed; it can only be destroyed."[64] Nor, clearly, can mere humans negotiate with Satan, not even with the ritual aid of a very long spoon.

The chief practical consequence of taking part in a cosmic struggle with a satanic enemy is that the enemy must be extinguished. The sentiments expressed by Hussein Mussawi, the founder of Hezbollah, are typical: "We are not fighting so that the enemy recognizes us and offers us something. We are fighting to wipe out the enemy."[65] A spokesman for Hamas likewise announced: "there are no such terms as compromise and surrender in the Islamic cultural lexicon." Or as Mohammed Mohaddessin, a spokesman for an opposition group in Iran, noted,

63. Juergensmeyer, *Terror in the Mind of God*, 10; Harmon, *Terrorism Today*, 188; Ruthven, *A Fury for God*, 30; Juergensmeyer, "Worldwide Rise of Religious Nationalism," 16.

64. Ruthven, *A Fury for God*, 34; Juergensmeyer, *Terror in the Mind of God*, 217.

65. Quoted by Hoffman, "Holy Terror," 275. See also Taheri, *Holy Terror*, 7–8.

"Moderate fundamentalists do not exist. . . . It's like talking about a moderate Nazi."[66] Similarly, the "Christian Identity" white supremacists in the United States are seeking some kind of racial and religious conflict to remove their polluted satanic enemies, as are the Sikh terrorists who kill for Khalistan, the "Land of the Pure." The pragmatic results of a murderous search for a pristine world are bound to be mass casualties.[67]

There are equivalent secular terms to such conflicts. Juergensmeyer recounted the following anecdote, which has been repeated in endless media reports: "an Israeli confirmed that he regarded innocent Arabs as enemies as well, since there were no such things as civilians in 'a cultural war.' Echoing this sentiment, a leader in the Hamas movement told me, 'no one is innocent in the war between Arabs and Jews.'"[68] Moreover, because the first reality is not changed by imaginary operations in a second reality of cosmic conflict, the circle of targets to be removed is bound to grow larger.

For terrorists participating imaginatively in a cosmic struggle, the purpose of what amounts to limitless killing is clear. "In a strange way," wrote Juergensmeyer, "the point of all this terrorism and violence is peace. Rather, it is a view of a peaceful world that will come into being when the cosmic war is over, and the militants' vision of righteous order triumphs." What is "strange" about mass murder in search of a righteous peace is, precisely, the pneumopathological projection by terrorist consciousness. The peace that comes at the conclusion of the cosmic war is "the peace that passeth all understanding" translated from heaven to earth, which is again an imaginative operation in a projected second reality. To use Voegelin's language, one might call this a metastatic peace, inasmuch as it requires a transformation of reality in order to be achieved.[69] Indeed, because the cosmic war is a projection into a second reality, only an equally imaginary metastatic peace could conclude it. The grave problem in reality, of course, is that magic operations do not work, which again indicates the centrality of the problem of pneumopathology.

We have drawn attention to the limitations of traditional terrorism.

66. Hamas spokesman quoted in Pipes, *Militant Islam Reaches America*, 39; Mohaddessin interview.

67. See Simon and Benjamin, "Real or Imagined Threats?" 171; Whitsel, "Ideological Mutation and Millennial Belief," 89–106.

68. Juergensmeyer, *Terrorism in the Mind of God*, 175.

69. Juergensmeyer, "Worldwide Rise of Religious Nationalism," 17; see Voegelin, *Israel and Revelation*, 506 ff.

It was technologically limited and thus there was a natural upper limit to the number of people that could be killed by conventional terrorist bombs—somewhere in the hundreds as opposed to the thousands. To move beyond explosives (at least prior to the use of fuel-laden civilian aircraft as bombs) entailed a search for weapons of mass destruction, but so long as terrorists had limited political purposes, this was an unlikely path to take. Once, however, an imaginary cosmic or world-transcendent purpose was added to the already spiritually disordered consciousness of a terrorist, the limits to destructiveness were also effectively removed. Before considering Islamist terrorists in this context, we will analyze a terrorist group, Aum Shinrikyo, the roots of which lie in a religious tradition far removed from that provided by the "Abrahamic divinity."

At approximately 8:15 a.m. on Monday, March 20, 1995, five trains in the Tokyo subway system were scheduled to arrive at Kasumigaseki station in downtown Tokyo, the most convenient stop for workers in the major bureaucracies that govern Japan. Five individuals, having swallowed an antidote to sarin, pierced vinyl bags containing the nerve gas and exited the trains about 8:00 a.m.

> Within minutes, commuters on the trains were coughing, choking, and clutching themselves in fits of nausea. As the trains stopped, passengers stumbled out, vomiting and writhing on the train platform in spasms. Still, the car doors closed and the trains moved on to Kasumigaseki. Passengers inside collapsed on the floors, twisting in agony, convulsing, foaming at the mouth, unable to breathe. Even those who managed to clamber outside and escape death were sick and blinded for days. Doctors and nurses who treated the contaminated commuters themselves developed sore throats and eye irritations. Eventually twelve died, lying in subway stations or perishing in hospitals soon after, and over 5,500 people were affected, many with permanent injuries.[70]

Had Aum been able to keep to its original production schedule and manufacture gas of greater purity, the casualties would have been enormously higher. Indeed, the March 20 attack had been preceded by at least nine less successful efforts using botulinum toxin and anthrax as well as sarin.[71] Aum was simply unable to manufacture an effective

70. Juergensmeyer, *Terror in the Mind of God*, 103.
71. Cameron, "Multi-track Microproliferation," 277–310.

botulinum toxin and their technicians were unable to turn the anthrax slurry into an aerosol, which is a relatively complex operation. This is one reason why terrorists using biological agents have usually preferred to contaminate food or water rather than mount a full-fledged biological attack.[72] In a dress rehearsal for the Tokyo attack the group succeeded in releasing sarin in June 1994 in the resort town of Matsumoto, which killed seven people and a large number of dogs and fish, and sent more than fifteen other people to the hospital. The deaths and injuries were blamed on an accidental release of a homemade pesticide.[73] After the attack of March 20, when Asahara and other members of Aum were evading police capture, a second subway attack took place. Had it succeeded, it might have killed 20,000 people.[74]

Following the subway attack, Senator Sam Nunn declared that "the world has entered a new era." The reason for this alarming assessment was clear: "Terrorists packing guns and bombs are frightening enough, but chills go down the spine at the thought of indiscriminate killers employing weapons that at times cannot be seen, heard, smelled or tasted: arbitrary death from an imperceptible cause is a nightmare if ever there was one."[75] Sarin had first been developed by the Nazis (though Aum copied a Soviet formula); its first significant use by terrorists, however, seemed to signal that they had crossed yet another moral threshold, akin to the mass murder of noncombatants or blowing up embassies.[76]

72. Carus, "The Threat of Bioterrorism."

73. Several lengthy studies of Aum Shinrikyo have been undertaken, including extensive hearings before the U.S. Senate. See U.S. Congress, Senate Committee on Government Affairs, Permanent Subcommittee on Investigations, *Global Proliferation and Weapons of Mass Destruction;* see also: Lifton, *Destroying the World to Save It;* Kaplan and Marshall, *Cult at the End of the World;* Kaplan, "Aum Shinrikyo (1995)," 207–26; Reader, *Poisonous Cocktail?;* Reader, *Religious Violence in Contemporary Japan;* Sale, "Nerve Gas and the Four Noble Truths," 56–71; Reader, "Spectres and Shadows," 147–86; Clinehens, "Aum Shinrikyo and Weapons of Mass Destruction"; Metraux, *Aum Shinrikyo's Impact on Japanese Society;* Trinh and Hall, "The Violent Path of Aum Shinrikyo," 77–110.

74. Senate Committee on Government Affairs, *Global Proliferation and Weapons of Mass Destruction,* 40; Kaplan and Marshall, *Cult at the End of the World,* 279.

75. Nunn quoted in Falkenrath, Newman, and Thayer, *America's Achilles' Heel,* 167; Smithson and Levy, *Ataxia,* 1.

76. In fact the first modern terrorists to use poison gas were the Tamil Tigers, in an attack in 1990 on a Sri Lankan army post. They were also the first to use suicide bombers. To use Jenkins's formula: few people were watching, and it received little attention.

In this analysis we will consider first how Aum was able to undertake the operation, the external story, and then we will examine the motives for doing so, the internal story.

The chief reason why Aum was able to muster the resources to conduct these attacks and to do so without attracting attention from either the Japanese police or any other intelligence service is that under Japanese law Aum was considered a religious organization and so screened from police surveillance. Article 20 of the postwar Japanese constitution was designed to separate the Japanese government from the Shinto religion and make it more difficult to forge the political and religious alliance that proved so effective in motivating Japanese military activities during the 1930s and 1940s. This article guarantees freedom of religion and prohibits any state involvement in "religious activity." The Japanese courts and police have interpreted Article 20 to mean they cannot examine the religious practices of any organization covered by the Religious Corporation Law nor enter any religious building without solid evidence of significant illegalities. This meant that even occasional and intermittent police surveillance of a "religious corporation" was unlikely. Moreover, in Japan there is no national police force such as the RCMP or the FBI to coordinate information from local police—who in turn are often ill-equipped to deal with major and sophisticated criminal activity outside the traditional underworld, the *yakuza*. Finally, American intelligence organizations were focused primarily on left-wing Japanese political groups, and Japanese authorities, which had responsibility for "right wing" political groups, considered Aum a protected religious group. Accordingly, Aum attracted next to no interest in what they did nor in what they believed. By 1995 Aum Shinrikyo had assets totaling over $1.4 billion.[77] It was, therefore, in a position to undertake significant political activity.

The story of the organizational growth of Aum began rather unpropitiously. In 1981, the founder, born Chizuo Matsumoto in 1955, joined a sect founded by Kiriyama Seiyn, a great popularizer of esoteric Buddhism. Kiriyama combined Buddhist teachings with yoga, and Matsumoto as a consequence adopted the Hindu god Shiva as his principal god, "which was rather strange and quite unusual for a Buddhist."[78] Shiva is the consort of Kali, whom the Thugs served, and is associated

77. Stern, *Ultimate Terrorists,* 53.
78. Watanabe, "Religion and Violence in Japan Today," 82.

with salvation through the destruction of the world. Matsumoto adopted some additional Buddhist teachings on the degeneration of humanity and announced that all human beings alive today would become either animals or *preta*, "hungry ghosts," in the next cycle of birth. Matsumoto also adapted, or departed from, Kiriyama's teaching on the removal of karma, which he based on his own interpretation of Tibetan Buddhism.

In 1982, Matsumoto was fined 200,000 yen, sent to jail for twenty days, and had his herbalist license revoked for selling a worthless infusion of orange peels as an herbal cure. He apparently confided to one of his assistants that "religion," not yoga or herbal medicine, was the way of the future. His studies of Nostrodamus, the sixteenth-century French "seer," introduced him to the importance of the Battle of Armageddon; his examination of American New Age teaching reinforced his career shift to retail religion. He later added some conventional anti-Semitism, noting that the Japanese emperor, the president of the United States, and the popular singer Madonna were all Jews.

In 1984 he founded his own group called Aum Shinsen no Kai. *Aum* (*om* in English) is Sanskrit for the fundamental powers of cosmic stability and change and often is chanted as part of a personal or community mantra. *Shinsen no Kai* means "circle of divine wizards." The implication of the name of Asahara's first group, therefore, was that they might magically command the basic cosmic forces. A year later, Matsumoto directly encountered Shiva, who told him that "it was his task to build the Kingdom of Shambala," that is, an ideal society consisting of people who have achieved psychic power.[79] The kingdom would fully come into being between 2100 and 2200. The next year, 1986, Matsumoto said he had become fully enlightened but did not provide any details concerning the content of his enlightenment. He recommended "out of body" experiences achieved by frequent masturbation or frequent sexual activity. Whatever else was implied by such "out of body" experiences, it contained a strong element of self-manipulation.

In 1987 Matsumoto changed his name to the more spiritually heroic Shoko Asahara. That same year he renamed his group Aum Shinrikyo. The latter word, *Shinrikyo*, means teaching of supreme truth. Taken together, Asahara was claiming to be a wizard with knowledge of the supreme truth, namely, that salvation demands the destruction of the world. Between 1988 and the early 1990s, the implications were gradu-

d., 83.

ally worked out in practice. Asahara also founded a commercial enterprise in association with his cult to operate a chain of yoga schools, and he published his writings. In his texts, he claimed to have received several visions indicating that he was a major prophet and that apocalyptic events lay just over the horizon.

Using the yoga centers as recruiting bases, Asahara's "neo-new religion" (shin shin shuko) grew rapidly. He was certainly correct about the market for "religions" and benefitted enormously from a general spiritual void in Japanese society that by the early 1990s had been filled by more than 200,000 registered cults with a membership of some 200 million, 70 million more than the population of the country, which indicates that considerable numbers of Japanese held memberships in more than one cult. At the same time, the requirement that members turn over large sums to the organization enabled Aum to grow and to grow wealthy. Many converts were *otaku*, individuals with a deep involvement in science and technology, limited interpersonal skills, and a strong taste for the peculiar genre of book-length, ultraviolent, graphic, and dramatic Japanese comics called *gekiga*. Internal discipline was maintained by a strenuous regime involving sleep deprivation, drugs, especially LSD, and rigorous indoctrination, along with violence (including murder) directed against anyone wishing to leave or criticize Aum or Asahara. Many of the converts were technically skilled, notwithstanding their *gekiga* view of the world, and a significant number were members of the police and Self-Defense Forces.

By the time of the subway attack Aum had more than 10,000 members in Japan and 50,000 across the world in half a dozen countries, including the former Soviet Union, where 30,000 Aum supporters lived, many of them, as in Japan, technically adept. There is evidence as well that the former Soviet Union was the scene of several attempts by Aum to acquire nuclear weapons, atomic demolition munitions (suitcase bombs), or uranium that would be useful for conducting radiological warfare, that is, large-scale radioactive contamination, and what Asahara called a "radioactive sunrise." Asahara also cultivated his contacts with the Japanese underworld gangs, the *yakuza*, much as the KGB had extended connections with the Russian mafia or the Nazis with German gangsters. As a result of these connections and organizational successes, Aum had become a multinational NGO with assets of a billion and a half dollars and control over a number of front companies engaged in purchasing raw materials, state-of-the-art equipment, and modern facilities. They were organized in a strict hierarchy and staffed by dedicated scientists and technicians. Moreover, the administrative structure of Aum essentially duplicated that of the Japanese government, with a Construction Ministry, Education Ministry, and so on.[80] By most ordinary measures of normality, Aum was a successful start-up company in the "religious market," as Asahara called it.

The product Aum delivered to that market, we noted above, was derived from a wide selection of esoteric sources. The actual contents consisted of a bizarre and syncretistic apocalyptic cocktail outlined above. By the late 1980s, however, it had become clear to Asahara that universal salvation would not be possible. Instead, there would be mass destruction that would result in a saving remnant—Aum Shinrikyo. At the center of the remnant sat Asahara, issuing the prophecy of a cataclysm scheduled to arrive in 1995 because Pluto entered the sign of Sagittarius on January 18. The next day a major earthquake struck Kobe, and Asahara used the occasion to explain the higher significance of the event to all who would listen: "The mysterious Great Power had set off the earthquake either with a small, distant nuclear explosion or by 'radiating high voltage microwaves' into the ground near the fault line." As a consequence of this "prediction," the profile of Aum, at least in the Japanese media, increased enormously. Perhaps more ominously, Asahara's sermons mentioned more frequently the danger of gas attacks from the U.S. Air Force, which in fact telegraphed his next move. As Inoue Yoshihiro, an Aum disciple, said at his trial, "Asahara's predictions were not just a forecast or a prophecy, but something that had to be realized."[81] Increasingly, therefore, Asahara determined that his new task was to initiate the final apocalyptic struggle for the good of a corrupt world and in order that Aum might then save it, starting with Japan. It became the task of his followers to ensure the prophecies of Asahara came true. That is, Aum would initiate the final events and in this way prove the truth of his apocalyptic vision.

We have encountered this logic before—in Stalin's remarks quoted in chapter 1, for example, on the status of the Kulaks as a dying class.

---

80. Mullins, "Aum Shinrikyo as an Apocalyptic Movement," 317. In this respect they are similar to Al Qaeda and the Communist Party of the Soviet Union: all showed "parallel structures" to the existing government. Only the CPSU was able to act as a true "vanguard party," shadowing the official office holder.

81. Sale, "Nerve Gas and the Four Noble Truths," 69; Inoue Yoshihiro quoted in Watanabe, "Religion and Violence in Japan Today," 91.

To ask if Asahara "really" believed what he was saying is meaningless because, within his consciousness, the meaning of reality was itself in play. Kaplan and Marshall expressed a conventional response: "A religious sect seizing control of a world economic superpower—it was a delusion of fantastic proportions. But for Aum's doomsayers, the coup plan [to follow the apocalyptic struggle] was real, or as real as anything else in their twisted cartoon world." Reader's appraisal was more circumspect: "Aum Shinrikyo produced from within itself, its doctrines, its ways of looking at the world, and its experiences, an internalized sense of reality that, while strikingly different from the external reality of the society around it, contained its own internal logic." In addition, however, Aum sought to be effective in the external world of common-sense reality. After all, Asahara and the members of Aum "believed" what they said to the extent that they acted in order to achieve it. On one occasion, for example, Asahara was reflecting on the inevitability of World War III, which he identified with the biblical Armageddon and which he (and not God, as in the Bible) was charged with bringing about, and remarked: "I stake my religious future on this prediction." Lifton commented on this passage: "We may assume that he was unaware of the irony of that statement. (Who, after all, would be around to affirm his 'religious future'?) But in his own theological terms the statement had a certain logic."[82] Indeed, the logic of this particular idea was compelling, once the premise was accepted.

The crucial event that led Asahara down the road to terrorism was the result of the February 1990 election for the Japanese parliament. Aum ran twenty-five candidates under the banner of Shinri-to, the Supreme Truth Party; they received 1,783 votes, and the self-described prophet was humiliated by his party losing their deposit in every constituency. Moreover, many members of Aum fled from the organization during the course of the campaign. Like a regular politician, Asahara repaired to a retreat on the Okinawan island of Ishigaki. He returned to Tokyo and announced a switch from Mahayana or "Great Vehicle" to Vajrayana or "Diamond Vehicle" Buddhism, which meant that only a few, not all beings, would be saved.[83] At the same time he issued a prediction that

82. Kaplan and Marshall, *Cult at the End of the World*, 156; Reader, *Religious Violence in Contemporary Japan*, 230; Lifton, *Destroying the World to Save It*, 44.

83. Wessinger, *How the Millennium Comes Violently*, chap. 5. See also Reader, "Imagined Persecution," 158–82.

Japan was about to suffer a disaster, which meant in commonsense language that he was about to cause one. He then enlisted Shiva, Nostrodamus, and esoteric tantric texts and practices in his cause and started an intensive search for sarin, botulinum, ebola, and other WMDs, including "surplus" nuclear weapons from the former Soviet Union. In terms of the second reality of Asahara's prophetic vision, the 1990 election was the last chance for the world. Kaplan called this a strategy of "defensive aggression." That is, by its own self-interpretation, Aum did not attack Japan "so as to precipitate a final war. Rather, an apocalyptic war will occur because of the external conspiratorial forces that are intent on destroying Aum."[84]

To common sense, however, it looked as if the Aum organization was used to defend the disordered consciousness of Asahara by destroying the source of his irritation, namely, the world. It was as if Asahara said, "The world will not listen to my prophecies; too bad for the world, for I shall bring disasters upon it. Then they will have to listen." Reader summed up the position of Aum and Asahara after the 1990 election disaster: Aum began on a path of righteousness with a promise of universal salvation but the refusal of the world to heed the new gospel increased the distance between the commonsense world and the salvific world of Aum.

> Its doctrines developed accordingly, sanctifying acts that were committed in order to protect the position and authority of its leader and to safeguard what it saw as its mission of truth. As it followed this path, Aum lost its grasp of external reality and turned inwards into a self-constructed world in which all who remained outside the movement were unworthy while those inside were transformed into sacred warriors who believed that they could kill with impunity and that in so doing, they could save in the spiritual sense those they killed.[85]

He went on to characterize this outcome as "tragic" because the exalted objective, the imaginary fight against evil that would save the world, turned into brutal and indiscriminate murder. It would be more accurate to say that once Aum embarked on the imaginary task of saving the world (in second reality) the killing of ordinary people who refused to be saved at the hands of Asahara (in first reality) became inevitable.

84. Kaplan, "Aum Shinrikyo (1995)," 260; Reader, "Spectres and Shadows," 162.
85. Reader, *Religious Violence in Contemporary Japan*, 248–49.

The pneumopathological substance of Asahara's remarks is self-evident when summarized in the commonsense language of a Reader or a Lifton. Only within the context of Asahara's second reality did the "logic" of his "theological terms" make sense. As with the existence of a dying class of Kulaks or of the altruism of terrorist killing, the spiritual disorder is evident enough to common sense. In the case of Asahara, commonsense reality was overshadowed not only by the *gekiga* comic book imagery favored by the adherents to Aum but also by an idiosyncratic interpretation of the Buddhist doctrine of *poa* or *pho-wa*.

A description of the technique of *poa* begins book 1 of the *Tibetan Book of the Dead*.[86] It is practiced chiefly by a sect of Tibetan Vajrayana Buddhists. According to the Vajrayana tradition, this jealously guarded and secret meditative practice transfers consciousness from the mundane world of existence to a transfigured world of postexistence. The meditation is undertaken with the intention of attaining a higher state of consciousness in the next rebirth. Asahara's version changed the meaning completely. Instead of an individual intentionally undertaking a disciplined, deathbed *poa*-meditation as a step toward nirvana, Aum would impose the benefit whether the individual sought it or not. *Poa* was for Aum not meditative exercise but, within the second reality created by Asahara, became an active, transitive verb. Thus, when Asahara ordered someone to be *poa*-ed, his or her time on earth was already up; by carrying out a death sentence, in the second reality of Aum, the victim would benefit in his next birth. Asahara added another touch: by "letting a person have his *poa*," which is to say, by murdering someone on the orders of Asahara, the world would benefit by the removal of "bad karma," the victim would benefit by gaining access to a higher state of consciousness, and the murderer would benefit by performing the service for the victim and for improving the world.[87] Because anyone could accumulate a great deal of bad karma simply by existing outside the Supreme Truth, namely, Aum Shinrikyo, Asahara was, in fact, announcing a program of large-scale killing.

The first murders began during the winter of 1988–1989 and were suffered initially by members of Aum who perished during "training" or felt remorse for those who did. In November 1989 a lawyer, Tsutsumi

---

86. *Tibetan Book of the Dead*, ed. Evans-Wentz, 85 ff. See also Evans-Wentz, *Tibetan Yoga and Secret Doctrines*, 167 ff., 237 ff.
87. Watanabe, "Religion and Violence in Japan Today," 84–85.

Sakamoto, and his family were *poa*-ed for criticizing Aum in the media.[88] Within the Aum second reality, opposition was *prima facie* evidence of bad karma. Killing altruistically meant that the murdered person would be prevented from accumulating more bad karma and even worse retribution in the next life. Asahara said that to *poa* meant "to transform a person doing bad things." In commonsense language, to *poa* meant to end the possibility of any transformation; to *poa* meant to murder, pure and simple. But for Aum *poa*-ing enhanced the immortality of both the killer and his victim. As Lifton observed, Aum took a step beyond even the Nazi killers: the Nazis "claimed no spiritual benefits for the Jews from being murdered. In Aum, the 'healing' embraced both the perpetrators and their victims: they merged into an all-encompassing immortalization."[89] In fact, however, in commonsense reality only the murderer was transformed: his victim was, in reality, dead, and nothing could be known or said about the consequences for the soul of the victim.

Poa, therefore, was more than a convenient rationalization of murder as a defensive tactic or a means of socializing individuals to the ordinariness of massive killing. Within the second reality created by the pneumopathological consciousness of Asahara and of Aum members, it was also a means to purify the world so that it might be filled with the "supreme truth," the "sacred carefree mind" that Asahara instilled in his followers through "training." This "sacred carefree mind" enabled the members of Aum to *poa* anyone Asahara marked for death. In commonsense language, killing "others," namely, everyone outside Aum who necessarily had not attained a "sacred carefree mind," would enhance the sentiment of immortality within Aum, would enhance their purity, and most of all would enhance their power as the only arbiters of life and death, truth and lie. Asahara's doctrine of *poa* became a recipe for altruistic genocide, and indeed a prelude to altruistic omnicide.

In the description of pneumopathological consciousness provided by Voegelin, emphasis was drawn to the self-assertive and aggressive aspects

---

88. Sakamoto charged that the "initiation of blood" ceremony, which required the initiate to drink Asahara's blood and pay a million yen for the privilege, was fraud and false advertising. Ibid., 89.

89. Lifton, *Destroying the World to Save It*, 67. At about the same time the Ayatolla Khomeini announced a similar doctrine: "if we kill the infidels in order to put a stop to their [corrupting] activities," he said, "we have indeed done them a service," for which, presumably, they should be grateful. Quoted in Taheri, *Holy Terror*, 113.

of an individual who claims an exceptional status, an exemption from the ethical or political constraints of ordinary people. The claims of Asahara and Aum are almost a caricature of the ordinary terrorist. Aum was the first group in history to combine an ultimate exceptionalism with a quest for ultimate weapons that might destroy the world but that somehow would not at the same time destroy them.

In one respect Aum followed a trajectory common to other terrorist groups that combined extreme exceptionalism with a search for extreme weapons. As we noted above, the appeal of WMDs is bound to increase with the transition toward "unlimited goals," which is to say goals for which there exists a world-transcendent element that, through magical operations in a second reality, can be brought within the imaginary power of a projector.[90] As Cameron put it, "On the assumption that terrorist demands and tactics have to be proportionate to one another, just as the scale of the group's objectives has increased, so too must the strategies employed to achieve them."[91] Moreover, within the logic of traditional terrorism, given the limited number of people that can be killed by explosions, if the shock of killing is thought by terrorists to be wearing off, because not enough people are watching, as McVeigh said, then graduation to weapons of mass destruction is a logical next step.

On the other hand, however, it is difficult for common sense to understand how "proportionality" is maintained between WMDs and grandiose transformative goals. Indeed, no goal can be "unlimited" and still remain a goal in any pragmatic sense. "Unlimited goals" can make sense only within the second reality of the imagination. Accordingly, when someone acts in the common world as if it were possible to achieve an "unlimited goal," the aforementioned friction between first and second reality is bound to arise.

In the example of Aum, many commentators have noted the inability of the organization to mount a serious lethal attack. Notwithstanding its many technical and material assets, the Aum scientists and technicians failed to produce sarin sufficiently pure to accomplish what Asahara intended. It has been suggested that one of the reasons for the failure of the biological weapons program was not that the scientists and technicians within Aum were incompetent but that they "seemed hampered by the cult's fickle and irrational leadership and by poor scientific

90. See Gurr and Cole, *New Face of Terrorism*, 251.
91. Cameron, "Multi-track Microproliferation," 297.

judgment and a lack of experience in working with agents such as
B. antracis and botulinum toxin."[92] That Asahara was "fickle" and that
his scientists had limited experience is undoubtedly true. It is also true
that the sarin program "was rife with life-threatening production and
dissemination accidents"[93] and that the judgment and effectiveness of
the scientists and technicians had been compromised by the physically
demanding and mentally destabilizing practices used by Aum to ensure
religious solidarity—sleep deprivation, hallucinogens, poor nutrition,
and so on.[94] It does not follow, however, that if only the leadership of
Aum had been more reasonable, or more careful, or less paranoid, they
then would have been able to carry out a more successfully lethal attack
on the Tokyo subways. The argument that Aum *could not* have been
more prudent and so *could not* have been anything other than a
"fickle," not to say paranoid, organization is as old as political science
and rests upon an equally antique philosophical insight: the realm of
action, power, and pragmatic rationality—what used to be called the
vita activa—is not autonomous. It is an integral part of human existence that, in its entirety, includes the rationality of the moral and spiritual order. It may be true, for example, that Aum "provided every critic
of Japanese society with avenues through which to vent their particular
agendas," and likewise true that Aum's violence was undertaken "to
defend the name and ego of its guru, and to strike out at and punish
those who had challenged him in any way,"[95] but it was equally true that
normal people do not reply to "challenges" with sarin attacks on a general population, many of whom may, indeed, have grievances they wish
to "vent."

Precisely *because of* their pneumopathology, their commitment to the
second reality of Asahara's vision, were the members of Aum incapable
of undertaking long-term pragmatically rational pursuits. In reality,
human beings are not capable of bringing about a spiritual Armageddon; they cannot "force the end," as Asahara sought to do. When spiritual rationality is replaced by a pathology such as afflicted Asahara,
then the pursuit of pragmatic goals will be controlled by irrational or
pathological spiritual aspirations. To put it bluntly: the coordination of

92. Rosenau, "Aum Shinrikyo's Biological Weapons Program," 296.
93. Smithson and Levy, *Ataxia*, 280.
94. Falkenrath, Newman, and Thayer, *America's Achilles' Heel*, 23.
95. Reader, *Religious Violence in Contemporary Japan*, 228, 219.

end and means was possible in the sense that Aum could murder people, but the action of murdering them was senseless because the goal for which the killing was undertaken had no connection to the reality of spiritual or any other kind of order. The spiritual irrationality of Aum, and hence the friction between Aum and Japanese society, was expressed with great clarity in the perverse doctrine of *poa* invented by Asahara and was enacted with equal clarity in the grotesque scene of Asahara's capture by the Japanese police, hiding in a secret room, sitting on a large pile of gold and cash.

In one sense, Aum Shinrikyo kept one foot on the ground of common sense. The organization remained concerned with the safety of the terrorists who carried out the attacks. Aum members were provided with anti-sarin pills as well as quick-reacting antidotes. That is, they were not so completely absorbed in the second reality that they were taken in by their own apocalyptic fantasies: the Tokyo killers wished to survive and kill again. The last step in the logic of pneumopathology was taken, not by Aum and the esoteric and syncretistic theology of omnicidal *poa*, but by spiritually disordered individuals acting within the entirely different religious world of Islam. The example of radical Islam, or jihadist Islam, or Islamism, will illustrate the difficulty of using the language of grievance and alienation, which was certainly part of the appeal of Aum to its membership, to enlist support to transfigure the structure of reality by violent action. It is to that question we now turn.

3 Genealogy of Salafism

The spectacular nature of the Aum attack led to a great deal of exaggerated rhetoric concerning its likely effects. The most obvious consequence lay not in the area of ideological inspiration, except perhaps in Japan, but in the significance that the event occurred. That is, once a large-scale terrorist attack had taken place, especially one that had the potential of being much more serious, the *fact* of such an event was itself important. By 1995, therefore, the Aum attack in Tokyo indicated to the world that a major terrorist event could and likely would sow mass confusion, demoralization, and terror. This is why Hoffman said the Aum attack "marked a historical watershed in terrorist tactics." It really was "a new kind of terrorist threat."[1] For the new terrorists generally, the success of Aum provided yet another reason to undertake further large-scale operations using WMDs if they could lay their hands on them.

Our concern in this study is not the history of modern terrorism but, broadly speaking, the spiritual or religious dimension to it. It is important never to lose sight of the fact that many ordinary individuals, with a great variation of talents and idiosyncrasies, seek and find political, economic, and military expressions to religious experiences. When the heart is sensitive to the things of the world and the mind is perceptive regarding their structure, one look is enough to indicate the misery and injustice as well as the grandeur and joy of human existence: when heart and mind are insensitive and dull, massive events will be required to engender even weak sentiments and modest insights. One person may see in suffering and injustice the essential attributes of humanity and search for meaning and deliverance beyond the world; another may

1. Hoffman, *Inside Terrorism*, 121.

experience the same realities as a flaw, a mistake, a grievance that must be remedied, right here and right now. In such matters the human spirit is free. Of course the freedom of the spirit raises a host of deep and complex questions, but not all of them need to be answered in order to continue the present analysis: it is sufficient to note that the action by Aum changed the context for future terrorist operations.

In the literature dealing with religious terrorism, the traditional sociological distinction between sect, cult, and larger religious organization is secondary, if it is mentioned at all.[2] Most analysts are content to use metaphors such as a "thread" that is said to link a wide range of religious groups, each with its own particular traditions and motivations, but all involving some element of purity and catharsis not unlike the imaginary goals of Aum.[3]

During the 1990s, for example, Sikh terrorists killed upwards of 20,000 people in their quest for Khalistan, the Land of the Pure.[4] White supremacists in the United States and associated "militias" have their own sacred texts such as *The Turner Diaries* that advocate a "racially pure" America in the context of a mythic renewal of the cosmos—a doctrine that apparently motivated Timothy McVeigh to bomb the Alfred P. Murrah Federal Building in Oklahoma City.[5] In 1994, Baruch Goldstein, a member of the Kach movement, emptied three 30-shot magazines into a crowd gathered at the Ibrahim Mosque in Hebron, killing 29 and wounding 150. He claimed he was enacting the role of Mordechai the revenger in the Purim story.[6] He was beaten to death by worshippers at the mosque, and his killing spree was invoked by Islamists as a reason for initiating a campaign of suicide bombing. Other Jewish terrorists had even more grandiose notions: enacting the magical dictum of Rabbi Meir Kahane, that "miracles are made," by blowing up the Dome of the Rock, the third holiest shrine in Islam, some of his followers expected to ignite a holy war between Jews and Muslims, which would compel the intervention of the Jewish Messiah.[7] There are reli-

---

2. See, for example, Laqueur, *The New Terrorists*, 80.

3. Hoffman, "Terrorism and Weapons of Mass Destruction," 47.

4. Hoffman, "Holy Terror," 279.

5. Barkun, "Racist Apocalypse"; Barkun, *Religion and the Racist Right*; Campbell, "The Cult"; Whitsel, "Ideological Mutation and Millennial Belief," 89–106.

6. Ranstorp, "Terrorism in the Name of Religion," 41.

7. Juergensmeyer, *Terror in the Mind of God*, 46 ff.; Benjamin and Simon, *Age of Sacred Terror*, 428 ff.

gious overtones to purifying terrorism in Ireland and in the Balkans, which after all gave the world the euphemism "ethnic cleansing." Among Islamist terrorists the names Hezbollah (Party of God) or Jund al-Haqq (Soldiers of Truth) indicate clearly enough their own religiously purifying purposes. We will see in detail below that "purity" of one sort or another is a recurring theme among Islamist terrorists.[8]

There are major differences between the way that the political implications of Islam have been worked out historically and the political order of liberal, constitutional democracy. It is as important not to ignore those differences as it is to begin from the self-evident consideration that, although Islam broadly considered does not provide a threat to Western liberal democracy, militant jihadist Islam, what we have been calling Islamism, most certainly does. That, quite simply, was the meaning, the significance, and the message of September 11, 2001.[9]

Let us begin to consider this problem with the commonsense observation of Max Weber: "Neither religions nor men are open books. They have been historical rather than logical or even psychological constructions without contradiction. Often they have borne within themselves a series of motives, each of which, if separately and consistently followed through, would have stood in the way of the others or run against them head-on. In religious matters consistency has been the exception and not the rule."[10] With respect to Islam, understood in as wide a sense as possible, we should not expect consistency between the pious traditional Muslim who seeks in his or her religion only to learn how to live in accord with God's will, and the fanatic who is clear that he knows God's will and that God's will demands that he attack the Great Satan by flying airplanes into buildings or by other murderous deeds. Our concern, however, is not with the wide spectrum of Islam and even less with whether Osama bin Laden, for example, has a sound grasp of Islamic spirituality. We are concerned, rather, with the genealogy of Islamism, the Islam of suicidal murderers. To be more precise, we seek to understand the spiritual experience that is expressed in language symbols derived from, or affiliated with, Islam, and how it motivates individuals to commit terrorist acts.

8. Ruthven, *A Fury for God*, 27.
9. See Pipes, *Militant Islam Reaches America*, 3, 245; Hiro, *War without End*, xxx.
10. Weber, "The Social Psychology of the World Religions," 291.

In the first chapter of this book we began by considering the obvious and external aspects of turmoil in the contemporary world. There are sound empirical reasons for beginning with external events because they are visible to all but the willfully blind, regarding whom persuasion is next to impossible. Moreover, as Voegelin observed in *The New Science of Politics,* the existence of a crisis has often been an occasion for "the fundamental problems of political existence in history" to come into focus.[11] Voegelin mentioned the establishment of political science by Plato and Aristotle as marking the Hellenic crisis, the appearance of Augustine's *City of God* as marking the crisis of Rome and Christianity, and Hegel's philosophy of law and history as marking the beginning of the modern Western crisis. There are other crises in other civilizational contexts, including Islam, with equivalent efforts at restoring a sense of order and of principled understanding of the source of order, and we shall consider them below.

A second commonsensical assumption can also be made explicit. In the previous chapter we drew attention to the large number of "neo-new religions" filling the Japanese spiritual landscape and indicated that this spiritual outburst was also an indication of spiritual instability for which cults such as Aum Shinrikyo provided a repose. Looking to the problem of Islamist terrorism, therefore, a similar commonsensical assumption would be that it is one expression of a crisis in the spiritual order of the Islamic community, the umma. In order to analyze this aspect of the problem of terrorism and modernity, it is necessary to make a further distinction, within Islam, between what may be called Islamic history, the paradigmatic story of God's relationship to humanity as experienced within Islam, and the pragmatic history of the society and religious community formed by the Muslim religion. There is also the problem of the historical origin of Islam and the transformation of the originary events into a paradigmatic history. We will discuss some recent analyses of this problem, which is not central to our primary concern, in the appendix to this study. With respect to all of these matters, it may seem preposterous for a non-Muslim, especially one for whom the sacred texts of Islam are available only in translation, to say anything about paradigmatic Islamic history. We do so, indeed, with hesitation: Ajami is no doubt correct to say that "it has been the besetting sin—

11. Voegelin, *The New Science of Politics,* 88.

and poverty—of a good deal of writing on the Arab world that it is done by many who have no mastery of Arabic. This has always seemed odd to me: to presume so much without hearing a people through their own words."[12] On the other hand, because the distinction between pragmatic and paradigmatic history is central to political science, we proceed in spite of this philological defect.

For purposes of the present analysis, we assume that, for Muslims, Islam is the religion of God, as for Jews and Christians are Judaism and Christianity. To put it the other way around, we begin from the assumption that God reveals Himself, that the fact of revelation is its content, as Voegelin once put it, and that the great religions of the world, which include the "Abrahamic" religions, Judaism, Christianity, and Islam, are human responses to those appearances of the divine.[13] Our interest, therefore, is in the human response, or, more precisely, in the experience and its symbolization. In principle, the question of the reality of God independent of the experience and symbolization of God is, from the standpoint of political science, a non-issue. As a merely human science, political science is capable of analyzing the origins and the structure of the several paradigmatic religious stories and of examining the implications of them for pragmatic politics, and even of pointing to equivalent meanings, symbols, and experiences. That is a sufficiently large task so that a refusal to judge the validity or veracity of the many varieties of religious experience is not so much an evasion of responsibility as an impossibility. To be more precise: if the analysis of a religious discourse is adequate to the experience expressed through it, the problem of judging does not arise. Religious experiences are not like swimsuit competitions in a beauty contest.

For a Muslim, then, to say that Islam is the religion of God means that Islamic history did not begin sometime in the seventh century of the common era but with the creation of the world or even before that event—and Muslim theologians, like other people, have debated the interesting question of "the beginning," or of the sense of the message of the Koran being "eternal." This is a question to which we shall return below because it has remained an issue in the history of the Muslim community. For the present, however, within the context of Islamic

---

12. Ajami, *Dream Palace of the Arabs*, xix.

13. Voegelin, *The New Science of Politics*, 151. See also Niebuhr, *The Meaning of Revelation*, esp. chaps. 3 and 4.

history, when God created the world, He prescribed both how natural events would take place and He declared there is a right way to live, even if humans disregard His message. Moreover, according to Islamic history, God has informed humanity on a number of occasions what that right way is, and starting with the first prophet or messenger from God, namely, Adam, humans have proved to be disobedient. Adam was followed by other prophets—Abraham, Moses, and Jesus in particular— and by other failures. According to Islamic history, then, Abraham was not a Jew and Jesus was not a Christian; both were Muslims.

Now, if Islamic history, the story of God's message and God's messengers, were simply a human story, that is, if it were simply a story of the human response to God, then the pattern of receiving and then abandoning God's message would have continued until the end of time. But God is also part of the story, and indeed is the center of the story. Because His compassion and mercy are infinite, he delivered a final and clear message through the angel Gabriel, an ethereal messenger, to a human one, the prophet Muhammad. Gabriel spoke the message in the language of Muhammad, so there could be no ambiguity or misunderstanding, and the Prophet created a community that faithfully preserved it and carried it to humanity. "Thus," writes Wilfred Cantwell Smith, "a new era in human history was born."[14] Moreover, year one of the Islamic era began not with the birthday of Muhammad, nor with his conversation with Gabriel, but with the *hijra*, the flight or exodus from Mecca to Medina prior to the triumphant return of the new community from exile. One may say, therefore, that the start of the paradigmatic Islamic era is marked by a pragmatic theo-political event. To be more precise, such is the traditional account of the origin of Islam. Muslim believers take it simply as truth; scholars of Islam take it as an account, a theological account, to be sure, but one that has a history. For political science, in other words, the beginning of what both conventional scholars and pious believers call a new era in human history is the point where the internal spiritual reality within which Muslims experience a personal relationship with God, which we have called paradigmatic Islamic history, touches the generally accessible pragmatic history of Islam, and of the Muslim community, which is informed by Islamic history. We will call this complex for simplicity, and without prejudice regarding its

14. Smith, *Islam in Modern History*, 15. See also Hodgson, *The Venture of Islam;* Cook, *Muhammad;* Rippin, *Muslims.*

veracity, the Islamic vulgate.[15] It can be summarized as follows: following the *hijra*, the Prophet defeated his own tribe in battle and thereby created the umma, humanity *in statu nascendi* obedient to God. The theological symbolism, both in terms of the Muslim vulgate and as a reworking of the exodus symbolism of the Bible, is therefore subtle and complex.

The most obvious characteristic of the early history of the Islamic community was its political success. Unlike Christianity, which penetrated an already existing political order, imperial Rome, Islam combined temporal and spiritual activity in a single act of imperial-religious founding. As Smith observed: "The success was comprehensive as well as striking. As we have said, the enterprise gained not only power but greatness. In addition to quickly attaining political and economic mastery, Muslim society carried forward into new accomplishments both art and science. Its armies won battles, its decrees were obeyed, its letters of credit were honoured, its architecture was magnificent, its poetry charming, its scholarship imposing, its mathematics bold, its technology effective." Moreover, it proved difficult and perhaps impossible for one participating in Islamic history, that is, the pious Muslim, to distinguish the political from the religious dimensions. As Fazlur Rahman put it, Muhammad "was duty-bound to succeed."[16] His success, for the community, was understood to be an intrinsic aspect of Islam, an element of Islamic history, proof, as it were, of God's favor. The victories of the Prophet were understood to be the victories of God. The difference between Islam and Christianity on this issue is fundamental. It is central as well for the present analysis.

According to both the pious and the traditional scholarly accounts, that is, according to the Islamic vulgate, Muhammad returned to Mecca to bring God's message to the city and to bring the city to submit to God's message. That was his "duty to succeed." Mecca was a religious center and would be instrumental in spreading God's message abroad. At the same time, however, there always existed the temptation of compromising God's message. This option, however, was strongly rejected, not least of all because Gabriel warned Muhammad against it.

15. The contemporary scholarship concerned with the historical origins of the Islamic vulgate is discussed briefly in the appendix to this study. For the present it is sufficient to accept this account, as the lawyers say, "without prejudice."

16. Smith, *Islam in Modern History*, 28; Rahman, *Islam*, 16.

Was it not the time to go ahead? Who will say it was not? And yet it is exactly at this point that the Prophet has been most misunderstood, especially by Western critics. They say they fail to understand the Prophet at this juncture: how can a preacher become pugnacious? We must confess we fail to understand this failure, prejudice apart, except on the hypotheses that so addicted are these writers to pathetic tales of sorrow, failure, frustration and crucifixion that the very idea of success in this sphere seems to them abhorrent.[17]

Notwithstanding his somewhat aggressive language, Rahman made an important point. In contrast with Islam, in this respect, Christianity, to use Smith's phrase, is "supremely a religion of adversity... at its best in times of distress." Perhaps more to the point, at least for political science, because Christianity was not concerned initially with founding a political order, from the beginning the allegiance of Christians has been divided, as Jesus said, between the things that are Caesar's and the things that are God's (Matt. 22:21), a message Augustine symbolized in terms of a dual citizenship in the earthly and in the heavenly city. One implication is that the ordinary concerns of diet and hygiene or of politics are not, for Christians, of great spiritual significance. When Christians have acceded to seats of power, this has not typically been regarded as proof of the truth of Christianity, and the end of any particular earthly city—the sack of Rome in 410 by Alaric, for example—has not typically been understood as a religious catastrophe so much as a political disaster—in 410, a disaster for the Romans, not all of whom were Christians. Not so with Islam. In the words of Bernard Lewis, "In Islam there was no such painful choice [between God and Caesar]. In the universal Islamic polity, as conceived by Muslims, there is no Caesar but only God."[18] In principle the duty of success extended to the whole of humanity. At the center of the theological-political unity was the law, the Sharia, which unified an Islamic civilization that, again in principle, was ecumenic. At the same time, the law unified in the life of each individual Muslim what to a Christian would seem both the trivial and ordinary matters of daily life as well as the most profound aspects of faith.

The success in actually spreading God's message to humanity seemed to confirm the meaning of Islamic history in the course of events, namely, the history of Islamic society and of the Muslim religion. That is,

17. Rahman, *Islam*, 19.
18. Smith, *Islam in Modern History*, 31; Lewis, *Crisis of Islam*, 6–7.

the gap between paradigmatic and pragmatic history or between Augustine's two cities seemed to be closing and perhaps even to be closed. For Muslims, God had spoken and told human beings how to live; those who submitted to God's will and lived the way God said were visibly blessed. The pragmatic triumphs of the Muslim armies were understood as the confirmation and triumph of paradigmatic Islamic history. Pragmatic events thus confirmed a symbolic meaning and then came to be understood as having themselves acquired a symbolic meaning. This is a fascinating story because, as Smith bluntly put the issue, "history, however, moves," which is a very brief way of dealing with a highly complex issue in what is conventionally called philosophy of history.[19]

The political dimension of the problem that concerns us came into view early in the history of Islam for the most basic of reasons: there was no obvious and self-evident way to organize the community founded by the Prophet. All Muslims agreed that God had chosen Muhammad, but who would choose his successor? When the Prophet died in 632, prior to the major conquests, the issue remained outstanding. The Companions chose the first leader (imam) and deputy (caliph) from his tribe, the Quraysh. During the reign of the third successor, Uthman (646–656), an internal division developed over the appropriate share of the spoils of war; Uthman was assassinated and was succeeded by the cousin of Muhammad, Ali. The followers of Uthman and Ali fought the "battle of the camel" in 656 near Basra, which Ali won; this was followed by the battle of Siffin the following year, after which one of Uthman's governors, Muawiya, obtained a truce with Ali through negotiation.

Some of Ali's followers objected to making an agreement with Muawiya on the grounds that human beings could not bargain over who would be caliph because the choice was for God, not humans, to make. These men, called Khariji, or "seceders," by Ali loyalists, elected their own imam, and one of them succeeded in assassinating Ali. Ali's son then acknowledged that Muawiya was caliph and the Umayyad Caliphate, and with it a kind of political unity, was established.[20] From this first conflict over who should lead the community and how he should be chosen are derived, in the vulgate version, the main divisions of contemporary Islam, between Sunni and Shia, and several other minor sects. The Sunnis, in particular, would later look back to the first four "rightly guided"

19. Smith, *Islam in Modern History*, 32.
20. See Madelung, *The Succession to Muhammad*.

(rashidun) caliphs as models of political rule; the Shiites, likewise, saw Ali as the sole legitimate successor to the Prophet, followed by his son Hussein and the successors to Hussein. Even more important for present purposes, the Umayyads effected a reconciliation so far as possible between the followers of Ali and the followers of Uthman and generally promoted tolerance and inclusiveness.[21] In contrast, the Kharijites emphasized the importance of religious purity, which they combined with an enhanced emphasis on jihad to be waged against all who disagreed with them. The combination of purity and military violence recurred in later Muslim thought—as, indeed, the combination is not unknown in other cultural orders.

Even before the expansion of Islam, therefore, there remained some important and unanswered political questions, along with additional issues about which we need only offer a few hints in order to indicate the outline of the problem. To see the full amplitude of the issue involved in undertaking what was provisionally termed closing the gap between the earthly city and the City of God, it would be necessary to begin with the original experience of what is currently termed history, namely, the Israelite covenant. It would then be necessary to summarize three millennia of defections, returns, reforms, restorations, renaissances, revisions, insights, and losses because, as Voegelin said, "we are still living in the historical present of the covenant."[22] This is a tall order, indeed. Fortunately, to see the bearing of this question on Islamic history it may be sufficient to sketch the experiential dynamics, or the dramatic action of the Israelite covenant alone. Again we follow Voegelin's account.

According to Voegelin, the experience expressed in Exodus told the story of the revelation of God from beyond the cosmos into the cosmos. This intrusion from a cosmic-transcendent beyond, and the response to it by Moses and then by the Israelites, constituted the Israelites as a people chosen by God to live according to his law presented to them as a covenant. The alternative, in the biblical narrative, was to remain in Egypt, which was understood by the Israelites to be a house of bondage and even of death, the Sheol. For the Egyptians, as for the other inhabitants of the empires of the ancient Near East, social order was maintained not by living in accord with a covenant but by living in accord with the rhythms of the cosmos—diurnal changes, seasonal changes,

---

21. See Black, *History of Islamic Political Thought*, 18 ff.
22. Voegelin, *Israel and Revelation*, 207.

even the precession of the equinoxes were all understood to be expressions of cosmic rhythms to which society had to attune itself. Public rituals typically integrated the divine cosmic order with social order.

The experience of the covenant obviously does not abolish the cosmic order; the sun still rises in the east. Rather, there is a change in the self-understanding, or in what Voegelin occasionally calls the inner form, of the society that responds to the revelation. Thus did Voegelin describe Egyptian society as existing in cosmological form and Israelite society as existing in historical form. The continued existence of Israel in historical form entailed maintaining experiential continuity with the three elements that constituted the dramatic action of the covenant. First, God promised to Moses that he would make Israel his own *(segullah)* among the peoples, a kingdom of priests *(mamlekheth kohanim)*, and a holy nation *(goy qadosh)*, provided that the people hear his voice and abide by the covenant. Second, when the people accepted God's message, they became "His people," the people chosen by God (Exodus 19). Third, the terms of the covenant were set forth in the Decalogue, which thus became the fundamental law. The three moments constitute a single dramatic whole: the people who received the message from Moses could not disobey the Ten Commandments without at the same time breaking the covenant; the people could not break the covenant without repudiating their status as chosen by God; nor could they refuse to be a holy nation without rebelling against the will of God.

Of particular importance to the present analysis is that the response of the Israelites to the revelation to Moses led the Israelite historiographers to interpret the past of the Israelite people as a series of successes and failures not with respect to the rhythms of the cosmos but with respect to their faithfulness to the covenant. Voegelin termed this change in consciousness *differentiation*. The aspect to be emphasized for our purposes, however, is its precariousness and uncertainty.

The events of the Exodus from Egypt, the dwelling at Kadesh, and the conquest of Canaan, the Promised Land, became infused with meaning because they were animated by a new form of consciousness. Egypt became the spiritual House of the Dead, the Sheol, and Moses led the children of Israel out of Egypt into the Desert. According to Voegelin's interpretations of this well-known biblical story:

> Through the illumination by the spirit [i.e., the revelation to Moses] the house of institutional bondage became a house of spiritual death.

Egypt was the realm of the dead, the Sheol, in more than one sense. From death and its cult man had to wrest the life of the spirit. And this adventure was hazardous, for the exodus from Sheol at first led nowhere but into the desert of indecision, between the equally unpalatable forms of nomad existence and life in a high civilization. Hence, to Sheol and Exodus must be added the Desert as the symbol of the historical impasse. It was not a specific but the eternal impasse of historical existence in the "world," that is, in the cosmos in which empires rise and fall with no more meaning than a tree growing and dying, as waves in the stream of eternal recurrence. By attunement with cosmic order the fugitives from the house of bondage could not find the life that they sought. When the spirit bloweth, society in cosmological form becomes Sheol, the realm of death; but when we undertake the exodus and wander into the world, in order to found a new society elsewhere, we discover the world as the desert. The flight leads nowhere, until we stop in order to find our bearings beyond the world. When the world has become desert, man is at last in the solitude in which he can hear thunderingly the voice of the spirit that with its urgent whispering has already driven and rescued him from Sheol. In the desert God spoke to the leader and his tribes; in the desert, by listening to the voice, by accepting its offer, and by submitting to its command, they at last reached life and became the people chosen by God.[23]

The precariousness of historical existence is suitably expressed by the uncertainty of life in the desert, the only place where to Israelite consciousness the voice of God was audible.

There is another kind of precariousness as well: even though they were a people chosen by God, a holy nation, and so on, the Israelites were, like every other people, compelled to live in the common world.[24] Voegelin used the term *derailment* to describe the merging of the goal beyond the history with historically attainable goals. "It found its expression," he said,

in the symbol of Canaan, the land of promise. The symbol was ambiguous because, in the spiritual sense, Israel had reached the promised land when it had wandered from the cosmological Sheol to the

23. Ibid., 153.
24. It should, perhaps, be reiterated that this account of Israelite self-interpretation, like the Muslim vulgate discussed above, is based on scripture, on a sacred story, and not on, say, archaeology.

mamlakah, the royal domain, the Kingdom of God. Pragmatically, however, the exodus from bondage was continued into the conquest of Canaan by rather worldly means; further, to a Solomonic kingdom with the very institutional forms of Egypt or Babylon; and, finally, to political disaster and destruction that befell Israel like any other people in history. . . . The kingdom of God lives in men who live in the world, but it is not of this world. The ambiguity of Canaan has ever since affected the structure not of Israelite history only but of the course of history in general.[25]

The complex of issues surrounding the revelation of God to Moses and the response to his message to the people, briefly sketched here, recurs in a recognizably equivalent way with the revelation of God to Muhammad. It is repeated as well in the history of Islam as well as of Western Christianity, and indeed in "the course of history in general."

Before proceeding with the analysis of the Islamic case, however, let us trace the Israelite issues one step further. When history is understood as the internal form of a society oriented toward the will of God, the actions of its members will be experienced as fulfillment or defection in a historical present. Moreover, the experience of existing in the present under God will tend to radiate into the past and over societies that did not understand themselves as "historical" in this sense, as well as into a future where the expectations of the present will be fulfilled. This means that history as a realm of meaning tends to expand to include the whole of humanity, from the creation of the world until the end of days. We noted this process as being already at work in Islamic history, which absorbed Moses and Jesus into the story as Muslim prophets.

The expansiveness of the internal historical form leads to a number of complex theoretical issues concerning the ontological status of the "humanity" that enacts this history (or to whom it happens): who is included? who is not? does humanity exist before it is conscious of itself as humanity? what is its origin? what is its end? what is the historically "moving" present between these two termini? Perhaps most interesting for the present analysis: what are the changes to the meaning of the term *history* when the original animating experience, symbolized as existence under God, is lost or forgotten or eclipsed? That is, like all symbols, the meaning initially conveyed can evaporate and may be replaced with experiences that have nothing to do with that mode of existence sym-

25. Voegelin, *Israel and Revelation,* 154.

bolized, for example, as existence under God.[26] On the occasion of the revelation of God to Moses and the instructions given by God through Moses to His people, the political result was the creation of a specific community the self-understanding of which was radically unlike those of its neighbors, even though it was compelled to coexist with them. When the original meaning has been lost, the stage is set for a spiritual crisis, a search to recover the lost experiences or to restate or resymbolize them in a language more meaningful than currently is available to the community.

In particular, the implications of God's revelation to Moses have reverberated into the present. On the one hand, the revelation of God to Moses altered the structure of the consciousness of the Israelites: they saw themselves as a people chosen by God, and not, for instance, as Pharaoh's people. On the other hand, the traumatic stress of an unaccommodating pragmatic environment "sealed the meaning of the event ineluctably with its concrete, circumstantial features."[27] As a result, the universalist implications of the divine revelation tended to be overwhelmed by highly particularist and increasingly literalist notions. Thus the exodus from Egypt became identified with a final exodus from the Sheol, and the Kingdom of God was increasingly identified with the geographic territory of Canaan.

Such a "derailment" carried with it another kind of uncertainty: the Israelite invasion of Canaan was not a smashing success, and the Philistines clearly were a serious threat to the continued existence of Israelite political power. By the time of King Saul, the better-organized Philistines had the upper hand and the loose coalition of the Israelite tribes was on the verge of being wiped out.[28] The response to this challenge, namely, the creation of a kingdom in place of the tribal confederation, was an effective organizational response and led eventually to the successful conclusion of the Philistine wars. Thus the creation of the community substance with God's revelation to Moses was followed by the organization of the community as a victorious pragmatic historical actor, a power organization about which a conventional history could be written, at least so long as it continued to exist.

26. Voegelin analyzed many of these problems in his later work. See in particular *The Ecumenic Age.*

27. Voegelin, *Israel and Revelation,* 207–8.

28. Malamat, "The Struggle against the Philistines," and Tadmor, "The United Monarchy."

The continued existence of the kingdom, however, was itself a double-edged problem. On the one hand, as soon as it came into being, it was obvious that the social structure that sustained the kingdom had nothing to do with the meaning of the covenant, let alone with its fulfillment. It was clear to the prophets that the people no longer heard or even listened to the voice of God, and the Decalogue, likewise, had turned into a set of regulations requiring legal or cultic conformity, as if it were a commercial contract akin to a promise to purchase hog bellies at an agreed upon price at a specified future date. But if it were such a legal document, as it was understood more or less widely to be, and if the covenant was no longer kept by the people, the question was bound to arise as to whether God was still bound by His promise: was Israel still His chosen people? The absurdity of the question is obvious because the covenant was not a futures contract. The failure of the Israelites to keep the covenant did not mean that God had deceived the people. Even less had He deceived Himself regarding the ability of the Israelites to hold up their end of the deal. Rather the covenant remained a symbol expressing the insight that the cosmic-transcendent God was the source of order. That insight of "differentiated" consciousness remained true, which is to say, it accurately accounted for the structure of reality, whether or not human beings agreed or disagreed, attended to it or ignored it—or, in the language of the Bible, whether they kept the covenant or not.

The second edge of the problem was just as sharp: granted that Israel had badly misbehaved—because that is what motivated the prophetic recall of the Israelites to abide by the terms of the covenant—granted, that is, in the language of the Bible, that the Israelites ignored the revelation of God, that they did not wish to be chosen by God to be His priests or His "aides,"[29] and at the same time that they were on the verge of being annihilated by an empire that was, if anything, even worse than they, what then? What did it mean that God would abandon or ignore His people and permit them to be destroyed by their enemies? The political answer to these poignant questions is that, by raising them and by formulating their resistance to the pragmatic kingdoms of Israel and Judea, the prophets gave expression, perhaps for the first time, to the brutal clash between the "divinely willed and humanly realized order of history." Eventually, when the Israelite kingdoms were destroyed, in 721

29. Buber, *Moses*, 182 ff.

and 586, the gap between the pragmatic course of political life and the paradigmatic Israelite history, namely, faithfulness to God's instructions revealed to Moses, could serve as an explanation for the pragmatic catastrophe. On the one hand, "the present under God had become a suicidal impasse when it was conceived as the institution of a small people in opposition to empires." But on the other, whatever happened pragmatically to the actual Israelites, it remained true that the divinely revealed order is unquestionably the order of history: human beings cannot undo what God wills. In short, what we have called the double-edged problem, and Voegelin described as "the relationship between the life of the spirit and life in the world," remains "unresolved." Moreover, it is unresolved in principle, because it expressed the meaning of God's revelation to Moses.

Following the catastrophic blows to the collective existence of the Israelite community, the prophets recovered, or at least struggled with, the meaning of God's message. They "knew" that God did not proceed through trial and error, so Israel must still be a holy nation chosen by Him. They also "knew" that the last kingdom of Israel was about to disappear from the face of the earth. Accordingly, the prophetic utterances evoked both the terrible day of the Lord, in order to induce a change of heart so as to avoid punishment, and the day of salvation that would follow the change of heart. The options were not to be understood as information about the future but as expressions of vividly existential options available in the present. The two kinds of prophecies were not historical alternatives so much as "the one symbolism by which the prophets articulated their experience of the conflict between divine order and human realization, of the mystery that God suffers human rebellion against his foreknown order in the distention of historical time."

The issue of prophecy thus raises a central problem in philosophy of history. We quoted Voegelin above on the brutal clash between the "divinely willed and humanly realized order of history." The distinction between the two is ontological: to begin with, there would be no chosen people, no defection from the Decalogue, no suspension between condemnation and salvation without God who knows His people and the prophet who "knows" God's purposes. Existence in historical form necessarily implies a cosmic-transcendent God who nevertheless undertook on a specific historical occasion to reveal Himself—to Moses, for example, or to one of the later prophets. As noted above, the people of Israel existed in historical continuity with the revelation of God to Moses, and even though the prophets could anticipate the historical catastrophe that would befall the empirical society around them, sustained by Israelite power and of which they were a part, there could be no doubting the meaning of the original message. "History," Voegelin said, "once it has become ontologically real through revelation, carries with it the irreversible direction from compact existence in cosmological form toward the Kingdom of God." That is to say, history meant the order of being or the structure of reality as it had become visible through revelation. Once the cosmic-transcendent God had revealed himself, there was simply no return to the cosmic-divine order, notwithstanding the imaginary and pneumopathological efforts undertaken to reverse the insights of revelation or of "differentiated" consciousness.[30]

Again considered from the perspective of political science, the destruction of the Israelite kingdoms presented a serious spiritual crisis with no obvious resolution. The victories of Cyrus and the exile to Babylon certainly presented difficulties to a people who understood they had been chosen by God and who expected that God's choice entailed some kind of assurance, if not of prosperity, then at least of continued existence. One response can be found in the text of Isaiah 40–55, conventionally called "Deutero-Isaiah." Here, to follow Voegelin's formulation, one finds a further "differentiation" from the Mosaic historical consciousness that had become institutionalized as the kingdoms, which was itself a consequence of the "mortgage" of Canaan. Voegelin used the term *Exodus of Israel from itself* to conceptualize this experience.

The meaning of this new term refers to a specific complex of historical experiences. So long as the Israelite kingdoms, or, beyond them, the great cosmological empires of Assyria, Lydia, and Babylon, lasted, it was relatively easy to pay the spiritual aspect of the "mortgage" by interpreting the covenant as a legal document and interpreting the political history of Israel as a reward or punishment for more or less faithfully keeping to the bargain. Even if the Israelite kingdoms ran into political troubles, the surrounding empires seemed stable enough. But when,

---

30. Voegelin, *Israel and Revelation*, 514, 406, 227, 516–18. Voegelin referred to the structure of consciousness prior to "differentiation" as existing in a "compact" mode. There are degrees of compactness and differentiation, of course, but the direction of articulation goes in one direction only: from compactness to differentiation. The effort of a "re-compacting" consciousness is invariably accompanied by indices of irrationality. This becomes a major problem in developing a comprehensive account of modernity.

during the course of a century, they had *all* disappeared, there emerged to the prophet the insight that, beyond the rise and fall of empire, only "the word of our God shall stand forever" (Is. 40:8). Moreover, since the power of the Israelites had perished as thoroughly as the more militarily effective empires, the people chosen by God "has to emigrate from its own concrete order just as the empire peoples had to emigrate from theirs."[31] The "concrete order" of the Israelites had been, precisely, the people chosen by God; with Deutero-Isaiah, however, the new Israel has become the light to the nations (42:6) and the servant of God (49:6)—symbols with a much lighter worldly mortgage than that of the chosen people.

There are other changes in Deutero-Isaiah as well. First, the empirical society of Israel has shrunken to the soul of the prophet. Second, the "exodus of Israel from itself" has already occurred, also in the soul of the prophet—for otherwise he never could have written what he did. And third, yet another impasse has come into the differentiated prophetic consciousness: if *no* empire or kingdom can institutionalize a life of righteousness before the Lord, if, indeed, the task of the new Israel, namely, the prophet who has gained this insight, is to bring this message to the world, then what has become of political order? Is the heretofore autonomous order of the world, that is, of kingdoms and powers and empires, reduced to hearing and then rejecting the prophetic word? Has it no more purpose than to inflict the suffering that somehow is related to the prophetic insight?

To these historically recurring questions, no simple answer can be given. A servant, indeed, a suffering servant (Isaiah 53) has a difficult missionary task ahead if even his fellow Israelites understand and hear his call to be a light to the nations. It may well be possible for an isolated individual or for a small community to enact the destiny of the servant of the Lord as being representative of Israel. But for those to whom the role of suffering servant held no appeal—as perhaps, on occasion, it was rejected by Isaiah himself—there seemed to be an alternative: God might decide to change the world, which was so recalcitrant and so reluctant to hear the word of God, all on His own. Voegelin introduced the term *metastasis* to describe this imaginary transfiguration of the structure of reality. "The constitution of being is what it is," Voegelin wrote, "and cannot be affected by human fancies. Hence, the metastatic denial of the

31. Ibid., 545 ff., 561, 506–8.

order of mundane existence is neither a true proposition in philosophy, nor a program of action that could be executed." It was simply an act of imagination undertaken in response to the experience of a reality that had become unbearable. For the imagination, relief would come with the abolition of the structure of reality, or in commonsensical language, by a miracle.

In keeping with the centrality of the historical form of Israelite symbolization, Voegelin classified these metastatic activities in terms of whether the imaginary acts of divine grace that were compelled by humans, or of the direct prophetic invocations of miracles, would take place in the future, the present, or the past. Less important than the choice of an eschatological, a mythical, or a historiographic fantasy is the common element of irrationality, or rather, of pneumopathology: the perversion of the experience of faith into an instrument of pragmatic political action. "This metastatic component," Voegelin observed, "became so predominant in the complex phenomenon of prophetism that in late Judaism it created its specific symbolic form in the apocalyptic literature." Finally, it is worth pointing out, the apocalyptic form was absorbed into Christianity and a host of gnostic and antinomian heresies, sectarian movements, and political ideologies.

Before returning to the question of Islamic history, there is one final issue about which it is important to be clear. There is a magical component to metastatic faith. More bluntly, demanding that God perform a miracle or alter the structure of reality does not work. The metastatic faith of the prophets cannot be fulfilled by any pragmatic organization, an insight made abundantly clear in Deutero-Isaiah. For metastatic prophets, the only thing to do is sit down and wait for the miracle to take place, from which experience arises the cry, "How long, O Lord? How long?" Prophets die waiting; generations of their disciples may die waiting as well. One might anticipate that eventually, after several generations died awaiting a metastatic transformation, someone would undertake a close and critical examination of what had become an article of faith. On the other hand, once the agency for the miracle is transferred from God to human beings, there is no reason to expect any end to it at all: futuristic dreams practically by definition have an indefinite shelf-life.

We have undertaken this analysis of Israelite problems because many of the issues raised by this first "Abrahamic" religious experience recur in Christianity and in Islam. What we have called the precariousness of God's revelation could hardly admit of any other outcome: the compromises of the Caliphate and the formular purity of the Kharijites look like two sides of the same coin.[32] Returning, then, to the history of Islam, it is clear from the vulgate account that Muhammad fulfilled his duty to succeed, at least in the sense that expanding Islamic power in the hands of his successors was able to encroach successfully upon the neighboring Byzantine Empire and conquer the Sassanid entirely. Modeled on its neighbors, the new religion combined conquest and spiritual apostolate, church and empire, to use contemporary Western language.

As noted above, Muhammad was the last messenger of God (Koran, 33:40) and the last apostle to the world (Koran, 7:157–58). Moreover, his mission was to enact the struggle between truth and falsehood through force of arms (Koran, 21:18, 9:29). If the nonbelievers refuse to abandon their ways, they will be dealt with appropriately until all the world submits (Koran, 8:40–41). We will have occasion to consider in detail the problem of jihad below; it should be clear from the outset, however, that the duty to succeed implied the duty to fight unbelievers and idolaters throughout all the world. The mood, to say the least, is far removed from that of the suffering servant who brings the word of God to an unreceptive world, like a light into darkness. The reason seems to be as much cultural as historical. "The right to conquer and plunder," observed Black, "was carried straight over from pre-Islamic nomadic tradition into Islam."[33] That is, from the outset, Islam was not simply a "re-compacting" of Israelite or Christian experience, notwithstanding the fact that it appeared to Christians, for example, as a heretical retrogression. It was, in addition, a "differentiation" in its own right, however Christians (or Jews or Buddhists, for that matter) might judge it from within their own experience.

Whatever the origin of the duty to succeed, the Prophet was not alone in having one. So, for example, did the Mongols, who in 1258 destroyed Baghdad and killed the last Abbasid Caliph, thus ending what is conventionally called the classic period in Islamic history.[34] The rules of engagement for the Mongol armies were even more brutal than those

---

32. Voegelin has discussed the Christian version of this issue in *The New Science of Politics,* chap. 4, esp. 187 ff., and in "The People of God," 131–214.

33. Black, *History of Islamic Political Thought,* 12; see also Crone, *Meccan Trade and the Rise of Islam,* 245.

34. See Voegelin's analysis of Mongol constitutional law, "The Mongol Orders of Submission to European Powers, 1245–1255," 76–125, and the analysis in Cooper, *Eric Voegelin and the Foundations of Modern Political Science,* 252–84.

of the Arabs: collective destruction was the consequence of resistance or insubordination, which on occasion might be literally enforced, and sometimes no living thing at all, no cat or dog, let alone human being, might be left to mark their passing or mourn the dead. More specifically, Hulagu, nephew of Genghis Khan, destroyed the dikes and irrigation system surrounding Baghdad, destroyed the mosques and libraries, the palaces and academies of the great city and then put it to the torch. Even so, estimates of nearly a million dead are greatly exaggerated, since the population of the city was much below its former greatness, and the story of the ceremonial trampling of the caliph and his sons beneath the hooves of the Mongol ponies is probably a literary trope rather than an event.

One response to this first great crisis of the established Islamic world was greater emphasis on a more mystic interpretation of Islam, which by about 1200 had crystalized as the "orders" or "brotherhoods" of Sufism. The great Sufi poet Rumi wrote his poem *Masnavi* shortly after the Mongols destroyed Baghdad, much as Augustine wrote *The City of God* following Alaric's conquest of Rome.[35] A second, and equally important, response was to convert the conquerors, which in turn led to a renewal of conquest and eventually to the relative stability of empire. A third response, of great importance for later Islamic political thought and especially for the Islamists of the twentieth century, and for them akin to a restoration of the Kharijites of the seventh, was formulated by Ibn Taymiyya (1263–1328).[36] Moreover, since Ibn Taymiyya lived in Mamluk Egypt-Syria, which defended itself successfully against the Mongols, his response also expressed a distinct Islamic alternative informed by a self-confidence that came from resistance to the Mongols.

The foundation of Islamic political thought was the religious jurisprudence based upon the Koran, collections of reported sayings and deeds of the Prophet and his Companions, and descriptions of his personality, conventionally called the Hadith. Together they conditioned the development of the law, Sharia, and the tradition, Sunna. Initially the laws of Islam applied only to Muslims living within a given territory, and their chief purpose was to teach human beings how to live in harmony

35. Rumi, *Tales from the Masnavi.*
36. In his testimony regarding the 1998 embassy bombings in east Africa, Jamal Ahmad al-Fadl, a former Al Qaeda member turned FBI informant, recounted how Abu Hajer, a senior member of Al Qaeda, instructed al-Fadl's group on ibn Taymiyya's teaching. See Benjamin and Simon, *Age of Sacred Terror,* 41–42.

with God's will. "Justice," wrote Black, "was defined independently of the political rulers or state authority. . . . This undermined the project of monarchical authority and world government for the House of Islam."[37] It also provided those who studied the texts, the ulama, with their own networks of authority outside the imperial political organizations.

One of the intellectual and spiritual tensions in the West is conventionally described as between faith and reason. Voegelin's contrast between noetic and pneumatic theophanies[38] is theoretically a more precise but clearly an equivalent version of the Platonic distinction of *mythos* and *logos,* as well as the reconciliation of the two in the philosopher's myth. One can find an analogous reconciliation between philosophy and Christian mysticism in Saint Thomas Aquinas. Within the Islamic world a somewhat different intellectual path was taken.

Between the eighth and eleventh centuries, practitioners of philosophy, the *falasifa,* introduced new political ideas, borrowed chiefly from Greek antiquity. The significance of the *faylasuf* is disputed. According to Black, "Philosophy was not allowed to question seriously the tenets of Islam," nor did Muslim philosophy entail the systematic investigation of nature or ethics. According to Leaman, the subject matter investigated in the West by philosophy had already been dealt with by theology and by jurisprudence. Likewise, Voegelin noted that philosophy in the Islamic world amounted to "a religion for an intellectual elite" informed by the high culture of the conquered societies of Syria, Persia, and Egypt, a culture that was alien to the "fundamentalism" of "Islamic orthodoxy, relying on a literal acceptance of the Koran." By this account, the partial or perhaps more than partial incompatibility of the *faylasuf* with Islam did not at first become apparent "because the content of philosophy was on the whole beyond the range of an undeveloped creed that did not argue." Not until Averroës (1126–1198) was the issue treated systematically with the argument that the philosopher should leave the doctrines of popular religion to the people in the service of public order, though he need not himself accept those doctrines.[39] In other words, it

37. See Rauf, "Hadith Literature," 271; Schacht, *Origins of Muhammedan Jurisprudence,* 58–59; Black, *History of Islamic Political Thought,* 33.

38. Voegelin, *The Ecumenic Age,* 305–8.

39. Black, *The History of Islamic Political Thought,* 58; Leaman, *Introduction to Medieval Islamic Philosophy,* 13; Voegelin, *The Middle Ages to Aquinas,* 185, 186; Averroës, "The Decisive Treatise," 164–86. See also the qualifications of von Sivers in Voegelin, *The Middle Ages to Aquinas,* 187–89n14.

would be difficult to say that Islamic philosophy sought to reconcile faith and reason, however understood. Rather, it looked more like a juxtaposition with the assumption being that, in any apparent conflict, the religious teachings, and thus the religious teachers, the ulama, were correct, and the *falasifa* were wrong. There was, so to speak, no need for philosophical elaboration of ethics or politics; "rather, all humans should adhere to the one true moral Code, the Muslim Shari'a."[40] Intellectually and spiritually, as well as militarily, negotiation between the domain of Islam, the *dar al-Islam*, and the domain of impiety, the *dar al-Kufr*, which was also necessarily the *dar al-Harb*, the domain of warfare, looked highly doubtful. And in fact the justification for a *dar al-Ahd*, a domain of contractual peace, did not arise easily. Indeed, one of the most common compromises was to negotiate a treaty that might licitly be abrogated when the Muslim side was stronger.[41] This may be a common enough practice of *Realpolitik*, but it can hardly be said to inspire confidence in the reliability of a religious oath.

We have seen in the analysis of the symbolism of God's revelation to the Israelites how the destruction of the kingdoms evoked, broadly speaking, a metastatic hope that God would fix things along with a reinterpretation of the symbolism of Exodus in the direction of greater differentiation between the mundane affairs of the world, Augustine's earthly city, and the existentially most significant problem for human beings, living in righteousness before the Lord, Augustine's pilgrimage toward the heavenly city. In the work of several Islamic thinkers, beginning with Ibn Taymiyya, one finds a rather different pattern of response to external threats, starting with the Mongols, and to the internal crises created by these threats. Apart from the Sufis, the major pattern reinforced the tendencies toward doctrinal and dogmatic expression already present in Muslim jurisprudence and the teachings of the *falasifa*.

Taqi al-Din ibn Taymiyya was born in Harran, an ancient town a few miles north of the current Turkey-Syria border. It was conquered early in the Arab expansion and six hundred years later conquered again by the Mongols, forcing Ibn Taymiyya's father to flee with his family to Damascus. By 1282, he had succeeded his father as a legal scholar at a local madrasa and as a preacher at the ancient Umayyad mosque in the city. Both men followed the Hanbali school of jurisprudence, named

40. Black, *The History of Islamic Political Thought*, 59.
41. See Esposito, *Unholy War*, 35 ff.; Bull, *The Anarchical Society*, 41–44.

for Ahmad ibn Hanbal, who, during the ninth century, advanced highly literalist interpretations of the Koran, the Hadith, the tradition, and the Law. In addition, the Hanbali school emphasized the independence of religious authorities from the Caliphate and "brought the potential for militant opposition to the Caliphate into the very core of Sunni Islam."[42] Ibn Taymiyya developed Hanbal's jurisprudence, particularly in opposition to the Mamluk government in Syria-Egypt. He was rewarded for his trouble with torture and several years in jail, where eventually he died.[43]

The significance of the Mongol attacks was more than a personal inconvenience to Ibn Taymiyya. They were also understood to be both a punishment sent by God to chastise the faithful for their errant ways and evidence that the Mongols were not true Muslims. The clearest indication of their true status was found in the continued adherence by the Mongols to the *Yasa,* the constitutional order formalized by Genghis Khan, and not to the true law, Sharia. Accordingly, the first thing to be done was to understand that the nominal Islam adopted by the Mongols was a sham. They were either apostates or infidels by this interpretation and so indistinguishable from the pagans of Mecca before the Prophet brought God's message to them. This was the time of *jahiliyya,* of ignorance, but also of barbarism and cruelty.[44] As we note below, the term has been reintroduced into Islamist discourse in the twentieth century.

Likewise, the appropriate response to God's scourge, both then and now according to the Muslim vulgate, has been to recover the purity of the early companions of the Prophet, the "rightly guided" first Caliphs or the *al-salaf al-salihin,* the venerable or pious forefathers. Spiritually considered, the return to the origins is a common theme in Judaism and Christianity as well. Central to that recovery of original purity for Ibn Taymiyya was a restoration of the true meaning of the entire corpus of Muslim scripture: the Koran, the Sharia, the Hadith, and the Sunna. Central as well was the importance of jihad. We shall, accordingly, refer

---

42. Lapidus, "Separation of State and Religion," 383.

43. See Laoust, *Essai;* Rosenthal, *Political Thought in Medieval Islam,* 51–61; Black, *History of Islamic Political Thought,* chap. 16. Hanbali jurisprudence is not merely of historical interest. It was a major element in the Abu Zaid affair at Cairo University in the 1990s. See Abu Zaid, "Divine Attributes of the Qur'an," 144; and Ruthven, *A Fury for God,* 39–42.

44. See Goldhizer, *Muslim Studies,* 219 ff.

to this position as "salafism" or as "jihadist salafism." It was an important constituent element in the spiritual complex of the terrorist attack
of September 11, 2001.[45]

Two significant implications followed. First, Ibn Taymiyya was drawn
into a polemical debate with the conventional ulama, for whom the
gates of independent interpretation of scripture *(ijtihad)* were closed:
"For Ibn Taymiyya they were wide open."[46] Second, it bears reiterating
that by Ibn Taymiyya's reading of the sacred texts, as with the Kharijites,
jihad became one of the "pillars of Islam," equal to prayer, the declaration of faith, the pilgrimage, and so on. Even though this position contradicted that of the Hanbalis, his reasoning was simple enough: because
jihad was so important to the Prophet and the venerable forefathers,
and because they were the source, jihad necessarily remained essential
to Islam—especially if directed against apostates or pagans. Moreover,
there was a domestic implication as well: because the goal of jihad was
God's victory, anyone who opposed this teaching thereby declared themselves to be enemies of God. The dictum clearly applied to the Mongols, whether they were considered apostates or pagans. Either way, the
penalty, as prescribed in the Koran, is death; the most important practical consequence, however, was to ensure that "rightly guided" violence
could be directed against Muslims with whom this particular interpreter
happened to disagree. By the late twentieth century, claiming the mantle of the venerable forefathers in order to evoke the piety of a salafist,
jihad became no more than a euphemism for terrorism.[47]

However that may be, for Ibn Taymiyya, once the infidels and apostates had been defeated the next task was to apply the Sharia to the
daily operations of government. The title of his book on this topic, *al-
Kitab al siyasa al-shar'iyya,* has been variously translated as the *Book on
the Government of the Religious Law* or the *Book on Righteous Rule.* The
application of Sharia to government, rather than to the traditional
sphere of personal conduct, was a significant expansion. Perhaps the
most important aspect, for our present analysis, is that such an application proved to Muslims who followed Ibn Taymiyya the superiority
of Islam over Christianity and Judaism because it prescribed "the conditions necessary for the existence of true religion: power, jihad, and

45. Armstrong, "War: Is It Inevitable?" 64.
46. Benjamin and Simon, *Age of Sacred Terror,* 45.
47. See Kepel, *Jihad,* 219–21.

wealth."[48] Indeed, it was as great an error to think it was possible to achieve power and wealth without piety—now including jihad—as it was to try to live piously and achieve spiritual purity without power, wealth, and jihad.[49]

Syntheses work miracles, and the result of this synthesis of power, wealth, and piety was bound to achieve what is indicated by the title of Ibn Taymiyya's book, which for simplicity we shall call "righteous rule." More simply still, the religious duty of "commanding good and forbidding evil" would become the law of the land. Naturally enough, a good deal of coercion will be required; or as Ibn Taymiyya put it, terror and love go together. So far as traditional Islamic institutions are concerned, Ibn Taymiyya was calling for an end to the offices of caliph and sultan. All good Muslims, which is to say, all followers of Ibn Taymiyya, can serve in the office of caliph and guide the affairs of the Muslim community. It is plausible, as Black pointed out, that "the idea, now emerging in [fourteenth century] Europe, of the state as a trans-personal entity is not far away, and was probably not inconceivable within Ibn Taymiyya's mental universe."[50] Equally plausible was the interpretation of contemporary, twenty-first-century Islamists: that righteous rule would be enforced by a self-appointed elite using whatever power and wealth was available.

Laoust reports that Ibn Taymiyya was largely ignored for four hundred years. Rosenthal explained that the chief objection to the practicality of his views, which is to say, the reason why he was ignored, was that social conditions had changed from the days of the "venerable forefathers" except, perhaps, in the land of the Prophet himself—or rather, in the remote interior of Arabia, where Muhammad ibn Abd al-Wahhab (1703–1787) was born. The village of Uyaina, on the Najd plateau, was remote from the relatively cosmopolitan centers of the Hijaz, which included the two holy cities, Mecca and Medina, and from the ports of Jeddah on the Red Sea and al-Hasa on the Persian Gulf—to say nothing of the centers of power, civility, and religious life, Ottoman Istanbul.[51] Moreover, by the mid-eighteenth century, administrative control from Istanbul had become more relaxed.

48. Laoust, *Essai*, 178.
49. Rosenthal, *Political Thought in Medieval Islam*, 54.
50. Laoust, *Essai*, 70, 14–16, 53; Black, *History of Islamic Political Thought*, 157.
51. Laoust, *Essai*, 477 ff.; Rosenthal, *Political Thought in Medieval Islam*, 60–61.

Al-Wahhab left Uyaina to study in Mecca, where he first encountered Hanbali jurisprudence and the writing of Ibn Taymiyya.[52] He visited other centers of Islamic learning in what is now Iraq and Iran and for a time was even a teacher of Sufism. On his return to Arabia al-Wahhab had reached the conclusion that Islam as practiced in the cities of the Ottoman Empire and in Persia was corrupt. Moreover, he identified that corruption with the waning of the Islamic power.

Indeed, generally speaking, the history of Islam prior to and during al-Wahhab's lifetime was one of spiritual decline and political humiliation. The large topic of the decline, or at least the decentralization, of the Ottoman Empire has been debated at great length both inside and outside the empire, starting in the sixteenth century. Much of the discussion has centered on the changing balance of power between the empire and the new states of the West, rather than between Istanbul and other Muslim states. From the battle of Lepanto in 1571 until the time of al-Wahhab, Ottoman power was, if not in retreat, then certainly undergoing reconfiguration in the Balkans, the Caucasus, the Crimea, southern Ukraine, and Hungary. At the same time, British, Dutch, and Portuguese ships were trading into the gulf. In the Ottoman homeland, these developments generated an extensive political literature dealing not just with themes of decline but also of religious reform.[53] For al-Wahhab, as for many other less successful reformers, the answer to political decay was a salafist restoration of the virtue and piety of the pristine early days.[54] As with all such movements, including those that have emerged from Judaism and Christianity, al-Wahhab's salafism was defined more by what he sought to destroy than by what he sought to build.

The list of errors and opponents was long. Bedouin cultural practices common to the Najd, such as sanctifying the dead or the practice of devotions at shrines, he said, was evidence of polytheism (*shirk*) and therefore was evil.[55] In his struggle against *shirk*, al-Wahhab relied on the Koranic instruction (9:5): "Wherever you find them, kill those who ascribe partners to God," which is to say, polytheists. By this interpreta-

---

52. According to one account he found Ibn Taymiyya so compelling he copied the *Book on Righteous Rule* by hand. See Nicholson, *Literary History of the Arabs,* 466.

53. See Black, *History of Islamic Political Thought,* chap. 24. See also Lewis, *What Went Wrong?*

54. Rahman, *Islam,* 196.

55. Hourani, *Arabic Thought in the Liberal Age,* 37.

tion, for example, the Christian mystery of the Holy Trinity was *shirk*. As part of his salafist program to recover the pristine ways of the pious ancestors, al-Wahhab restored the archaic punishments, such as execution by stoning for female adulterers.[56] As did Ibn Taymiyya, al-Wahhab criticized the traditional ulama for their prohibition of independent interpretation, *ijtihad*. He also argued in favor of strict and exclusive reliance on the Koran and the Sharia, to which he added strictly prescribed times for prayer that must be practiced according to equally strict and prescribed postures. Eventually he was such a nuisance to the ulama in Uyaina that he was expelled.

He found refuge with Muhammad ibn Saud at Diriyah, near modern Riyadh, and in 1744 formalized an agreement or covenant, *mithaq*, under the terms of which Ibn Saud established a political community the religious practices of which were determined by al-Wahhab. The new community was animated by "the call to the doctrine of the oneness of God" *(al-da'wa ila al-tawhid)*, which subsequently was known simply as Wahhabism.[57] The *mithaq* was further solidified by the marriage of Ibn Saud to the daughter of al-Wahhab. The chief practical benefit of the *mithaq* was that the tradition of tribal raiding could be carried on in the name of jihad and booty could be sanctified as a charitable payment, *Zakat*, one of the "pillars of Islam." So far as al-Wahhab was concerned, he was simply emulating the conquests of the salafis. Similarly on the hermeneutic front, al-Wahhab determined that those who refused to follow his version of Hanbali legal interpretation showed thereby their unbelief and so were no better than pagans and apostates.

Smith drew attention to an addition al-Wahhab made to the doctrinal strictness taught by Ibn Taymiyya. Like his predecessor, al-Wahhab said that Muslims owed their allegiance to the Koran as it was originally and correctly implemented in practice. There was nothing nostalgic or idealistic about the salafist approach, in the sense that it might be impractical. On the contrary, "the Wahhabis rejected the actual practice, but not the conception that Islam is a practice, is essentially a divine pattern in this-worldly, historical motion." Or, as Haddad observed, for salafists, "the mission of Muslims is not to accommodate the guidance of the Qur'an to prevailing or borrowed social systems; rather, the revelation itself provides a revolutionary ideology that seeks to transform

56. Brockelmann, *History of the Islamic Peoples*, 352.
57. See al Rasheed, *History of Saudi Arabia*, 17.

society and liberate people from bondage to human systems." Accordingly, they appealed to their own understanding of the Sharia but also to the necessity of establishing a society that would embody the decrees of God. That is, the Wahhabis recaptured the Prophet's duty to succeed but directed it in a much more astringent direction. Resistance did not inspire anyone to reconsider because adversity was a test and compromise apostasy. Difficulties were simply reasons to simplify further and to try harder. As Meddeb observed, "The objective of all forms of Wahhabism is to make one forget body, object, space, beauty; these obscurations mean to impose a generalized amnesia, one of the symptoms of the sickness that has afflicted the disciple of Islam."[58]

Because the Wahhabis began their work in a region geographically remote from Istanbul, they were able to proceed more or less unmolested. By the early nineteenth century the alliance between the Wahhabis and the Saudis had given them control of Mecca, from which pilgrims on the hajj would return home with news of the strict but exhilarating Islam they had encountered. At the same time Wahhabi armies conducted raids into Iraq and Syria, even though the region was at least nominally part of the Ottoman Empire.[59] The Ottoman subjects, however, were likely to see the Wahhabi victories as evidence of God's will. In more conventional terms, the Wahhabis posed a religious as well as a political challenge to the sultan, who also claimed to be caliph and thus protector of Sunni Islam. But with the two holy cities in Wahhabi hands, he was no longer their custodian.

Accordingly, in 1811, the vigorous Egyptian governor Muhammad Ali entered the Hijaz at the head of an Ottoman army and, despite an initial defeat, restored the two cities to Ottoman hands by 1813. Five years later an Ottoman army under the command of the son of Muhammad Ali, Ibrahim, captured the Saudi leader, Abdullah, grandson of Ibn Saud, and removed him in chains to Istanbul for execution. The consequence was not the extinction of Wahhabism so much as a renewed radicalization and a gradual recovery and consolidation of Saudi power in the Najd.

The story of the declining power of the Ottomans, and the rising power of the British, and the skill with which Ibn Saud worked the seam between them to become the first king of Arabia is less important

58. Smith, *Islam in Modern History*, 43; Haddad, "Qur'anic Justification for the Islamic Revolution," 17; Meddeb, *Malady of Islam*, 121.
59. Hitti, *History of the Arabs*, 741.

for our current concerns than the growth of yet another religious movement within the Wahhabi spiritual dominion. North of Riyadh a descendant of al-Wahhab, Abdulla bin abd al-Latif, reenacted the exodus of the Prophet from Mecca to Medina and established the first *hijra* agricultural communes, where settlers could live according to Wahhabi rules and avoid any polluting contact with outsiders. Calling themselves the Brotherhood, Ikhwan, by 1920 more than fifty such *hijra* settlements had been founded. Most of these colonies failed because they were exposed to the danger of drought and could not become self-sufficient. Thus they were subsidized by Ibn Saud and eventually brought into his tents, where they subsequently became the religious, political, administrative, and educational centers of Wahhabism. He also turned them into a formidable army that eventually destroyed Hashemite rule in the Hijaz.

At the same time, however, Ibn Saud was compelled to treat with the infidel British, which "put the Ikhwan and Ibn Saud on a collision course, for the latter had to practice realpolitik," and the former did not.[60] The collision took place in 1929, at the battle of Sibila, and the Saudis, with the assistance of the RAF, won. The British, exercising both their discretion as mandated by the League of Nations as well as their power, established the new borders between Iraq and Transjordan in such a way that they provided a common barrier to the northern spread of Wahhabism.[61]

The British strategy succeeded in reducing the raids by the Ikhwan north of what was now the border of a new Arabian state, but it was powerless to prevent the spread of sentiments of great approbation for Wahhabi achievements. Chief among them was the undeniable fact that Saudi Arabia was formally independent of foreign, and thus infidel, rule. Because Saudi Arabia had experienced neither Western colonization nor rule by a Westernized elite, the Saudi rulers could easily and genuinely believe that Islam was socially, morally, and religiously superior. Moreover, the absence of Western imperial rule meant that the sense of Wahhabi superiority would not be diluted by nationalism or nationalist particularity. This is why the appeal of Wahhabism was equally strong

---

60. Gold, *Hatred's Kingdom*, 50. Gold's book, as the book by Schwartz, *The Two Faces of Islam,* are highly critical analyses of the Saudi regime. They do, however, direct attention to aspects of Saudi history that are understated or ignored by most other accounts.

61. Lewis, *British Empire in the Middle East,* 176.

across the Red Sea in Egypt, where the political balances were even more ambiguous and the sense of living at the center of a great but battered civilizational order was even more pronounced. It is also why, when Wahhabism is left alone in its religious superiority, it can become remarkably obscurantist.[62] According to Meddeb, Wahhabism "extols a kind of Islam that is not even traditional but has gone through a series of reducing diets from which it emerges anemic and debilitated."[63]

A verbal insistence on religious superiority, to say nothing of moral superiority, has precious little impact on political realities. "To many observers," wrote Rahman, "the history of Islam in modern times is essentially the history of the Western impact on Muslim society, especially since the 13/19th century." The failure to meet economic, technological, military, or political challenges sustains the image of Islam as a "semi-inert mass receiving the destructive blows or the formative influences from the West."[64] It is no surprise, perhaps, that the impact of the West, far from opening the Muslim, and especially the Wahhabi, world to new influences, has appeared as a threat.

The asymmetries of political power have changed the terms of the Muslim response to crisis from an emphasis on a religious recovery of the pristine Islam, from which political success would follow, to direct political action. We noted above that the distinction between political action and religious practice was not as sharply drawn in Islam as in Christianity. This is why the arguments of Ibn Taymiyya or al-Wahhab could as easily appear to be legal and political as they appeared to be religious. The post-Wahhabi response to Western domination was not only political, in the sense of unrest at the intrusions of foreigners and resistance to their rule, but also had a spiritual dimension to it. The reason was obvious enough: the West posed a spiritual as well as a political challenge or threat. In addition to the old religious challenge posed by Christian missionaries, there were new ones in the form of modern and secular political thought, and the study of Islam by Westerners,

---

62. The *locus classicus* is probably the fatwa issued by a Wahhabi imam, Abdul-Aziz bin Baz, in 1969 that declared the earth was a flat disk around which the sun moves. It was not until he was informed by Prince Sultan, who had witnessed the roundness of the earth from the space shuttle in 1985, that he withdrew the fatwa. See also the problem that Wahhabi ulama had in making sense of the radio in Hiro, *War without End*, 127.

63. Meddeb, *Malady of Islam*, 39.

64. Rahman, *Islam*, 212.

usually referred to as "Orientalism." It made no difference whether the modern political notions were understood as liberating or not; neither did it matter whether the Orientalists were hostile or sympathetic: either way they were challenges that demanded a response simply because they came from outside the *dar al-Islam*. As we shall see, the series of responses increasingly mirrored the modernity of the West.

The first such response is conventionally called modernism.[65] Modernists typically held that the real sources of Western triumphs were Islamic and that the Muslim world can overtake and, indeed, outperform the West once it understands both itself and the sources—the genuinely Islamic sources—of Western achievements. The modernists took from the premodern Islamic reformers such as Ibn Taymiyya the doctrine of *ijtihad,* or original interpretation; and after criticizing the traditional authority and teachings of the ulama, instead of arguing that the regeneration of Islam would result from a salafist recovery of the pristine ways of the forefathers, they proposed to replace the traditional teachings with "the intellectual products of modern civilization."[66]

There are a number of theoretical issues involved in distinguishing between what is modern and what is Western. To begin with, both terms are ambiguous. However, because it is far from certain that, even if the terms could be clarified sufficiently, they might serve as concepts in political science, the results would hardly be worth the effort. Accordingly, for present purposes it is sufficient to illustrate rather than analyze the problem: Bernard Lewis observed that a Muslim man in a suit embodied modernization, but a woman in a suit was an example of Westernization.[67]

More broadly speaking, *modernism* meant both what we now call technology and liberal constitutionalism. As certainly became true toward the end of the twentieth century, technology was understood chiefly in terms of hardware that could be bought either on the open or on the black market. It is probably fair to say that the link between science, technology, free enquiry, and secularism, which is to say, technology as a way of thinking, has not been well thought through by Muslim modernist thinkers. For Meddeb, Islamist ideologues have championed

65. See Hourani, *Arabic Thought in the Liberal Age;* Enayat, *Modern Islamic Political Thought;* Black, *History of Islamic Political Thought,* chap. 25.

66. Rahman, *Islam,* 215.

67. Lewis, *What Went Wrong?* 75.

a "cohabitation of archaic regression and active participation in technique and technology" that is simply incoherent.[68]

Additional obstacles made it difficult to persuade the Muslim community that they should adopt modern political forms. The most obvious is that, along with Christian missionary schools, modern social and political institutions were "experienced by the intellectual circles of Muslim countries as a result of colonial occupation."[69] Indeed, the very notion of the state, which emerged in the West as a compromise as well as a conclusion to the wars of religion, soon after claimed to be sovereign and eventually had to become secular. Secularism necessarily destroys the foundations of Islam by denying the sovereignty of God over the Muslim community and by turning Islam into a private creed and practice existing between the individual and God.

The spiritual challenge of modernity, even when unencumbered by Western dress, leaves the modernists in Islam vulnerable to criticism both from traditional religious leaders and later from jihadist and salafist revolutionaries on the grounds that their modernism was both ineffective and "un-Islamic." Thus a modernist such as Al-Afghani (1837–1897) or Muhammad Abduh (1849–1905) whose views might be considered unexceptionable and even mainstream in the salons of Mayfair or the cafés of Paris look in retrospect as if they were in a kind of limbo or halfway house on the way to radical, fundamentalist, or jihadist Islamism.[70]

Political institutions created after the destruction of the Ottoman Empire opened a number of political possibilities. In Turkey, the abolition of the caliphate in 1924 by Mustafa Kemal, the hero of the defeat of the Allies at Gallipoli, laid the foundation for what is arguably the most successful state whose citizens are chiefly Muslim.[71] In contrast, in Egypt the foundations were laid at about the same time for a renewal of salafist and jihadist Islam by Hasan al-Banna, who in 1928 founded the Muslim Brethren, the *Jamiyyat al-Ikhwan al-Muslimin,* in direct emulation of the Ikhwan of Arabia.

The Egyptian Ikhwan may have adopted the name of the Arabian agriculturalists, but they were "a new *type* of Islamic community,"

68. Meddeb, *Malady of Islam,* 40.

69. Haddad, "Qur'anic Justification for an Islamic Revolution," 15.

70. See Keddie, *Sayyid Jamal ad-Din "Al-Afghani";* Kerr, *Islamic Reform;* Rahman, *Islam,* 222–35.

71. See Lewis, *Emergence of Modern Turkey.*

namely, "the first mass-supported and organized, essentially urban-oriented effort to cope with the plight of Islam in the modern world."[72] Al-Banna was distressed at the abolition of the caliphate in 1924 and angered at the declaration two years later by the ulamas at al-Azhar University in Cairo that, absent a true caliphate, Muslims could not live properly as Muslims. He also rejected the position of the Western-izers and argued in favor of what would later be called an Islamic state, as distinct from an Islamic society within a secular state, as provided by the example of Turkey. At the end of the day, this "magical and mil-lenarian attitude" would require "the intervention of a supernatural power, an apocalyptic upheaval" to come into being.[73]

Al-Banna's position was similar to that of another intellectual and revolutionary, his older contemporary, Rashid Rita. Rita argued in sup-port of a familiar theme, that only a salifist Islam, purged of Western influences, could end Western colonialism and that it could be recov-ered by *ijtihad,* by exercising individual judgment in opposition to the traditions of the ulama. Rita also reintroduced the symbol *jahiliyya.* The Prophet used the term to refer to pre-Islamic Arabia; Ibn Taymiyya used it to refer to the Mongols. Rita was the first to apply the term to the Muslim lands of his own time. Soon enough, as Haddad observed, *jahiliyya* came to mean "any system, order, world view or ideology that is considered un-Islamic" by the salafist interpreter.[74] The chief differ-ence between Rita and al-Banna, apart from doctrinal issues, about which revolutionaries typically quarrel, was that Rita remained isolated and ineffective despite his ambitions and al-Banna led a social and polit-ical movement.

Like their predecessor, the Egyptian Ikhwan exalted their leader, though al-Banna and his organization did not come to the attention of the British authorities in Egypt until 1936, "the year that witnessed the beginning of large-scale revolt in Palestine against British occupa-tion, Zionist policies, and Jewish immigration."[75] Opposition to British authorities about the same time in India took a similar and, it turned out, highly portable form.

72. Black, *History of Islamic Political Thought,* 318; Mitchell, *Society of Muslim Brothers,* 326–27.

73. Meddeb, *Malady of Islam,* 40.

74. Haddad, "Qur'anic Justification for an Islamic Revolution," 27. See also Sivan, *Radical Islam,* 101; Kerr, *Islamic Reform.*

75. Choueiri, *Islamic Fundamentalism,* 39.

Mawlana Mawdudi, a vigorous participant in the prewar debates in India regarding the future of the subcontinent, made a number of dogmatic assertions based on the arguments of Rita and on the traditions of Indian Wahhabism. He asserted once again the unity of religious and political life and wrote a lengthy comparison of Islam with capitalism, fascism, socialism, and communism—and notably not a comparison with Judaism or Christianity. Like the other revolutionaries, he endorsed *itjihad* against the ulama and asserted a literalist reading of an unchanging Sharia. His organization, the Jamaat-I Islami or Islamic Association, was the "counterpart" of the Ikhwan in the Arab world.[76] Like the Ikhwan, he sought an Islamic state. Following partition, this stance placed him in opposition to Mohammed Ali Jinnah, the founder of Pakistan, who like Ataturk had established, at least in principle, a secular state that might shelter an Islamic society, but also non-Muslims.

In Egypt, political events followed a more or less similar path. In 1948, one of al-Banna's followers murdered the Egyptian prime minister, Mahamud al-Nuqrashi. As a consequence, the Ikhwan was dissolved and al-Banna was himself murdered within the year. The loss of their leader was a genuine decapitation, and his followers were unable to create any coherent political strategy.[77] The 1952 coup by the Free Officers Association led by Gamal Nasser introduced something like a secular state, which has remained intact ever since. The Ikhwan did not share the Arab nationalism of the new regime, and eventually they made a highly incompetent attempt on Nasser's life. The government then suppressed the Ikhwan by arresting its members, many of whom were subsequently tortured and executed.

The most intellectually important member of the Ikhwan, the "godfather to Muslim extremist movements around the globe," was Sayyid Qutb.[78] We will analyze his views in the following chapter. Let us conclude this chapter by summarizing the argument. We noted at the outset that the experiential dynamics of living in accord with the message of God are precarious and existentially demanding. The analysis of the Israelite experience indicated this clearly. Moreover, the same pattern emerged in the history of Christianity.

Historically, Christianity began as a Jewish messianic movement torn

76. Smith, *Islam in Modern History*, 234.
77. Choueiri, *Islamic Fundamentalism*, 42.
78. Esposito, *Unholy War*, 56.

between the expectation of the Parousia that would usher in the Kingdom of God as a historical event in the world and an awareness that the
faith of the community of believers constituted the continuing revelation of Christ in history. That is, from its origin Christianity contained
both an eschatological notion of community and the understanding
that the Messiah has already appeared and that his presence is continued in the community of the faithful. This new community, described in
Paul's Letter to the Hebrews, is centered on faith, is unified by the Holy
Spirit, and is guided by the Decalogue and the law of the heart.[79] The
transformation of an eschatological community into a Christian community, the beginnings of which are recorded in Acts,[80] had the effect of
toning down the expectation that the existing order of the world would
soon be transfigured into the Kingdom of God. Even so, during times
of crisis—such as the persecutions of the Christians by Roman authorities—expectation of the coming of the Kingdom of God could easily
be restored, as, for example, in the contemporary Revelation of Saint
John. The structure of the existential issue is notably similar to that of
the Israelite prophetic communities and the issue of metastatic faith
touched upon above. In Voegelin's words:

> If Christianity consisted in the burning desire for deliverance from the
> world, if Christians lived in expectation of the end of unredeemed his-
> tory, if their destiny could be fulfilled only by the realm in the sense
> of chapter 20 of Revelation, the church was reduced to an ephemeral
> community of men waiting for the great event and hoping that it
> would occur in their lifetime. On the theoretical level the problem
> could be solved only by the tour de force of interpretation that Saint
> Augustine performed in the *Civitas Dei*. There he roundly dismissed
> the literal belief in the millennium as "ridiculous fables" and then bold-
> ly declared the realm of the thousand years to be the reign of Christ in
> his church in the present saeculum that would continue until the Last
> Judgment and the advent of the eternal realm in the beyond.[81]

The Augustinian understanding of the Church, which remained intact
until the end of medieval times in the West, simply declared the revolutionary expectations of a second coming to be ridiculous.

79. See Heb. 6:4–5; 11:1; Eph. 4:4–7; Rom. 13:9–10. See also Voegelin's account in
Hellenism, Rome, and Early Christianity, 163–72.
80. See Acts 2:22–36.
81. Voegelin, *The New Science of Politics*, 176. The quotation is from *The City of
God*, xx, 7.

And yet, human beings are perfectly at liberty to believe in ridiculous fables. Moreover, the temptation to do so is likely to be particularly strong, as we have indicated, during periods of crisis and change, when historical institutions are challenged and individuals long for relief from suffering, from evil, from the effects of the famous apocalyptic horsemen.[82] Voegelin has called the experiential phenomenon the "fall from faith." In the Christian world, the probability of such a fall increased with the spread of Christianity to ever-larger numbers of individuals who, at the same time, lacked the existential stamina to endure the uncertainties and precariousness of faith. When such a fall is experienced on a socially widespread scale, the consequences will depend on the surrounding historical and, broadly speaking, religious culture into which the individuals are falling. "The fall could be caught," Voegelin wrote, "only by experiential alternatives, sufficiently close to the experience of faith that only a discerning eye would see the difference, but receding far enough from it to remedy the uncertainty of faith in the strict sense."[83] The history of Islam, from the Kharijites to the Ikhwan, recapitulates a structurally similar fall from faith in response to a series of historical crises.

The original crisis in the Prophet's "duty to succeed" was the exodus, the *hijra* from Mecca to Medina in 622. His triumphal return and the evocation of the umma was understood by his followers as the prelude to further triumphs—and especially the transformation of the umma from the potential of humanity living in submission to God to the actual establishment of an ecumenic Islamic world. The expansion of Islam was, of course, remarkable, but so too were the crises, most notably the Mongol depredations of the mid-thirteenth century. The response of Ibn Taymiyya began a pattern that has not yet come to an end: if Muslims were unable to fulfill their duty to succeed, the reason lay in their having neglected the message of the Prophet. Only by recalling the pristine Islam of the pious forefathers, the salafa, could their triumphs be repeated. On the one hand, success required a new interpretation of the Koran, *ijtihad,* and thus a struggle with the existing interpretive authority of the ulama. On the other, it meant enacting the rule of God, the

---

82. See Voegelin, *The New Science of Politics,* 187 ff., for an analysis of the problem in the Christian context. See also his more detailed treatment of the post-medieval reintroduction of eschatology into politics in "The People of God," 131–214.
83. Voegelin, *The New Science of Politics,* 188.

Sharia, by combining power, wealth, and jihad to command the good and forbid the evil.

Likewise the crisis of the "decline" of the Ottoman Empire motivated the restorative work of al-Wahhab. And again it was a salafist program of recovery that focused even more intently on puritanism, on political jihad, on dogmatic *ijtihad* in service to the Sharia. The setback of 1813, which ended with Abdullah's head on a pike in Istanbul, was followed by redoubled efforts and the consolidation of Saudi-Wahhabist power. The help provided by the British introduced yet another layer of complexity: the modern experience of imperialism and Western domination. This time there was no mystic reappropriation of the Prophet's message, such as may be found in the Sufism of Rumi. Nor, with the Saudi suppression of the Ikhwan (again with British help), was a genuine salafist response, namely, the formation of *hijra* communities in the desert, a serious possibility. Instead, with the increasing simplification of Islamic discourse with Mawdudi and al-Banna, and particularly with the reintroduction of *jahiliyya* as a means to stigmatize fellow Muslims who were political opponents, the response of Islamic thinkers was as modern as the Western intruders they found so objectionable.

By the mid-twentieth century, something like the following doctrinal complex informed the salafist enterprise. First, Islam is a complete and all-encompassing way of life both for the individual and for the community; its chief antagonists are communism, capitalism, and fascism. Second, the Koran, rightly interpreted according to the salafist *ijtihad*, is a complete guide to individual and communal action. Third, the Sharia, the law of God, is a detailed guide to the right order of human life. Fourth, abandonment of the pristine ways of the ancestors and reliance on the West has caused the decline of Islamic power, wealth, culture, and righteousness; only a return to the old ways can change this. Fifth, science and technology are available from the West but must be appropriated without Westernization. And, last, jihad is central to the revival of Islam and the final conquest of the world for God and against Satan.[84] In the following chapter we examine the further transformation of salafism into an ideology fueled less by love of one's own than by hatred of the other.

---

84. Esposito, *Unholy War,* 52–53.

4 Genesis of a New Ideology

The emphasis on jihad in contemporary Islamist discourse as well as in Islamist action is probably its most prominent characteristic. As with so many aspects of Islam, the history and meaning of the term *jihad* is rich and complex. The Islamist doctrine derived from it, however, moves in a single direction, toward dogmatic simplicity and transfigurative violence. A preliminary problem is to outline the appeals of simplification. It is probably fair to say that the experiential exclusivity of Islam and the expression of universalist sentiments in particularist language began with the end of the Koranic revelations upon the death of the Prophet in 632. The universalism of a general and open monotheism received expression in the first part of the first pillar of Islam, the declaration of faith: "There is no god but God." Such a profession could as easily be made by a believing Christian or Jew as by a Muslim. Only with the second part, the specifically Muslim profession "and Muhammad is His messenger," is the emphasis placed on the primacy, *de jure* as it were, of Muhammad's revelation. The meaning of *jihad* in a juridical and theological sense is conditioned by this wider experiential context, the *de jure* primacy that crystallized as the doctrine that Islam superseded the two previous "Abrahamic" revelations.

Turning, then, to jihad as doctrine: according to Khadduri, the general sense of jihad is the "exertion of one's power in Allah's path, that is, the spread of the belief in Allah and in making His word supreme over this world."[1] Indeed, *jihad* shares the etymology *ijtihad*, the "effort" or "struggle" of interpretation needed to understand the revelation and the law of God. The general sense of *jihad*, therefore, is effectively synonymous with the duty to succeed, but at least theoretically, it does not

1. Khadduri, *War and Peace in the Law of Islam*, 55.

necessarily mean war. Broadly speaking for the salafists, it does, however, mean war, pure and simple, whereas for mystics it also means spiritual and intellectual struggle.

In the Koran there are some obvious passages, 6:108 or 22:77, for instance, where *jihad* is used to mean "effort" or "exertion." In the most often cited passages, 4:95 or 61:10–13, *jihad* clearly means "warfare on the path of God." Other passages stress defensive war (22:39–40) or defending the faith (6:125), and still others preserve the very ancient view that God manipulates the outcome of battle (33:25). There are also a large number of interesting philological issues that can modify just about any generalization about the Koranic usage. We ignore them not only on the aforementioned grounds of philological incompetence but because there seems to be widespread agreement among salafists and traditional scholars of Islam and the Middle East that, in the earlier revelations at Mecca, the emphasis was on persuasion, which later was called jihad of the tongue (see Koran 39:5), and that, in the later revelations at Medina, *jihad* has much more the sense of fighting and warfare, which later was called jihad of the sword (see Koran, 2:215, 9:41, 49:15). Additional distinctions were subsequently drawn: "jihad of the heart" meant resisting the temptations of Satan; similarly, "jihad of the hands" was fulfilled chiefly by supporting what is right and changing what is wrong. At the same time, however, contemporary scholars have questioned the distinction between early and late suras in the Koran because of the problem of origins, noted in chapter 3, and the problem of assigning a date to the final redaction of the Koran, the influence of Christian sources, and so on.[2] For salafists and for those who believe in the "eternal" or "uncreated" Koran, none of this mere scholarship matters a bit: *jihad* means war.

The contemporary attribution of primacy to armed conflict over spiritual struggle was also influenced by Western operations in the Middle East during World War I. During that war, the British and the Central Powers both encouraged their Muslim allies to declare a jihad, in the sense of armed warfare, against their enemies, namely, the Central Powers and British respectively. At the same time in contemporary Persian and Arabic, the word can be used to refer to any major undertaking—a construction jihad, for example, much as in English one can speak of a "crusade" against poverty or AIDS.

2. See the appendix for a brief discussion of these issues.

Given the wide range of meaning, it perhaps is not surprising that there has been considerable controversy in the popular media following the terrorist attacks of September 11, 2001, about the meaning of *jihad* in this context. Much of it has been focused on a distinction between the lesser and the greater jihad. The distinction is drawn from a hadith that tells a story of the Prophet returning from a raiding party and announcing "we have now returned from the lesser jihad to the greater jihad," which, he explained, was a "jihad against oneself." For our purposes, this no doubt edifying story is beside the point. As contemporary salafists and Islamists have pointed out, the story has not been included in any of the authoritative compilations of hadiths.[3] These and other subtleties clearly have no authority for them.

A second reason why the issue of the "true meaning" of *jihad* need not concern us can be found directly in the probable history of early Islam. Assuming the condition of pre-Islamic Arabia was similar to other parts of the world between the desert and the sown, armed conflict among nomadic tribes as well as between the nomads and settled populations was more or less continuous.[4] Typical as well were the consequences of such modes of conflict: the redistribution of wealth in the form of sheep, horses, and camels; access to pasture; revenge and prestige. Indirectly, such comparatively primitive war was also a means of population control.[5] It seems likely that the notion of holy war (apart from a few Jewish and Christian tribes) was effectively nonexistent in pre-Islamic Arabia.

Whatever the tribal habits of the Arabs under Muhammad, it is certainly true that by the tenth century or so a legalistic understanding of *jihad* had been successfully projected onto seventh-century events. By this interpretation, which has been adopted by salafists without question, Islam clearly made a major difference not in the external behavior of the nomadic warriors of Arabia but in their self-understanding, in the spiritual significance attributed to mounting raids on caravans or slaughtering the foe. From the perspective of Islamic history, the revelation to the Prophet changed everything at once. From the perspective of the history of Islam "the actual transition may not have been as complete or as sudden as suggested by Islamic historiography, for the com-

---

3. Peters, *Islam and Colonialism*, 16.
4. Donner, "The Sources of Islamic Conceptions of War," 59–60n5.
5. See Keeley, *War before Civilization*, chap. 6.

ing of Islam simply marked a watershed in a long process of cultural, social, and religious change. Part of this process included a marked revaluation of violence and warring."[6] That is, the progress of Islam in Arabia did not appreciably change the style of warfare and probably did not markedly increase its tempo, considering the general bellicosity of typical nomad life. War did, however, change its meaning from mere intertribal raiding to an act of piety.

Two aspects of the transcendental sanctification of war dating from the classic period remain significant today in the context of Islamist terrorism: belief in the proximity of a final conflict, which we may call an apocalyptic sensitivity, and belief in the posthumous rewards and consolations of dying during a jihad. We consider these two problems in order.

During the seventh century, Christians, Jews, and Zoroastrians all undertook apocalyptic speculation. The Christians noted that a symbolic seven centuries had passed since the resurrection of Christ and God had passed judgment on the Byzantine Empire for its numerous failures; major changes therefore must be coming. The Jews noted the liberation of Jerusalem from Byzantine Christian rule, a sign that the Temple might be rebuilt, which in turn would signal the imminent appearance of the Messiah.[7] Zoroastrians were caught up in the enormous problem of making sense of the thirty-year conflict between the eastern Roman Empire and the Persian Sasanid Empire.[8] Increasingly, scholars of early Islam have connected these non-Islamic expectations to those shared by contemporary Muslims.[9] There is, moreover, plenty of evidence to indicate that apocalyptic expectations were harnessed by early Muslims

6. Firestone, *Jihad*, 41.

7. Sprinzak, "From Messianic Pioneering to Vigilante Terrorism," 194–216.

8. Whittlow, *The Making of Byzantium;* Fowden, *Empire to Commonwealth;* Palmer, Brock, and Hoyland, eds., *The Seventh Century in West-Syrian Chronicles;* Hoyland, *Seeing Islam as Others Saw It.*

9. Cook, *Studies in Classical Muslim Apocalyptic.* See also: Madelung, "Apocalyptic Prophecies in Hims," 141–85; Bashear, "Early Muslim Apocalyptic Materials," 173–207; Cook, "Eschatology, History, and the Dating of Traditions," 23–48; Cook, "Moral Apocalyptic in Islam," 37–69; Hellhom, ed., *Apocalypticism in the Mediterranean World;* Donner, "The Sources of Islamic Conceptions of War," 43–46; Blankinship, *End of the Jihad State;* Cook, "Muslim Apocalyptic and Jihad," 66–104; Landes, "What Happens When Jesus Doesn't Come," 243–74; Koren and Nevo, "Methodological Approaches to Islamic Studies," 103–4; Nevo and Koren, "Towards a Prehistory of Islam," 108–41; Crone and Cook, *Hagarism.*

to mobilize support, win converts, and release the energy and power to undertake the splendid conquests of the Muslim armies. "Fighting," wrote David Cook, "was what enabled the Muslims to conquer unimaginable tracts of territory, and forced the peoples around the Mediterranean basin and the Iranian plateau to take the despised Arabs seriously." Moreover, "this fighting is closely connected to the apocalyptic aspirations of the early Muslims.... The apocalyptic foundation of Islam is clear from the Qur'an, from the numerous predictions and prophecies in the early literature, from the doctrine of *jihad,* from the ecumenical spirit of the Believers, and from the rule of peace they sought to extend throughout the known world during the first century of their existence."[10] Cook went on to suggest that jihad was roughly equivalent in its redemptive qualities for the early Muslims to the doctrine of the cross for the early Christians, with the obvious political differences being, first, that the Roman armies ensured public order so the gospel might be preached throughout the Mediterranean basin and, second, that the chief political message of the gospel was that the Kingdom of Jesus was not of this world.

Just as traditional Muslim scholars have avoided considering the problem of origins, so too have they downplayed the importance of apocalyptic elements in Islam, concentrating instead on the exegesis of the Sharia within the context of one or another of the legal interpretative schools. At the same time, however, more radical contemporary salafist and jihadist writers have tried to enhance the apocalyptic themes that undoubtedly can be found in the Koran and in other Muslim scripture. These issues have become central not only with the declarations of a terrorist such as bin Laden but with a wide range of Islamist documents dealing with Israel.

The doctrine of Muslim supercession toward Judaism, the sentiment that no country that has become Muslim can ever revert to being non-Muslim, and the fact that Israeli control over Muslim holy places are issues on which Muslims cannot easily compromise, enhances the attractiveness of apocalyptic "solutions" to what is for common sense merely a pragmatic political impasse. Equally, there are utopian proposals to redeem the world with no realistic or even unrealistic account of how

10. Cook, "The Beginning of Islam as an Apocalyptic Movement"; Crone and Cook, *Hagarism,* chap. 9.

the redemption is to take place. Somehow, if the Sharia is imposed on the world, all will be well. Nor, of course, can Jews with messianic expectations find a common ground with their Muslim neighbors. Some contemporary Jewish apocalyptics, for example, see no reason why they should not build the Third Temple even if it means the Dome of the Rock is obliterated. After all, they argue, God granted Israel jurisdiction after the 1967 war. In response, Muslims have updated the classical apocalyptic materials to provide themselves with a guide to events in the modern world, most of which are seen to be highly disagreeable, and to events to come, which promise redemption.[11]

Friction between the imaginative evocation of an apocalyptic transfiguration of the world and the pragmatic day-to-day affairs of mundane and commonsense reality appeared early in the history of Islam. Behind both jihad and apocalyptic lies the experience of an imaginative anticipation of a test that will purify the believer from the evil of the world. It is not enough to fight and die for one's faith: one must fight with a pure heart. Accordingly, the spiritual preparation for war is at least equal to military preparation. Jihad, said Cook, "is literally a spiritual exercise." The apocalyptic jihadist "must be willing to give up everything, even actively desire to give it all up, in order to bring about the messianic age."[12] Initially the conflict was between apocalyptic jihadists and ordinary religious administrators and clerics who saw the need to build mosques and palaces to establish some kind of world-immanent order. The jihadists, in response, withdrew in a kind of continual *hijra* from established society; any particular withdrawal was then followed by a quest for ever greater jihads, jihads without end, until at last the

11. For an extensive treatment of this problem see Cook, *Contemporary Muslim Apocalyptic Literature*. Much of the popular material is both bizarre and highly syncretistic. For example, Hisham Kamal Abd al-Hamid argued that the Jews are extraterrestrial aliens in his book *The Appearance of the Anti-Christ Is Nearing: The Zionists and Other Satan-worshippers Are Preparing the Way for the Anti-Christ with Flying Saucers from the Bermuda Triangle*. According to al-Hamid, Jews are beamed down to earth with secret instructions for their Masonic followers. A similar view is expounded by Muhammad Isa Da'vd in *Warning: The Anti-Christ Is Invading the World from the Bermuda Triangle*. Cook discusses this material in "Taking the Apocalyptic Pulse of Muslims in Israel and Egypt." See also Benjamin and Simon, *Age of Sacred Terror*, 426; Juergensmeyer, *Terror in the Mind of God*, chap. 3.

12. Cook, "Muslim Apocalyptic and Jihad," 77–78.

jihadists were killed and became martyrs. The great desire to repudiate the order of the world is common to Jewish, Christian, and Muslim apocalyptic, but only with the last was the emphasis placed so heavily on fighting and dying as the ultimate and self-certifying proof of one's devotion.

Apocalyptic and jihadist groups were not always allied. During the eleventh century, for example, the destruction accompanying the conquests of the Seljuk Turks, which was relatively moderate compared to the extensive wreckage later left by the Mongols and Timur, was nevertheless understood as the execution of God's judgment on Muslim society as a result of its many sins. This apocalyptic reading of events was not easily assimilated to that of the fighter who desired nothing so much as to meet God through death in battle. That is, so long as the enemy was external, jihadists and apocalyptics could work together, jihadists invoking apocalyptic traditions and apocalyptics looking upon jihad as a means to actualize their visions. In reality, the apocalyptic desire to purify society entirely could never be satisfied, which in turn was understood by apocalyptics as further evidence of the continued failure of Muslim society. For their part, however much jihadists might sympathize with a project to purify society, the fundamental posture of the jihadists faced outward against the infidel. The apocalyptics were not limited in this way and had several traditions that could be deployed against Muslim authorities as well as infidels. As we shall argue below, modern Islamist thinkers such as Qutb or bin Laden easily combine jihadist and apocalyptic traditions in the expectation that a final and ecumenic conquest requires a pure society, which in turn is a bridge to the end time, an essential element in a grandiose redemptive event prior to the end of the world.

In addition to these free-floating apocalyptic themes, a second element of transcendence, introduced during the classical period and transmitted to the modern one, concerns the posthumous consolations a warrior receives for his death in the midst of jihad. Such consolations are necessarily transcendent to the conduct of warfare because they are posthumous and thus must be a matter of faith rather than a direct experience. In the prophetic traditions, there are several hadiths about the importance of jihad, almost always taken to mean "fighting in the path of God." One of the most highly respected collections, "The Book of Jihad," opens with a story of the Prophet being asked what is the best deed. He answers: prayers offered at the right time. Next is filial piety, and third is jihad in the path of God.[13] Later in the same collection: "A man came to God's messenger and said, 'Show me an act equal to jihad.' [The Prophet] replied: 'I cannot find one.'" It is reasonable to conclude, therefore, that in both the Koran and the early tradition, great merit is ascribed to raids and war on behalf of the umma. According to Firestone there are "virtually no dissenting traditions."[14]

Taking part in jihad is a means to great rewards. Those who are with the Prophet are hard against the infidels and merciful among themselves (Koran, 48:29); their ecumenic expansion may be profitable, but armed missionary work is not undertaken, as it was in the pre-Muslim days, as a business enterprise (Koran, 8:67). Taking prisoners for ransom is allowed, after a suitable slaughter, though a fifth of the booty was reserved for God, his Messenger, and good works of various kinds (Koran, 8:41).

More important, however, were the spiritual rewards that a warrior would gain if wounded or killed on jihad. The most important of these is entry into paradise: "Paradise lies under the shade of swords," declares a well-known hadith.[15] Even if the warrior is not killed in battle but was nevertheless on active duty, he will gain Paradise along with seventy of his kin who otherwise would have been doomed to hell. Indeed, the rewards of martyrdom are so great that one so killed will seek to return to earth so that he may be killed again. In order to be integrated into the modern understanding of the posthumous consolations for a warrior who dies on jihad, this austere but still powerful motivation for courageous action received some further touches, which are considered below, in the context of the Shia contributions to doctrines justifying Islamist terrorism.

We may summarize these preliminary remarks regarding the classical understanding of jihad in the following way: first, the classic reconciliation of the several ambiguities in the Koran, including the apparent shift from persuasion to war, postulated an evolution of God's revelation. At the beginning of his mission, when the Prophet was weak, God told him to avoid war and conflict; then, following the *hijra* to Medina, God allowed the Prophet to wage defensive war; finally, as the

13. See Firestone, *Jihad*, 99–100; Wensinck, *Handbook of Early Muhammadan Thought*, 246, for references to the primary texts.

14. Firestone, *Jihad*, 100.

15. Akbar, *The Shade of Swords*.

community grew in size and strength, additional revelations indicated that Muslims could wage war against infidels at any time and place. "The logic," wrote Firestone, "is superb." It indicates that God revealed His instructions regarding war only when the Muslims were strong enough to act on it: as the community grew stronger, so did the spiritual motivation to wage war. "God was, in effect, preparing and guiding his community for the role of world conquerors and propagators of the greatest and most profound religio-cultural system in history."[16] Firestone modified this interpretation on philological grounds and suggested a new reading of the evidence to account for the transition from pre-Islamic to Islamic warfare, but generally speaking his argument is consistent with what we called the Muslim vulgate tradition.

Second, we noted that pre-Islamic war, *harb*, was motivated by economic concerns and by the spirituality embodied in kinship structures. Islamic war reversed the emphasis: the spiritual responsibilities derived from religious commitment might require Muslims to fight even against their infidel kin. Thus, one of the connotations of *hijra* came to be not so much physical flight, as the Prophet undertook from Mecca to Medina, but a spiritual exodus and abandonment of one's tribe followed by attachment to the umma.[17] Whatever the pragmatic difficulties that might accompany the transition from tribe to umma, there was, third, the *result* of a spiritual *hijra*, namely, the transfer to the new religious affiliation all the emotional attachment previously accorded kinship. "War and revenge could therefore be motivated more out of a sense of common identity through the brotherhood of believers, the supertribe of Islam."[18] The energy that had been dissipated in kinship feuds and raids was spiritualized, enhanced, and externalized against the infidels, which in turn enhanced the internal strength and cohesion of the religious community.

Finally, once the ecumenic umma had become established as a political community capable of historical action, jihad became an essential instrument for its continuation and expansion, a political activity that may or may not be endowed with an apocalyptic meaning, namely, the transition to the last days, the end of the world, and so on.[19] Until the

16. Firestone, *Jihad*, 100–101, 50.

17. Watt, *Muhammad at Medina*, 242.

18. Firestone, *Jihad*, 121.

19. Khadduri, *War and Peace in the Law of Islam*, 51, and Cook, "Muslim Apocalyptic and Jihad."

world submitted to God, until the ecumenic caliphate was established, which might be seen as a clear utopian goal surrounded by ambiguity regarding the means to get there, jihad would be a permanent formal obligation imposed on the community, even if the community is not actually engaged in the permanent conduct of war. Hence the well-known distinction noted above between the realm of Islam and the realm of war: for mystical jihadists, argument and interpretation can bridge the gap; for others, for whom jihad was simply war, it became the means to negotiate the transfer of a people and a territory from one to the other.[20] Much like the doctrine of peaceful coexistence created by the communists, the world already belonged to Islam because the Koran calls upon humanity to submit to God, and eventually humanity will obey God's will. Christians and Jews must submit to God's will if they are to be good Christians and Jews, which is to say, they must become good Muslims.

The logic of the two worldly realms, the realm of war and the realm of submission, certainly accords a central place, if not primacy, to jihad. For Islamists, the issue is simple: in Muslim terms, the five pillars of Islam (profession of faith, prayer, the fast of Ramadan, pilgrimage, and charity) amount to a spiritual preparation for war against the enemies of God. More important, for purposes of this analysis, the index of spiritual movement has shifted from striving to live in accord with God's will or striving to understand God's law to striving militarily against some very worldly enemies. That is, the limitations on what can be achieved by worldly action or on what that worldly action may mean, which is established by the world-transcendent dimension of Muslim spirituality, tends to be eclipsed. A pivotal thinker in the process of immanentizing the world-transcendent dimension of Muslim thought, to whom we now turn, was Sayyid Qutb (1906–1966).

Qutb was born into an educated family in a small village in Upper Egypt, Musha. Like so many educated men of his generation, Qutb's father was able to combine support for modernization and for the secular National Party with great personal devoutness. The son, no less devout, had memorized the Koran by age ten. Qutb was a gifted child, but economic hardship in his family required that he be sent to live with an uncle in Cairo for his education. He attended a nonreligious teacher-training college, the Dar al-Ulum, where he was introduced to Western

20. Kelsay, *Islam and War,* 61.

literature and to modern women, whom he found to be of insufficient "moral purity and discretion" to interest him.[21] During the 1930s, Qutb was able to publish poetry, journalism, and critical essays, which in turn gave him sufficient literary repute to be appointed to the Ministry of Education as a school inspector.[22] He might therefore have remained a minor functionary with a modest literary reputation. A combination of political events and his own personality led him in quite a different direction.

Qutb was an enthusiastic proponent of modernizing Egypt's educational system, but much to his regret his plans were not accepted by his superiors. During World War II he objected to the influence of the British in Egypt, and afterward he grew even more bitter over the Jewish immigration to Palestine. He came to the attention of the Egyptian authorities, but instead of being sent to jail he was sent to the United States on a commission to study American post-secondary pedagogy and curricula. It became a defining event in his life.

Qutb was appalled by his shipboard companions, especially the Christian missionaries. He was particularly offended by an apparent encounter with an amorous drunken woman. When he arrived in New York, he was appalled by the noise and movement of the city. He fell ill in Washington, D.C., and was appalled by the women who nursed the forty-something virgin back to health:

> He explains how, while recuperating at the George Washington Hospital, a nurse had attempted to excite him by relating to him the characteristics she desired her lovers to have. Disapprovingly, he draws a picture of the American woman's seductive appearance ("thirsty lips...bulging breasts...smooth legs...") and flirtatious demeanor ("the calling eye...the provocative laugh..."). He castigates those fellow Arab "mission students" who gave in to these wiles and dated American girls.[23]

He was even appalled by Greeley, Colorado, a town characterized by "the moral rigor, temperance and civic-mindedness of its founding

21. Calvert, "'The World Is an Undutiful Boy!'" 98. See also Shepard, *Sayyid Qutb*, xiv–xxxiv.

22. Abubakar, "Sayyid Qutb's Interpretation," 57–65.

23. Calvert, "'The World Is an Undutiful Boy!'" 98. The quotations are from an essay Qutb published in Egypt after his return home.

fathers."[24] In Greeley, Qutb attended the Colorado State College of Education. He disliked the lawns of Greeley because they were "symptomatic of the American preoccupation with the external, material, and selfishly individual dimensions of life." He was amazed at the number of churches but disgusted at church socials and dances held in their basements. The Christian ministers facilitated shamelessness by dimming the lights, which increased the fury of the dance, "inflamed by the notes of the gramophone." As a result, "the dance-hall becomes a whirl of heels and thighs, arms enfold hips, hips and breasts meet, and the air is full of lust." Lewis added that Qutb also quoted the Kinsey Reports "to document his description and condemnation of universal American debauchery" and suggested that Qutb's evaluation may help explain why Islamist terrorists have targeted dance halls and nightclubs such as the Sari Club on Bali, which was bombed in October 2002.[25] For good measure, Qutb also hated football, jazz, American social etiquette, and American barbers. In this respect, Qutb looks like so many whose resentments toward America and the West, as Ajami observed, were born of an unacknowledged attraction to it.[26] Prudishness for Qutb as for his successors "has become a criterion of respectability."[27]

As with so many of the young men whom he later influenced through his writing, including the terrorists who carried out the attacks of September 11, 2001, there is no record that, notwithstanding his familiarity with Western literary culture, he ever visited any of the centers of art or music in New York or Washington. His aestheticism seems to have been focused entirely on *ijaz*, the ability of the Koran to move the souls of readers.[28] "He saw what he wanted to see," wrote Ruthven. "He noticed the pigeons which, like the people, he saw as being condemned to live joyless lives amid the traffic and bustle. His vision was 'occidentalist.'"[29] As Calvert put it, he developed a cartoon view of American culture. His personality seemed incapable of the imaginative extension required to understand America on its own terms, and he clearly found American women to be a major problem. For whatever reason, Qutb drew the

24. Calvert, "Sayyid Qutb in America."
25. Lewis, *Crisis of Islam*, 79.
26. Ajami, *Dream Palace of the Arabs*, 165.
27. Meddeb, *Malady of Islam*, 116.
28. See Binder, *Islamic Liberalism*, 170 ff.
29. Ruthven, *A Fury for God*, 77.

political conclusion that American culture was creating in Egypt an "American Islam" devoted only to opposing communists and corrupting the Muslim world.

Yvonne Haddad argued that Qutb adopted Islamism as a response to a long-standing political crisis in Egypt. By this reading, Qutb was searching for "a comprehensive ideological solution to Egypt's faltering political and economic order."[30] In the event, whatever his motives, upon his return to Egypt in 1951 he joined the Muslim Brotherhood, the Ikhwan, renounced his literary production, and plunged into Egyptian politics. The event that colored Qutb's politics was the founding of the Israeli state. In 1946 he had criticized the United States along with the European powers for permitting and then encouraging Jewish immigration to Palestine. In 1951, following the defeat of Egypt and the other Arab states by the Israelis, the Muslim Brotherhood, including Qutb, called for a jihad against the British. In the resulting riots, entire districts of Cairo were destroyed; not until July 1952, when the Free Officers under Nasser took control of the government, did things settle down. Qutb was engaged by Nasser's government to take part in the renegotiation of the Anglo-Egyptian treaty. For a time he sat on the Revolutionary Command Council but left when the Free Officers rejected Qutb's argument that the ethical foundation for the new state had to be the Koran and the Sharia.[31] Following an assassination attempt on Nasser in October 1954, which implicated members of the Ikhwan, Qutb was arrested along with many other members. He was tortured, tried, convicted, and sentenced to twenty-five years at hard labor. He was released in 1964 because of his deteriorating health but was rearrested, tried, and convicted in 1965 for plotting against the state. He was hanged in August 1966.

During his decade in jail Qutb produced two major works, an eight-volume commentary on the Koran and a shorter tract, *Signposts along the Way.*[32] The importance of these works lies less in the originality of the author's interpretation than in the effectiveness of his rhetoric and the influence and impact it had. According to Kepel, "Qutb devised a new way of writing about Islam that was simple and straightforward,

30. Haddad, "Sayyid Qutb," 69–70.
31. Haim, "Sayyid Qutb," 147–56.
32. The full commentary exists only in Arabic. *Signposts* has been translated a number of times. We examined the version entitled *Milestones* (Damascus: Holy Koran Publishing House, 1978). See also Moussalli, *Radical Islamic Fundamentalism,* and Euben, *Enemy in the Mirror,* chap. 3.

very different from the complex rhetoric of the ulemas, which was laden with traditional references and pedantic commentary. Qutb spoke directly to his readers, using the modern idiom to get simple points across."[33] Indeed, simplification to the point of Manicheistic duality is the most prominent characteristic of Qutb's discourse.

As with other revolutionaries, Qutb experienced a world in crisis. He opened *Signposts* with the announcement that "humanity is standing today at the brink of an abyss," not because of nuclear weapons but because of a nihilism that is manifest as the inability of the West or of Western-derived ideologies such as nationalism and socialism, the Nasserite synthesis, to provide meaning and order. His most powerful organizing symbol, jahiliyya, which Qutb took to mean the usurpation of divine sovereignty, *hakimiyya*, by humans, had, as noted in the previous chapter, been reintroduced to Islamist polemics by Mawdudi. Put positively, the sovereignty of God was the fundamental premise as well as the proof of the truth of Islam. On the surface, Qutb looks like an ordinary salafist revolutionary: jahiliyya is the problem; the solution was to establish the rule of God and to spread it by jihad.

There is a good deal of truth to this straightforward and conventional interpretation of Qutb's writing. The British had introduced the new jahiliyya into Egypt, but the Egyptians had adopted it as their own. The salafist recollection of the purity of the original umma was less a historical return than the recovery of an eternal message, the long-standing attribute of utopian thought. In the Prophet's day, the umma responded properly; in Qutb's day, he would recall them to the same truth. At the core of the new jahiliyya is the Western understanding of reason and knowledge, which, he said, ignored the basic truths expressed in Islam, the "true allusions to truths which are inaccessible to us."[34] Moreover, the new jahiliyya is universal: "everything about us is jahiliyya. The ideas of mankind and their beliefs, their customs and traditions, the sources of their culture, their arts and literature, and their laws and regulations." As Euben remarked, jahiliyya "is at once the embodiment and instrument of slavery, alienation, fragmentation and cosmic disharmony; it is also the veil that cloaks such evils in the language of freedom, progress and personal fulfillment."[35] The results have been clear for all to see:

33. Kepel, *Jihad*, 26.
34. Moussalli, "Sayyid Qutb's View of Knowledge," 332.
35. Qutb quoted in Binder, *Islamic Liberalism*, 179; Euben, *Enemy in the Mirror*, 72.

poverty, corruption, military defeat, and political fragmentation of the umma.

It is not a simple question of reversing direction and restoring the Sharia because of the strength and aggression of jahiliyya. Western rationalism, Choueiri said, was for Qutb the source of the "ever-recurring conspiracy" at the heart of the war to destroy Islam.[36] The basic structure, God's sovereignty and human disobedience, is expressed in several different ways. For the Western rationalists, there is no deception and no division. On the contrary, the unity of theory and practice is the source of the strength of jahiliyya. In contrast, the separation of Islamic consciousness and Islamic action, the conventional salafist notion that the umma must return to the ways of the utopian early days, is a source of weakness and is itself an expression of jahiliyya. "Rather than characterize Islam in terms of the absolute determinations of idealized theory," Binder said, Qutb "defines the Islamic understanding of the world and of religious action in terms of existence and movement." The world therefore is not understood as a field of action, a space for the actualization of Islam but the setting for the self-actualization of religious truth by means of religious practice, of which Qutb is himself an instance.

The family resemblance to traditional salafist arguments is there, but Qutb's formulations carry a more radical message as well. For example, because God is sovereign, only the Koran, which mediates God and His creation, is authoritative. Any other authority is necessarily illegitimate and bogus, *taghut*. "The purpose of Islam is to remove taghut and replace it with Islamic or divine authority. Human beings are totally bereft of any liberty vis-à-vis Allah and therefore, since all are equally slaves of God, none has any shred of authority over other human beings." Being a slave of God means that the individual who understands himself in that way is radically freed from all connection to the world of jahiliyya, which is to say the world of politics in the ordinary sense of the term. Binder summarized the chief implication: "When we consider once again that the absolute foundation of Islam, and of the freedom of the individual Muslim to act, is the hakimiyya [sovereignty] of God, then the characteristic Islamic act becomes the defiance of jahili activity. Thus is the groundwork laid for acts of martyrdom which appear to be suicidal and/or hopeless acts of political terrorism."[37]

36. Choueiri, *Islamic Fundamentalism*, 91.
37. Binder, *Islamic Liberalism*, 180, 203, 176, 201.

In order to move from the sovereignty of God to the justification of terrorism against a world filled with jahiliyya, it is necessary to have a clear grasp of the religious truths actualized in Qutb's writing, on the one hand, and in his very existence, on the other. In this respect, Qutb combined the supreme humility of a slave of God with the supreme certainty of knowing God's will. Indeed, for Qutb, only a slave of God could be fully conscious of God's will, which is to say Qutb's certainty and his humility are but two aspects of the same mode of existence.

Qutb advanced several ancillary arguments and assertions to support his attitude. In *Social Justice in Islam*, for example, he announced: "what we are saying about Islam is not a new fabrication, nor is it a reinterpretation of its truth. It is simply Islam."[38] There is no sense of irony, no awareness of any problems of reflexivity or error, or even of the possibility of "false consciousness." That is, Qutb did not advocate any form of ijtihad but an entirely novel doctrine, that Islam is a *tasawwur*, which can be translated as "vision," "intuition," or "idea." In any event, it is a "direct, personal, intuitive understanding of revelation."[39] Doubt is excluded, therefore, because, for Qutb, the revelation is the direct experience of truth. This is why he made the statement that he was not in the business of offering an interpretation of Islam but Islam itself. For the analyst, however, Qutb's Islam has ceased to be a thing to be known or understood and has been turned into a mystical vision and a product of the visionary's imagination.[40]

The division of political reality into Islam and jahiliyya and the assertion that jihad defines the relations between the two does not mean that the outcome is seriously in doubt. Provided that humanity recovers the message of the Prophet that Qutb was delivering to the umma, God would guarantee the final victory to the righteous. That is why his "signposts" were such clear markers of the path to God. This did not mean that the oppressors of God's servants and the usurpers of God's authority would give up their power because they had been out-argued. It simply meant that the outcome of the jihad was already known because the slaves of God were also willing martyrs.

One of the most important texts in the Koran (2:256) states: "There is no compulsion in religion." For Qutb, this text did not forbid religious

38. Shepard, *Sayyid Qutb*, 9.
39. Moussalli, *Radical Islamic Fundamentalism*, 86.
40. Binder, *Islamic Liberalism*, 189; Black, *History of Islamic Thought*, 322–23.

war against the West. On the contrary: because the West is the source of jahiliyya, because Islam means freedom from jahiliyya, and because jahiliyya means slavery to human beings, the end of jahiliyya will mean the freedom to choose Islam, and to become a slave of God. The logic, driven by the premise that postulates the sovereignty of God, is impeccable: an individual can adopt whatever belief she wishes, but the only belief that follows the way of God is Islam; accordingly, there is no compulsion in religion after the rule of men and of human institutions has been ended and the Sharia, the rule of God, has been established. Euben summarized Qutb's doublethink: "Islam, he says, attacks institutions and traditions to liberate humanity, but does not force individuals to accept its beliefs. But, of course, Qutb's understanding of the nature of those institutions precludes such a space for freedom of faith: the political community is premised upon an act of belief," but "belief is never just a matter of individual conscience, but [is] an issue of [human vs. divine] sovereignty."[41] As a consequence, the outcome cannot be in doubt.

In commonsense terms, Qutb has concocted a recipe for endless violence directed against both non-Muslims and nominal Muslims who are jahili, which is practically everyone who has not yet become a martyr. Qutb used the language of the Koran to express his experience of prison and of a repressive political regime, but also to give voice to a personality gifted in finding fault with others. It is, perhaps, no surprise that a genuine scholar such as Smith would dismiss Qutb as an angry dilettante.[42] A comparison with Marx indicates a more subtle appeal as well. Much as Marx promised that a classless society would emerge from the revolution that transformed reality, so too did Qutb create a doctrine that promised to transfigure reality once the jihad against jahiliyya is successful, which, of course, it never can be. Like other revolutionary thinkers, Qutb added to his vision of Islam the notion of a clandestine armed vanguard who would actually carry out the terrorism[43] as well as the notion of an "objective enemy," namely, the "Jewish agents" who would lead the umma in any direction other than that indicated by the

41. Euben, *Enemy in the Mirror*, 75.

42. Smith, *Islam in Modern History*, 159n203. Likewise Meddeb dismissed the intellectual content of these political radicals as evidence only of their bottomless mediocrity. Meddeb, *Malady of Islam*, 99.

43. See Moussalli, *Radical Islamic Fundamentalism*, 244; Choueiri, *Islamic Fundamentalism*, 158–60; Black, *History of Islamic Political Thought*, 323.

vision of Qutb, thus providing him with ever-renewed pretexts to continue on a violent course.[44]

The basic structure of Qutb's position is, in short, a conventional ideological conceit: the experience of revolution is supposed to bring about
a new reality that exists only in the imagination of the revolutionary. To
use the conceptual terminology introduced above in chapter 2, the pneumopathological nature of the animating emotions would not be obvious until the damage was done. It may be, therefore, that preemptive
violence, which has its own risks and consequences, is the only way to
extinguish the pathos of Qutb's murderous eschatological heroism.
Certainly that was the course adopted by the repressive Egyptian government. On the other hand, the government was not concerned with
transfiguring reality so that it conforms to the imaginative visions of an
embittered misogynist. It was repressive, not pneumopathological.

Qutb was hanged on August 29, 1966. Less than a year later Israel de-
cisively defeated Egypt, Syria, and Jordan in the Six-Day War. "Against
war," wrote Nietzsche, "one can say: it makes the victor stupid, the vanquished malignant."[45] Both effects were felt in the years following, especially among the vanquished.[46] The Islamists' responses were complex
and not a little contradictory. The monthly publication of al-Azhar University in Cairo stated that the humiliation resulted from neglecting
Islam whereas the Jews remained faithful to their beliefs.[47] Others indicated that God was simply using Israel to punish the umma for its sins,
an old image of the victor as the *ira Dei* and *ultor peccatorum*, common
to Christianity and Judaism as well.[48] For these people, the defeat of
the Arab armies was an apocalyptic judgment of God: socialism and
nationalism had been destroyed, and, as Kepel said, "the modern Islamist
movement, rebuilt around the ideas of Qutb, was at last able to command a hearing."[49]

44. Ayubi, *Political Islam*, 143; Zeidan, "Islamic Fundamentalist View of Life."
45. Nietzsche, "Human, All Too Human," 60.
46. A splendid military analysis on the side of the stupid, who saw their victory
as proof not only of the superiority of their arms but of their culture and their
understanding of God as well, is van Creveld, *The Sword and the Olive*, esp. chaps.
11–12.
47. Quoted in Hiro, *War without End*, 68.
48. Esposito, *Unholy War*, 96; Pipes, *Militant Islam Reaches America*, 3; Lewis,
What Went Wrong? 44–45.
49. Kepel, *Jihad*, 32, 63; Black, *History of Islamic Political Thought*, 310.

Qutb's doctrines filled an ideological vacuum that was especially pronounced in Egypt. It had been created in part by the failure of Egyptian and Arab arms that had been inspired by Arab nationalism, but also by the economic distress imposed by Nasserite socialism. There were new demographic challenges as well, not just in the inability of Egypt to feed so many new Egyptians but in the form of a new generation of young men who had grown to maturity entirely within a postcolonial context. They had never experienced the legitimizing struggles of their elders, and they were too late to inherit the jobs and abandoned wealth and property of the now-long-departed colonial administrators. The 1973 war against Israel restored something of the pride of the Egyptian army as a result of their successful and difficult attack across the Suez Canal, but the major short-term victor was Saudi Arabia. The "oil weapon" translated into extensive support for Wahhabite financial and educational networks focused upon young un- or under-employed men. For Wahhabi salafists, the outcome of the war confirmed their understanding that oil was a gift from God, additional proof of God's favor.[50]

Qutb's influence was felt most directly in Egypt during the presidency of Anwar Sadat (1970–1981).[51] Many of the individuals opposed to Sadat, and especially to his accommodation with Israel, had been members of the Ikhwan and had been arrested with Qutb in 1954 and 1965. Jail provided them with time and opportunity to deepen their radicalism and learn the techniques of clandestine organization. After a few attempts at "direct action," which led to the execution of the plotters, the survivors formed a number of loose jihadist networks, the most important of which was guided by Abdal Salam Faraj.

Faraj wrote a pamphlet in 1981, which was widely distributed in the early 1980s, variously translated as "The Hidden Imperative," "The Missing Obligation" or "The Neglected Duty," which criticized the Egyptian government and President Sadat in the strongest possible language: it was the embodiment of jahiliyya. It was not, therefore, the government that had neglected its duty or obligation, but the ulama. They had failed to declare jihad against those, whether nominally Muslim or explicitly non-Muslim, who refused to live by the Koran and the Sharia. In support of his views, Faraj quoted at length from Ibn Taymiyya, arguing

50. Ruthven, *A Fury for God*, 140.

51. See Kepel, *Muslim Extremism in Egypt*, 70–102; Ibrahim, "Anatomy of Egypt's Militant Groups," 423–53.

that the contemporary crisis in Islam was very close to that which existed in Ibn Taymiyya's time as well as in the time of the Prophet. In particular, Faraj noted that the Prophet removed the Jews from seventh-century Medina. Likewise, the faithful must do the same to the Jews today. President Sadat, however, had made peace with Israel and acknowledged the occupation by infidels of holy Muslim lands.

Worse, the ulama at al-Azhar University justified peace with Israel on the same grounds that Faraj opposed it. The conflict between Qutb's radicalized ijtihad, which gave primacy to the imagination, and the prudent scholarship of the ulama henceforth became central to salafist arguments.[52] Faraj, like the later terrorists, was not religiously educated. He was trained in electrical engineering. Like them as well, his doctrine of the neglected duty provided a ready-made argument against religious education and against the ulama. They were part of the problem, and like a good engineer confronting a problem, he looked for a solution and found it in Qutb's notion of a direct "vision" of Islam.

On this basis, Faraj declared a jihad against the Egyptian government and President Sadat, whom he denounced as an apostate of Islam nourished at the tables of Zionism and imperialism. His timing could not have been better: within weeks of publishing *The Neglected Duty*, Sadat was murdered.[53] The assassination was supposed to spark a revolution. Once again, however, the Islamists were disappointed: the new government of Hosni Mubarak quickly established its authority and drove the jihadists underground. They responded with increased terrorist attacks, this time on infidel tourists, and were in turn censured by the ulama as contemporary Kharijites. Hiro compared Faraj to Trotsky, the proponent of "permanent revolution," as opposed to Stalin's preference for "socialism in one country."[54] As historical analogy, the comparison is otiose: Qutb can as easily assume the Trotsky mantle.[55] Even so, comparing the writings of Faraj to the likes of Trotsky and Stalin does indicate a level of commonality, at least in terms of slogans.

52. Rapoport, "Sacred Terror," 113. See also Jansen, *Neglected Duty*.

53. Probably the new law regulating family matters, championed by Sadat's wife, Jihan, was equally offensive to the salafists because it authorized rights not found in the Sharia.

54. Hiro, *War without End*, 79.

55. In fact, Trotsky was not the inventor of the term. That honor goes to the early-nineteenth-century French liberal and editor of *Le Censeur*, Charles Comte. See Voegelin, *Crisis and the Apocalypse of Man*, 216 ff.

The importance of Qutb and Faraj for purposes of this analysis is that they were able to purge the religious discourse of Islam of its serious remaining spiritual content, its mysticism, and any experiential concern for a world-transcendent God. Islam is thus changed into a uniform, single, and dogmatic social, political, economic, and cultural blueprint, revealed by God to an electrical engineer who sets about to impose his vision by the sword.[56] By turning Islam into an ideological political program, the new generation of jihadists has robbed the ulama of their traditional role, "the preservation, systemization, and dissemination of religious ideas and concepts." Political violence is, somehow, a means to reverse "centuries of decline and enfeeblement to effect a renaissance without recourse to the ulama and their culture."[57] The fact is, enshrining ignorance of Islam in the political vanguard made no difference to the revolutionaries.

> What did matter to them was the plight of politically underrepresented and economically marginalized Egyptian Muslims. Alienated from the Westernized values of the establishment culture, and angered by the Egyptian government's Western-leaning policies, these organizations' members fastened onto those symbols of their Islamic culture that distinguished them from the hegemonic order, thus providing their quest for empowerment with a "cultural affect" grounded in basic sentiments of pride and identity.[58]

What gave their concern for the politically underrepresented its edge of violence, however, was the religious fervor imparted by the subjective certainty of doing God's work. Faraj was executed in 1982 for his part in the assassination of Anwar Sadat.

We noted above that, despite the significant achievements by Egyptian arms, the chief beneficiaries of the 1973 Arab-Israeli War were the noncombatant Saudis. They had laid the foundations for leadership with the creation of the Islamic Conference in 1969; the petro-dollar triumph after 1973 reinforced their status as guardians of the holy sites of the Arabian peninsula. Qutb's denunciation of jahiliyya looked to the Saudi Wahhabis as the reverse of their own puritan exclusivity. Moreover, the Saudi model had for many years provided an alternative to the

---

56. Ruthven, *A Fury for God*, 94.
57. Abu-Rabi, *Intellectual Origins of Islamic Resurgence*, 217, 219.
58. Calvert, "Islamist Syndrome," 340–41.

secular and republican regimes of Egypt, Syria, and Iraq. The Saudis also provided refuge for Egyptian jihadists, including Sayyid Qutb's brother, Muhammad, and Abdulla Azzam, both of whom taught at King Abd al-Aziz University, from which bin Laden graduated in 1979 with a degree in engineering and business.

Two other major events took place in 1979 that bear upon this analysis. In November of that year, several hundred armed men, organized under the name Ikhwan,[59] took control of the Grand Mosque in Mecca, turning hundreds of pilgrims into hostages. A young Saudi man, Juhayman bin Muhammad bin Sayf al-Utaybi, announced over the mosque public address system that his brother-in-law, Muhammad bin Abd Allah al-Qahtani, was the Mahdi, the Islamic messiah who had appeared, as promised in a hadith, on the first day of the year 1400 after the *hijra*. Al-Utaybi said he was inspired by Ibn Taymiyya and ibn Abd al-Wahhab, as his brother-in-law was inspired by God. He proceeded to challenge the Islamic credentials of the Saudi royal family by denouncing them for failure to rule by the Sharia, by pointing to the corruption brought by the oil boom, and especially by blaming them for the presence of Westerners in Arabia. The Saudis, in short, were apostates and deceivers. By implication the Mahdi, al-Qahtani, had the task of killing the apostates, restoring the Sharia, and instituting the final caliphate.

Recapture of the mosque took the efforts of ten thousand troops, including several hundred infidel French, who needed a special dispensation to enter the sacred precincts. The Saudis responded in two ways. First, they accorded the ulama greater domestic control and supervision of the internal affairs of the kingdom, thus abruptly ending the previously pervasive rhetoric about defending Islam by economic and technological changes. Second, the Saudi government decided that the jihadists, salafists, and other apocalyptic revolutionaries presented a genuine danger to the kingdom that best could be met by keeping them outside the country.[60] The anti-Soviet campaign in Afghanistan, which also escalated in 1979, allowed the Saudis to export troublemakers as remittance men and export Wahhabi doctrines at the same time, thus turning the revolutionaries into missionaries. Thus were the revolutionary

59. These people had no direct connection to the earlier Saudi Ikhwan nor to its Egyptian derivative. The term *Ikhwan* seems to have become a free-floating symbol of Islamist revolution rather than an organization with historical continuity.
60. Esposito, *Unholy War,* 72–73; Kepel, *Jihad,* 299.

teachings of Qutb sponsored by recycled Saudi petro-dollars from the industrial West.[61]

The other great event of 1979 took place earlier in the year: the return of the Ayatollah Khomeini to Tehran in February. The new Islamic republic provided a direct challenge to Saudi leadership that was exacerbated by the strong anti-Shiite views of the Wahhabis. Notwithstanding their differences, the Shiite contribution to terrorism was twofold. First, the effect of Khomeini's fatwa against the novel by Salman Rushdie, *The Satanic Verses,* broke with the long-standing tradition of Islamic law. Previously, no fatwa had extended beyond the lands of a Muslim government where the Sharia was applied. "Now, at a stroke, the ayatolla had placed the entire world under his jurisdiction."[62] This act had a remarkable consequence so far as Islamic law was concerned: not only were both Sunnis and Shiites of the umma affected, which was unusual enough, but citizens of European states, or of the West more broadly, who happened to be Muslims were also subject to Khomeini's pronouncement. No longer did such people live in the *dar al-Ahd,* or the *dar al-Sulh,* the realm of contractual peace or truce, but were, de facto, part of the *dar al-Islam.* This is why, in the late 1980s, for example, some of the Muslim citizens of France argued that they should be governed by the Sharia and Muslim women should be veiled.

A second Shiite contribution was even more significant. We noted above that individuals such as Qutb or Faraj were not religiously educated. They made up for this limitation by attacking the religiously learned but conventional ulama and by issuing their own fatwas; but by so doing they also divided themselves from pious middle-class Muslims who still accorded the ulama great respect. As did the highly religiously educated Khomeini before him, an educated imam, Muhammad Fadlallah, met the objection that the jihadists were religious ignoramuses. Indeed, he developed a doctrine that the ulama were to become a revolutionary vanguard with the task of exposing the rich and powerful as the agents of oppression and fear.[63] For Fadlallah, history is a quasi-Marxist struggle between the oppressors and the oppressed, the former taking the latter into account only to inflict endless pain upon them. As

61. Rubin, "Arab Islamists in Afghanistan," 179–206.

62. Kepel, *Jihad,* 190.

63. Abu-Rabi, *Intellectual Origins of Islamic Resurgence,* 230 ff. An early and naïve appraisal of Fadlallah is Carré, "Quelques Mots-clefs de Muhammad Husayn Fadlallah," 478–501.

Frantz Fanon had argued a few years earlier in Algeria, violence was at the heart of the struggle. For Fanon, the murder of a settler both rid the native of his oppressor and created a free man,[64] whereas for Fadlallah violence was both self-defense and the path of martyrdom. His greatest contribution to terrorist doctrine was, in fact, to connect martyrdom and suicide.

Within what might be called "orthodox" or mainstream Islam (both Shiite and Sunni) a martyr, *shahid*, is one who bears witness to truth, which is a common enough sentiment that is hardly confined to Islam. Article 8 of the (Sunni) Hamas Covenant, for example, states that "death for the sake of Allah is its most sublime belief."[65] Such sentiments are common to Judaism and Christianity as well as Islam, and although they may be unusual or even disagreeable, there does not seem to be anything particularly unorthodox, metastatic, magical, or pneumopathological in them. It is also true that, just as jihad is usually a community obligation, not an individual one, so by tradition the umma assigns or awards the status of martyr not simply to those who die on its behalf but to those whose death provides proportionate benefits to the community.[66] It is comparatively rare for the ulama to endorse actions in defense of the community that have a high probability of death for the individual warrior, but it is far from unknown.[67] Fadlallah's initial formulation of the problem was a variation on the traditional teaching. The faithful can become martyrs, he said, if they die fighting "to advance the collective cause of Islam and Muslims." They cannot simply die in a futile gesture, all on their own, because that would offend God. Accordingly, they must, "in principle, meet the approval of a theological body," which in turn Fadlallah was willing to provide.[68]

It is an innovation, therefore, to think of martyrdom in terms of an individual act undertaken without reference to the community and without reference to the practical issue of the defense of the community. It is also an innovation to identify as martyrs those who kill civilians rather than soldiers who are more worthy and more equal opponents. By 1990, however, it was clear from a study of Shiite terrorists that

64. See Fanon, *The Wretched of the Earth.*

65. Quoted in Ranstorp, "Terrorism in the Name of Religion," 52.

66. Khadduri, *War and Peace in the Law of Islam,* 61–62.

67. The Koranic sources are extensive in the justification of martyrdom, as one might expect, as are the hadiths. See, for example, Koran 3:164.

68. Abu-Rabi, *Intellectual Origins of Islamic Resurgence,* 236–37.

none of the sample interviewed had the slightest interest in including any communal constituency or changing anyone's mind. They were acting without reference to the practical commonsensical realities of politics and were concerned only to serve God individually by killing and dying.[69]

To see how these terrorists came to this self-understanding, we may recall the traditional teaching that martyrdom suffered while on jihad carries such great consolations that a man who dies fighting in battle against the infidel and on behalf of the umma must be considered especially fortunate.

> The Messenger of God said, "A martyr has six privileges with God. He is forgiven his sins on the shedding of the first drop of his blood; he is shown his place in paradise; he is redeemed from the torments of the grave; he is made secure from the fear of hell and a crown of glory is placed on his head of which one ruby is worth more than the world and all that is in it; he will marry seventy-two of the houris with black eyes; and his intercession will be accepted for seventy of his kinsmen."[70]

For some, the specifics of posthumous repose are no doubt appealing on their own; for others, the angelic promise may be a source of strength. The contemporary interpretation, however, is heavily weighted in favor of redeeming a contractual promise. In the words of one of the commanders of the 1983 bombing of the Marines barracks: "none of us is afraid. God is with us and gives us strength. We are making a race like horses to see who goes to God first. I want to die before my friends. They want to die before me. We want to see our God. We welcome the bombs of Reagan."[71] The terrorists, that is, welcomed death, even sought death, because they expected to be rewarded as well as consoled.

It is a short step to transform the rewards and consolations of martyrdom into the appeals of martyrdom. That is, if you are importuned by seventy kinsmen and find the prospect of marriage to seventy-two black-eyed houris appealing, then an angelic message can become a

69. Schbley, "Religious Terrorists," 240.
70. Quoted in Rapoport, "Sacred Terror," 117–18.
71. Quoted in Wright, *Sacred Rage*, 54. To this attitude General Norman Schwartzkopf is said to have replied with equal brutality a few years later: "They say they want to meet their God? I guess our job is to arrange the introduction."

piece of sympathetic magic: in order to avoid the torments of the grave, obtain a free pass to Paradise for your relatives, or gain access to the black-eyed houris, get yourself killed in action.

This magical brutality is so transparently simpleminded that it has led to considerable debate both among the learned ulama and in the Western media. Much of the controversy has centered on the meaning of the word *houri*. On August 19, 2000, the CBS program *60 Minutes* aired a story dealing with Hamas and the rewards of martyrdom that, CBS said, included "seventy virgins." This translation of the Arabic text led the Muslim Public Affairs Council to demand a retraction from CBS, and CBS then sought clarification of the proper way to translate *hur'ayn*. The executive director of the Muslim Public Affairs Council, Salaam Al-Maryati, said that the issue was "about fighting aggression and occupation, not about opportunities for sexual fantasies." Maryati's colleague Maher Hahout, resident scholar at the Islamic Center of Southern California, added that the term *houri* really means "angel" or "heavenly being" and that "there is nothing in the *Koran* or in Islamic teachings about 70 virgins or sex in Paradise. This is ridiculous and every true Muslim knows that."[72] Whatever he may have meant by "true Muslim," it soon became clear that for many Muslims, at least as well educated in Islamic doctrines as Hahout, matters were more complex.

For example, in response to the question, "if men [in Paradise] get 'the black-eyed,' what do women get?" the deputy director of the Center for Islamic Studies at al-Azhar University in Cairo, Sheikh Abd Al-Fattah Gam'an, replied with due solemnity:

> The Koran tells us that in Paradise believers get "the black-eyed," as Allah has said, "And we will marry them to 'the black-eyed.' "The black-eyed" are white and delicate, and the black of their eyes is blacker than black and the white [of their eyes] is whiter than white. To describe their beauty and their great number, the Koran says that they are "like sapphire and pearls" (Al-Rahman 58) in their value, in their color, and in their purity. And it is said of them: "[They are] like well-protected pearls" in shells (Al-Waqi'a 23), that is, they are as pure as pearls in oysters and are not perforated, no hands have touched them, no dust or dirt adheres to them, and they are undamaged. It is further said: "They are like well-protected eggs" (Al-Safat 49), that is, their

72. Hahout, *Final Call*.

delicacy is as the delicacy of the membrane beneath the shell of an egg. Allah also said: "The 'black-eyed' are confined to pavilions" (Al-Rahman 70), that is, they are hidden within, saved for their husbands.

He went on to answer the specific question as well.[73] In addition, Abd Al-Hadi Palazzi, head of the Cultural Institute of the Italian Islamic Community, cited several "Islamic teachings" in the form of commentary and hadiths that support the notion that seventy-two houris are, indeed, part of the posthumous rewards for those who dwell in Paradise.[74]

However *hur'ayn* is translated,[75] whether information concerning "the black-eyed" is theology or folklore, in the context of recruiting terrorist suicide bombers, at least until very recently, the appeal seems to be literal enough. Nasra Hassan reported the instructions given by a Hamas "dispatcher" to a potential suicide bomber: "We focus his attention on Paradise, on being in the presence of Allah, on meeting the Prophet Muhammad, on interceding for his loved ones so that they, too, can be saved from the agonies of Hell, and on the houris." And it clearly works: Hassan spoke to a young man who was about to become a "martyr" but who for some reason did not kill himself or murder others, and he told her of his sense that Paradise was "very, very near— right in front of our eyes. It lies beneath the thumb. On the other side of the detonator." *Al Risala,* an official publication of Hamas, made public the will of Said Al-Hutari whose June 1, 2001, suicide attack on a Tel Aviv disco killed twenty-three people, mostly teenage girls. He wrote: "Call out in joy, O my mother; distribute sweets, O my father and brothers; a wedding with 'the black-eyed' awaits your son in Paradise." There are many other examples of precisely the "sexual fantasies" that Maryati dismissed because, as one sixteen-year-old "youth leader" of Hamas

73. Abd al-Fattah, http://www.lailatalqudr.com/stories/p1260503.shtml (accessed January 3, 2003), quoted in Feldner, "'72 Black Eyed Virgins.'" The answer is that, if a woman's sole husband is in Paradise they are reunited; if her husband is not in Paradise, she is given to one suitable for her station; if she has more than one husband in Paradise she gets to choose the best.

74. Palazzi Abd Al-Hadi Palazzi, http://jerusalempost.com/06092001.html (accessed May 23, 2002), quoted ibid.

75. According to a report in the *New York Times* by Stille, "Scholars Dare to Look into Origins of Quran," Christoph Luxenberg (a pseudonym) argued in *Die Syro-aramaeische Lesart des Koran (Syro-Aramaic Reading of the Koran)* that the houris are, in fact, white raisins, a prized culinary delicacy. See appendix herein.

told Jack Kelley of *USA Today,* "most boys can't stop thinking about the virgins." In the current (2002–2003) intifada, however, as Tabet Mardawi, also a Hamas "dispatcher," pointed out, there are enough recruits already. "We do not have to talk to them about virgins waiting in Paradise," he said.[76]

Whether an appeal or a consolation, suicidal martyrdom introduces additional variables into the understanding of terrorist motives and adds new complexities to counterterrorism. There are two distinct aspects of the new attitude. The most obvious practical consequence of undertaking terrorist acts with a high probability of getting killed is that antiterrorist measures would have to change in response. In the words of Lord Chalfont: "The whole time that I have been involved in terrorist operations, which now goes back to 30 years, my enemy has always been a man who is very worried about his own skin. You can no longer count on that, because the terrorist [today] is not just 'prepared' to get killed, he 'wants' to get killed. Therefore, the whole planning, tactical doctrine, [and] thinking [behind antiterrorism measures] is fundamentally undermined."[77] Changes in the practical business of delivering terrorist violence as well as counterterrorist measures are, of course, important, and we will consider some of the problems involved in the following chapter. Our present concern is to specify the theoretical or theological step that extends the notion of martyrdom to include suicide, which brings us back to Fadlallah.

According to Abu-Rabi, Fadlallah is "the spiritual and intellectual leader of Hizbollah." Carré also indicated that Fadlallah was one of the spiritual guides, indeed the principal guide, of Hezbollah.[78] This Shiite group rose to prominence with suicide bombings in Lebanon against French, American, and Israeli targets from 1983 through 1985. Most of these attacks were undertaken by Islamic Jihad; Hezbollah disavowed its complicity but praised the results and benefitted politically. The chief ethical and theological problem with such attacks is that they involved,

76. See Hassan, "An Arsenal of Believers"; *Al-Risala,* July 7, 2001, quoted in Feldner, "'72 Black Eyed Virgins'"; Kelley, *USA Today,* June 26, 2001; Margalit, "The Suicide Bombers."

77. Kidder, "Terrorist Mentality."

78. Abu-Rabi, *Intellectual Origins of Islamic Resurgence,* 244; Carré, "Quelques Mots-Clefs de Muhammad Husayn Fadlallah," 479. Many other subsequent analyses agreed.

not premeditated killing, but premeditated suicide, *intihar,* which is necessarily premeditated. And *intihar* is usually considered a grievous sin.

Following a thorough analysis of the relevant passages in the Koran, Rosenthal concluded, in an authoritative study undertaken many years before the advent of suicidal terrorist attacks: "it may be said that there is no absolutely certain evidence to indicate that Muhammad ever discussed the problem of suicide by means of a divine revelation, although the possibility remains that *Qur'ân* 4.29(33) contains a prohibition of suicide. It is, however, certain that from the early days of Islam on this and some other passages of the *Qur'ân* were considered by many Muslims as relevant to the subject." If one looks to the hadiths rather than the Koran, one finds that the Prophet many times is recorded as having said that a person who commits suicide will never enter Paradise but, on the contrary, will repeat his suicidal agony in the flames of Hell. Moreover, the canonical literature containing the fatwas of judges also indicates that suicide is unlawful. Thus, according to Rapoport, the Shiite teaching that suicide bombers go to paradise with the six privileges of a martyr is simply "a perversion."[79] For one reason or another, therefore, the ulama had to confront the issue of suicide bombers.

Fadlallah was the cleric who provided the most extensive analysis of the problem. Initially he denied that his organization was terrorist at all. "We don't believe in terrorism," he said. "We don't see resisting the occupier as a terrorist action. We see ourselves as *mujahideen* (holy warriors) who fight a *jihad* (holy war) for the people."[80] He then modified his position and argued that the suicide attacks of Islamic Jihad should be abandoned because they were ineffective. In the event, however, they proved highly effective—after all, the infidels left Lebanon—so he had to confront and deal with the basic theological question. For a time, he resisted efforts to get him to provide a decisive ruling or explicit judgment, a fatwa, and instead reflected on the plight of Muslims and the need to fight, even using "unconventional" methods. This was, of course, fair enough as a political complaint, but it did not address the theoretical or theological issue of suicide. As Martin Kramer said, "One could not simply argue extenuating circumstances to a constituency devoted

---

79. Rosenthal, "On Suicide in Islam," 243. See also Lewis, *Crisis of Islam,* 153–54. Rapoport, "Messianic Sanctions for Terror," 195.

80. Carré, "Quelques Mots-Clefs de Muhammad Husayn Fadlallah," 479.

to the implementation of Islamic law."[81] Finally, Fadlallah denied that the commonsensical difference between suicide and martyrdom is valid: "There is no difference between dying with a gun in your hand or exploding yourself. In a situation of struggle or holy war, you have to find the best means to achieve your goals."[82] On another occasion, he asked, rhetorically: "what is the difference between setting out for battle knowing you will die *after* killing ten [of the enemy], and setting out to the field to kill ten and knowing you will die *while* killing them?"[83] More recently still he has been quoted as condemning suicide bombers.[84]

Whatever his inconsistencies, there is a significant difference between setting out for battle knowing you will die after killing ten of the enemy and knowing you will die while killing them. First of all you can never *know* that you will die after killing ten of the enemy; you might kill nine or eleven or you might be killed first. Second, from the perspective of the military commander, he does not know *who* will be killed in battle, though he knows some will die; the dispatcher of a suicide bomber knows both that his "soldier" will die and precisely who it will be. Accordingly, such an individual cannot absolve himself of personal responsibility for the bomber's death by appealing to the will of God, fate, statistics, luck, or the Clausewitzian fog of war. The reason, moreover, is obvious: even within the context of jihad as armed struggle against unfavorable odds, there is an important and unexpungible difference between risking one's life in the service of religious truth in such a way that one may or may not become a martyr, and blowing oneself up. There is, to be blunt, no risk in blowing oneself up, only the certainty of death. By any commonsensical understanding, such an act is suicidal.

For Fadlallah, however, death by suicide was merely "a step that leads to reaching the martyr's goals. That is why the believer, when he achieves self-martyrdom, lives through spiritual happiness."[85] Not every religious scholar and cleric agreed with Fadlallah's position. In April 2001, for

81. Kramer, "The Moral Logic of Hizballah," 145.
82. Ranstorp, "Terrorism in the Name of Religion," 55.
83. Kramer, "The Moral Logic of Hizballah," 145–46.
84. Quoted in Ruthven, *A Fury for God*, 101.
85. Abu-Rabi, *Intellectual Origins of Islamic Resurgence*, 242. For Abdul Aziz Rantisi, a founder of Hamas, suicide bombers were matter-of-factly called self-chosen martyrs. Rantisi is a medical doctor. See Juergensmeyer, *Terror in the Mind of God*, 72–73.

example, the mufti of Saudi Arabia, Sheik Abd Al-Aziz bin Abdaallala al-Sheik declared he was unaware "of anything in the Sharia regarding killing oneself in the heart of the enemy, or what is called 'suicide.' This is not part of jihad, and I fear that it is merely killing oneself."[86] His fatwa was immediately criticized on two general grounds. First, the difference between suicide and martyrdom was fundamental but could not be determined by outward behavior—since blowing oneself up only *looks* like suicide. Rather, the decisive factor was the motive of the bomber: "The mentality of those who carry out heroic operations of martyrdom," said Sheik Yussuf Al-Qaradhawi, a spiritual leader of the Sunni Muslim Brotherhood, "has nothing to do with the mentality of someone who commits suicide." He explained the difference: "He who commits suicide kills himself for his own benefit, while he who commits martyrdom sacrifices himself for the sake of his religion and his umma. While someone who commits suicide has lost hope with the spirit of God the Mujahid is full of hope with regard to God's spirit and mercy. He fights his enemy and the enemy of God with this new weapon, which fate has put in the hands of the weak so that they would fight against the evil of the strong and arrogant."[87]

A second argument also began with an examination of motives. Sheik Muhammad Sayyed Tantawi, of Al-Azhar University, declared that "suicide operations" were acts of self-defense "and a kind of martyrdom as long as the intention behind them is to kill the enemy's soldiers, and not women and children." He later changed his mind.[88] In any event, Sheik Al-Qaradhawi had already declared that "Israeli society is militaristic in nature." Thus, killing women is acceptable. As for children and old people, that would be a mistake, but "a result of military necessity," and "necessity justifies the forbidden." Besides, as Tawfiq Al-Shawi, an Egyptian professor of Islamic law, explained, there is no contradiction between the Saudi mufti and the others because the fatwa of the former applies the Sharia only in peacetime "and not in a state of

---

86. Interview in the London Arabic-language paper *Al-Sharq Al-Awsat,* quoted in Feldner, "Debating the Religious, Political, and Moral Legitimacy of Suicide Bombings, Part I."

87. This and quotations in the following paragraph, unless otherwise identified, are from Feldner, "Debating the Religious, Political, and Moral Legitimacy of Suicide Bombings, Part I."

88. Tantawi, "Leading Egyptian Government Cleric Calls for 'Martyrdom Attacks that Strike Horror into the Hearts of the Enemies of Allah.'"

war, as is currently the case." These two positions of opposition to any criticism of the identity of martyrdom and self-martyrdom were reiterated, at decreasing levels of sophistication, in the columns of journalists and even on TV by one Adel Sadeq, chairman of the Arab Psychiatrists Association.[89]

As with the question of the black-eyed houris, the simplifiers and vulgarizers clearly dominated the current popular debate. It is now dogmatically established and lies beyond question self-martyrdom, *istishad*, is not suicide, *intihar*, but indeed the highest form of martyrdom. End of story.

For purposes of this analysis, the significant point is not that a collection of ulama invented a new doctrine, istishad, and defended it with a torturous theology that contradicted all the evidence of Muslim scripture as well as common sense, but that any argumentation at all ceased to be necessary once suicide bombing (whether described as self-martyrdom or anything else) became a more or less normal practice. In 1988, the suicide-bombing campaign in Lebanon was abandoned for tactical, not theological, reasons—the opportunity for success ended with the withdrawal of the troops of the Multilateral Peacekeeping Force. It has never fallen from favor among Hamas and Islamic Jihad, terrorists operating against Israel, and was revived in a spectacular fashion with the attacks on New York and Washington. As we shall see, by the time bin Laden was involved, the distinction between suicide and martyr had become meaningless. He sent his terrorists on "martyrdom operations" with the same equanimity a mother would send her child on an errand to fetch yoghurt.

There is a psychological dimension to the spiritual perversity of "self-martyrdom" operations similar in its way to the psychology of sixteen-year-old boys dreaming of glorious black-eyed virgins. Abu-Rabi is of

---

89. See Feldner, "Debating the Religious, Political, and Moral Legitimacy of Suicide Bombings, Part II"; Feldner, "Debating the Religious, Political, and Moral Legitimacy of Suicide Bombings, Part III"; "Debating the Religious, Political, and Moral Legitimacy of Suicide Bombings, Part IV." See also "Suicide, Martyrdom, Terrorist Attacks, or Homicide: A Debate in the Arab Media." Dr. Adel Sadeq's remarks were published as "Class Isn't over Yet, Stupid" in the form of an open letter to President Bush, the "Stupid" of his title, and were broadcast over Iqraa, a Saudi-Egyptian satellite TV channel. See "Chairman of the Arab Psychiatrists Association Offers Diagnoses: Bush Is Stupid; Perpetrating a Suicide/Martyrdom Attack Is Life's Most Beautiful Moment; We'll Throw Israel into the Sea."

the opinion that there is nothing irrational or immoral about self-martyrdom, because to use such terms would be to be guided by "psychology," which is insufficiently profound for these deep issues. He explained: "What gives the martyr the right to die is not merely a cause in a theoretical sense but the practical conditions that give rise to that cause." But what, other than "psychology," could link the "practical conditions" to a "cause" for which someone might die? For Abu-Rabi, who was trying to provide an analysis, and not to advocate an ideological position, "suffering is mainly caused at the hands of Israelis, and the only answer to this suffering is martyrdom."[90] This is evidently untrue. Martyrdom, in the sense of suffering at the hands of others, in this instance the Israelis, is *one* response, a passive one. Negotiating, engaging in politics, fighting back is another. But fighting back is in no sense passive: it is most emphatically going into action. Considered in that context, the psychological aspect has a clear enough meaning.

In chapter 1 we drew attention to the perverse logic of terrorism whereby someone acts in such a way that by killing a third party he seems to be sacrificing either his moral personality or, indeed, his life for the sake of another who, nevertheless, has never requested such a sacrifice and would likely be opposed to the initial murderous action. We noted that the killers were not victims and could lay no claim to any moral high ground: they were simply asserting their own power in such a way that the aggressiveness of an ordinary assault was masked, at least temporarily, by the experience of horror at the fact of the terrorist action. Empirical studies of groups and of individual suicide bombers confirm this interpretation. Religious terrorism, Ranstorp argued, offers "more hope and a greater chance of vengeance against the sources of their historical grievances than they otherwise would have ... violent acts give these [terrorist] groups a sense of power that is disproportionate to their size."[91] The same argument applies to studies of individual terrorists.

Ruthven, for example, addressed the issue of posthumous rewards and roundly declared the whole issue to be spurious. "The suicidal martyrdom they embraced in their final, horrendous act of destruction was not so much the result of some naïve faith in a paradisiacal future, but

90. Abu-Rabi, *Intellectual Origins of Islamic Resurgence*, 242. See also Stern, *Terror in the Name of God*, 50–53.

91. Ranstorp, "Terrorism in the Name of Religion," 53.

the final solution they found to a profoundly tragic personal predicament."[92] In his analysis of the exit videos of Palestinian suicide bombers, Margalit reached a conclusion that indicated that the individuals who made these documents, along with their sponsoring organization (usually Hamas), both asserted their power and solved their problems.

The Palestinian suicide bombers have all been Muslims, notwithstanding the sizeable Christian Palestinian population and the fact that, during the 1970s and 1980s, many of the PLO terrorists were Christians. The most obvious reason for this is because Hamas and Islamic Jihad have stated that suicide bombing is a religious duty. Secular Palestinian nationalists, until recently, with the formation of the Al-Aqsa Brigade, affiliated with Fatah, have not used suicide bombers. The introduction of the Al-Aqsa Brigade, moreover, has made the problem of controlling suicide bombers and ensuring they would be politically effective more difficult. From the point of view of Hamas, the newcomers, who were also the first to use women and the elderly, look like undisciplined freelancers simply solving their personal problems. The majority of suicide bombers, however, are dispatched by religious Islamists, and according to Margalit, their main motive "is revenge for acts committed by Israelis, a revenge that will be known and celebrated in the Islamic world."[93] Both aspects are important: because there are other ways to take revenge than by blowing oneself up, the actual act must be sufficiently spectacular that it will be noticed, remembered, and celebrated by the community from which the suicide bomber comes. When one adds in the appeal of instilling fear in the Israeli audience, the assertiveness, indeed the power, of the act is obvious. At the same time, as we shall argue in the next chapter, the moral perversity associated with such modes of self-assertion requires a highly imaginative response, both for the terrorist and for the community that offers support.

Following the terrorist attacks of September 11, 2001, several accounts of the origin and development of Al Qaeda and biographies of Osama bin Laden have appeared.[94] In the personality of Osama bin Laden and in his organization, Al Qaeda, many of the themes discussed separately so far in this chapter come together. We begin, therefore, with a conven-

92. Ruthven, *A Fury for God*, 132.

93. Margalit, "The Suicide Bombers."

94. See, for example, Bodansky, *Bin Laden*; Bergen, *Holy War, Inc.*; Jacquard, *In the Name of Osama bin Laden*; Corbin, *The Base*; Lewis, "License to Kill," 14–19; Boroumand and Boroumand, "Terror, Islam, and Democracy," 5–20.

tional historical reprise. The broad context of bin Laden's intellectual and spiritual formation is familiar: secular, liberal, democratic, Western civilization is devoid of spiritual substance, which makes it the antithesis of God's final and unambiguous revelation. Because of this ever-present threat, the faithful must resist the West as strongly as possible and destroy the regimes that defend it or are allied with it—especially in the Islamic world. History is the simple story of the waxing and waning of Islamic truth until the last apocalyptic events, which establish a final, ecumenic, and peaceful Muslim world.

In 1977, bin Laden enrolled in an engineering and business course of study at King Abd al-Aziz University in Jeddah. He was required as well to take a course of study on Islam, which refined his Wahhabism under the guidance of Abdulla Azzam and Muhammad Qutb, the younger brother of Sayyid, a member of the Egyptian Ikhwan, and editor and publicist for his brother's work. Azzam was a member of the Palestinian Ikhwan and a founding member of Hamas. He fought in the Six-Day War in 1967, received his doctorate in 1969, and became a professor of Islamic law at the University of Jordan. He was expelled a few years later and began teaching at Abd al-Aziz. His understanding of jihad and of the question of recovering the lands of Islam was straightforward and crystal clear: "Jihad and the rifle alone: no negotiations, no conferences, no dialogues."[95] Any land once ruled by the caliphate, even if it is as small as the span of one's hand, must be recaptured. Such opinions for bin Laden were axiomatic.

According to one account, bin Laden was deeply affected by the occupation of the Grand Mosque in 1979.[96] A far more important event for him personally was the war against the Soviet Union in Afghanistan. The significance of Afghanistan apparently dawned on bin Laden's teacher Azzam after he met some Afghan pilgrims in 1980 in Mecca. In 1984 he moved to Peshawar and established the Bureau of Services to the Mujahideen. In Saudi Arabia, bin Laden had already been collecting funds for the jihad in Afghanistan. He subsequently joined his mentor in Peshawar and, unlike many of the volunteers from the Middle East, actually fought Soviet troops in Afghanistan. His experience in Afghanistan and his association with Azzam impressed upon bin Laden the

95. Quoted in Bergen, *Holy War, Inc.*, 53.
96. *The Observer* (London), October 28, 2001, quoted in Hiro, *War without End*, 191.

importance of jihad. For both men it was not a rhetorical measure or a means of exhortation but a concrete, empirical activity, suffused with divine purpose that eventually would ensure the restoration of the caliphate. Bin Laden returned to Saudi Arabia in 1989, convinced that God had won a great victory in Afghanistan and that additional triumphs lay ahead.

In 1988, bin Laden created a set of computer files to track all the volunteers who had passed through Azzam's recruitment facilities in Peshawar and the training camps inside Afghanistan that he had established. This database, in Arabic *al Qaeda*, became the nucleus for the notorious terrorist network.[97] Later that year, for reasons that are not entirely clear but that probably involved a difference of opinion concerning the relative priority of attacking Israel or destroying jahili Muslim regimes, bin Laden and Azzam dissolved their working relationship; a year later Azzam was dead, blown up by an anonymous car bomb along with two of his sons. Meanwhile bin Laden had recruited an impressive number of senior associates, including Ayman al-Zawahiri, a medical doctor and a leader in Egyptian Islamic Jihad who had spent time in jail following the killing of Sadat. Sheikh Omar Abdel Rahman, later convicted for his part in the first attack on the World Trade Center, was also in Peshawar at the time. Two of his sons later joined Al Qaeda. In addition to a number of technical experts in weaponry, explosives, and other tradecraft, bin Laden's council, or *shura*, also included Abu Muaz al-Masry, who specialized in the interpretation of dreams.[98]

The returning soldier who cannot reintegrate with civilian society is common throughout the world. This conventional problem applied to the "Afghan Arabs," as they were called, when they returned from the battlefields of Afghanistan to their homes in the Middle East. This was certainly true of bin Laden. Moreover, the Iraqi invasion of Kuwait in August 1990 made matters worse. Because of the prominence of his family, bin Laden had access to the highest levels of Saudi leadership. He offered King Fahd his Afghan veterans for service in defense of the kingdom against the blaspheming apostate secular nationalists from Baathist Iraq, but the Saudi government turned him down and opted for infidel GIs. The meaning of these events was clear to bin Laden: after God had defeated the Soviets in Afghanistan and then caused their athe-

97. Kepel, *Jihad*, 115. See also Meddeb, *Malady of Islam*, 141–43.
98. Benjamin and Simon, *Age of Sacred Terror*, 105.

ist empire to disintegrate, the Americans had taken their place. God, accordingly, would attack and destroy America as well, along with the Saudi stooges.

As had Qutb before him, bin Laden identified the Americans with the eleventh-century Crusaders, the timeless enemy of Islam. Likewise, when the Saudi ulamas issued a fatwa giving permission for the Americans to stage troops in the kingdom, this was evidence of their supine apostasy. The Saudis responded to these charges the way the Egyptians did to those of Qutb, by harassing and repressing the author of them. It took the assistance of his family to enable bin Laden to escape the Saudi authorities. He went first to Pakistan and then to Afghanistan before ending up in the Sudan, practically the sole Islamist refuge in the region.

The Gulf War and its aftermath seem to have constituted another major turning point for bin Laden. In organizational terms, he built up Al Qaeda as a network of, but also for, Afghan veterans, finding them jobs in his Sudanese agricultural operations and in the family construction business. He also helped facilitate the exit of his jihadists from Pakistan, where they were no longer welcome, and some of them he redeployed to Somalia, the Balkans and Chechnya, East Africa, and the Philippines. He had created in Al Qaeda a new international brigade of Islamist jihadists, salafists trained to fight and to train others. They were cut off from conventional social realities, "the free electrons of jihad" who looked at the world solely through the lens of "religious doctrine and armed violence."[99] The returning veterans, far from being Saudi or even Arab nationalists, were deracinated fanatics.[100]

Bin Laden also enhanced the ability of Al Qaeda to transfer funds around the world. As Benjamin and Simon observed, "Al Qaeda's future was beginning to come into focus."[101] That future turned out to involve forming alliances with Shiite terrorist organizations, developing an extensive training regime, carrying out attacks on American and Saudi targets, and eventually relocating once more to Afghanistan. About this same time, during the summer of 1996, bin Laden started referring to himself as "Sheikh." He also began issuing documents, which he called

99. Kepel, *Jihad*, 219.
100. Hiro, *War without End*, 156. See also Gause, "The Kingdom in the Middle," 112.
101. Benjamin and Simon, *Age of Sacred Terror*, 117.

fatwas, to provide direction, justification, and self-interpretation to the organization. Like his predecessors Qutb and Mawdudi, bin Laden lacked formal scholarly qualifications and so, properly speaking, did not deserve to be called Sheikh bin Laden, nor did he have the authority to issue fatwas. But again like Qutb, he considered the religiously educated ulama to be corrupt: he needed no instruction from them to interpret the word of God.

It is, of course, possible to interpret bin Laden's activities and those of Al Qaeda in terms of conventional terrorism—propaganda by deed, and so on. Psychological explanations are always available as is the suggestion of Kepel that bin Laden is defending the "great merchant" class of Arabia against the oppression of the Saudis.[102] It also seems clear, however, that the standard "root cause" argument is entirely inapplicable. Poverty was the least of the concerns of the Al Qaeda terrorists. To begin with, bin Laden comes from a very wealthy family; moreover, fifteen of the nineteen terrorists identified in the September 2001 attacks were also Saudi citizens, many of whom were well educated and from reasonably prosperous families. It is also evident from bin Laden's statements over the years that his alleged concern for Israeli insults to the ethnic pride of the Palestinians is entirely contingent upon his more grandiose schemes for the "Islamic nation," the umma. To the extent that bin Laden is in pursuit of what might be called the ordinary goals of international politics, he seeks to control the oil wealth of Saudi Arabia and the nuclear arsenal of Pakistan.[103] He has indicated in interviews with *Time* (December 23, 1998) and *Newsweek* (January 6, 1999) that he had long been seeking weapons of mass destruction, including atomic demolition munitions or "suitcase bombs" from the former Soviet Union, chiefly Kazakstan.[104] Even so, the point of obtaining such assets is subordinate to his "religious" vision—or more accurately to his pneumopathological expectation of an ecumenic transfiguration of human life.

The accounts of bin Laden's expectations are found in the pseudofatwas he began issuing shortly after he decided to style himself a sheikh. Following his expulsion from the Sudan, in August 1996, for example,

102. Kepel, *Jihad*, 13.
103. Berger and Sutphen, "Commandeering the Palestinian Cause," 124.
104. Cameron, "Multi-track Microproliferation," 288.

bin Laden issued his "Declaration of War against the Americans Who Occupy the Land of the Two Holy Mosques."[105] The "fatwa" begins with formular invocations of praise to God, a selection of texts from the Koran, and a summary of several hadiths. It seems that the "Zionist-Crusader alliance" is responsible for massacres of Muslims from Bosnia to Burma. These massacres have been carried out and ignored because of a conspiracy between the United States and the United Nations, the worst expression of which is "the occupation of the land of the two Holy Places" by infidel Crusader troops.

At the same time, bin Laden continued in his "Declaration," a "blessed awakening" is sweeping the Islamic world, much as in the days of Ibn Taymiyya and the Mongol depredations. Even though the Americans have killed Azzam, he said, and imprisoned the "blind sheikh," Omar Rahman, bin Laden himself can still carry on their work from the place of the destruction of "the largest infidel military force in the world," Afghanistan. Bin Laden emphasized the *hijra* theme, as if he were re-enacting the Prophet's migration from Mecca to Medina, by calling Afghanistan "Khurasan." The reference is not to the modern province of northeast Iran but to the medieval word for the land east of Persia, at the center of the Parthian Empire, and from the perspective of bin Laden, a land located on the farthest rim of civilization. For bin Laden, Benjamin and Simon observed, "the campaign against the infidel is something out of the great age of Islamic chivalry,"[106] which at least establishes his salafist credentials.

The Americans did not get the message when the Khobar Towers were attacked in 1996, he went on. To ensure the enemy knew what was at stake, he repeated a litany of complaints against the Saudis: the corrupt House of al-Saud had allowed the Crusaders into the country; they refused to follow the Sharia, preferring instead man-made laws; they did not answer petitions to change their ways. Indeed, the situation is so bad that it is necessary to attack the root of the problem, which, as Ibn Taymiyya taught, was to destroy pagans and infidels as the Mongols had been destroyed. "What bears no doubt in this fierce Judeo-Christian campaign against the Muslim world, the likes of which

105. See the excerpts in http://www.pbs.org/wgbh/pages/frontline/shows/ binladen/who/edicts.html. See also the appreciative analysis of Lewis, *Crisis of Islam*, 158–60.

106. Other commentators have speculated that Azzam was murdered by bin Laden. Benjamin and Simon, *Age of Sacred Terror*, 104, 143.

has never been seen before, is that the Muslims must prepare all the possible might to repel the enemy on the military, economic, missionary, and all other fronts." An unprecedented attack clearly requires an unprecedented response.

When the task is finished, when the campaign against Islam is defeated, the emerging Islamic state will command great wealth and power and will extinguish the Zionists. In the meantime, because the Saudis opened the Arab peninsula to the Crusaders, they have "voided" their right to call themselves Islamic and so must be removed along with the Crusaders.

> The regime is fully responsible for what had been incurred by the country and the nation; however the occupying American enemy is the principle and the main cause of the situation. Therefore efforts should be concentrated on destroying, fighting and killing the enemy until, by the Grace of Allah, it is completely defeated. The time will come—by the Permission of Allah—when you'll perform your decisive role so that the word of Allah will be supreme and the word of the infidels (Kaferoon) will be the inferior. You will hit with iron fist against the aggressors. You'll re-establish the normal course and give the people their rights and carry out your truly Islamic duty. Allah willing, I'll have a separate talk about these issues.

Bin Laden continued to remind the world of his presence from his retreat in "Khurasan" by granting interviews to several Arabic language as well as Western media. In March 1997 his PR campaign enlisted CNN in its service.[107] On February 22, 1998, in *al-Quds al Arabi*, an Arabic newspaper published in London, he promulgated his famous edict and fatwa, the "Declaration of the World Islamic Front for Jihad against the Jews and the Crusaders."[108]

The text has remained central to Al Qaeda doctrine. It begins with a formular invocation of God's name, a quotation from the Koran exhorting the faithful to slay pagans, and a passage from a hadith where Muhammad said he had been sent with a sword to ensure that no one but God is worshipped. It goes on: "The Arabian Peninsula has never—

107. Excerpted at http://www.pbs.org/wgbh/pages/frontline/shows/binladen/who/edicts.html.

108. The text was widely reprinted; this version is from the Federation of American Scientists, http://www.fas.org/irp/world/para/docs/980223-fatwa.htm. See analysis of Lewis, "License to Kill."

since God made it flat, created its desert, and encircled it with seas—been stormed by any forces like the crusader armies spreading in it like locusts, eating its riches and wiping out its plantations." As a result of this desecration of Arabia, "we should all agree on how to settle the matter."

Before indicating how things are to be settled, however, the edict makes three points. First, the United States "has been occupying the lands of Islam in the holiest of places, the Arabian Peninsula" and using Arabian wealth; second, to fight Muslims, especially Iraqis, who historically have occupied the center of the Islamic world; third, this "crusader-Zionist alliance" aims "to serve the Jews' petty state" by diverting attention from Israeli atrocities, by destroying Iraq, by dividing and weakening the other Muslim states, in order "to guarantee Israel's survival and the continuation of the brutal crusade occupation of the peninsula." All these crimes, listed in order of importance, the edict says, "are a clear declaration of war on God, his messenger, and his Muslims," for which an armed jihad is the only acceptable response. The text of the fatwa then states: "The ruling to kill the Americans and their allies—civilians and military—is an individual duty for every Muslim who can do it in any country in which it is possible to do it, in order to liberate the al-Aqsa Mosque [in Jerusalem] and the holy mosque [in Mecca] from their grip, and in order for their armies to move out of all the lands of Islam, defeated and unable to threaten any Muslim." The edict then quotes again from the Koran and returns to the theme of war: "We—with God's help—call on every Muslim who believes in God and wishes to be rewarded to comply with God's order to kill the Americans and plunder their money wherever and whenever they find it. We also call on Muslim ulema, leaders, youths, and soldiers to launch the raid on Satan's U.S. troops and the devil's supporters allying with them, and to displace those who are behind them so that they may learn a lesson."

The "declaration of war" was signed by four other individuals besides bin Laden on behalf of a "World Islamic Front." The implication was clear: several dispersed Islamist organizations were coordinating and perhaps consolidating their capabilities. Second, it was an indication that the Islamists were going to strike at the United States as soon as it was judged to be possible and prudent.

In May 1998, a few months prior to the spectacular bombings of the American embassies in Kenya and Tanzania, bin Laden was interviewed by ABC reporter John Miller, at which time he further clarified some of the issues.[109] The original declaration of war, he said, was purely defensive. Thus any use of "guerilla tactics" and indeed of terrorism was legitimate. The terrorism of Al Qaeda is "commendable" and "blessed" because "it is directed at the tyrants and the aggressors and the enemies of Allah," including Muslim apostates and traitors. "We do not have to differentiate between military and civilian. As far as we are concerned, they are all targets and this is what the fatwa says. The fatwa is comprehensive." On the positive side, bin Laden said, he was simply reiterating the call to all mankind that was revealed to Muhammad, the call of Islam, the invitation to all nations "to embrace Islam, the religion that calls for justice, mercy and fraternity among all nations, not differentiating between black or white, or between red and yellow except with respect to their devotedness. . . . We fight the governments that are bent on attacking our religion and on stealing our wealth and hurting our feelings." He reiterated the message conveyed by the attack on the Khobar Towers and added that, so far as the Jews are concerned, "the enmity between us . . . goes far back in time and is deep rooted. There is no question that war between the two of us is inevitable." As for the "American Crusaders," it matters not what they say: God determines how long bin Laden will live and the Americans can do nothing about that. His first task, he said, is to liberate Mecca from the Crusaders and Jerusalem from the Jews.

The Jews are not, for Islamists, merely the citizens of Israel and unwelcome neighbors of the Muslim states of the region. Nor are they merely the repository of a long-standing hostility. Later in the interview bin Laden explained why he was so confident of victory: "We are certain that we shall—with the grace of God—prevail over the Americans and over the Jews, as the Messenger of Allah promised us in an authentic prophetic tradition when He said the Hour of Resurrection shall not come before Muslims fight Jews and before Jews hide behind trees and behind rocks."

This "authentic prophetic tradition" is one of many apocalyptic themes surrounding relations between the two religions, Islam and Judaism.[110] Article Seven of the (Sunni) Hamas Covenant, for example,

---

109. See http://www.pbs.org/wgbh/pages/frontline/shows/binladen/who/interview.html.

110. See Cook, *Studies in Classical Muslim Apocalyptic,* and *Contemporary Muslim Apocalyptic Literature* (forthcoming).

states: "The time [of Resurrection] will not come until Muslims fight the Jews and kill them, and until the Jews hide behind rocks and trees, whence the call is raised: 'Oh Muslim, here is a Jew hiding! Come and kill him.'"[111] During the apocalyptic Hour of Resurrection, therefore, the common world is transfigured, and even the rocks and trees cry out to assist in the process of extermination of the enemies of God.

The purpose of this large-scale killing is akin to Asahara's purpose of ordering large-scale *poa*-ing: to bring about a peaceful world of triumphant justice.[112] As with the example of Aum Shinrikyo, common sense has difficulty grasping how an apocalyptic war of extermination can achieve an endless peace of righteousness. Thus, as Juergensmeyer said, with some perplexity, there are no "simple answers" that terrorists alive to apocalyptic expectations can give when they are asked "simple questions," such as: "What kind of a state do you want? How do you plan to get it? How do you think you will get along with the rest of the world?"[113] Juergensmeyer's commonsense questions are easily dismissed by terrorist pneumopaths because such people are concerned, not with getting along with the rest of the world, but with changing the structure of reality, with "changing the world" as Marx put it, so that an apocalyptic conflict will give rise to a metastatic peace.

Even within the world of commonsense, when an operation with the grandiose title of the World Islamic Front issues such a high-octane document as the "Jihad against Jews and Crusaders" and lays such emphasis on the urgency and inevitability of the coming conflict, it takes on a life of its own. Something had to be done, the more spectacular the better, if only to preserve the voice of the World Islamic Front and of "sheikh" bin Laden in the Muslim world. The bombings of the American embassies in Nairobi and Dar-es-Salaam on August 7, 1998, were directed at relatively low-risk targets but carried a high reward if successful. Both also showed Iranian "signatures" on the explosives. More important, however, the simultaneous, multiple, and indiscriminate nature of the attacks demonstrated great organizational skill, a capacity to innovate, and murderous lethality.

111. Quoted in Hoffman, *Inside Terrorism*, 98–99. See also Benjamin and Simon, *Age of Sacred Terror*, 193.

112. Rapoport, "Messianic Sanctions for Terror," 197. See also Ruthven, *A Fury for God*, 48.

113. Juergensmeyer, "Worldwide Rise of Religious Nationalism," 17.

By 1998, at the latest, it was clear that bin Laden had created an Islamist argument to authorize an extensive and ruthless terrorist attack on the West, not in response to the ongoing political problems between Israel and the Palestinians nor even as a reaction to the crisis in Iraq after the Gulf War. He had done so initially with the help of Iran, and his World Islamic Front served the interests of that country by providing a screen to ensure "plausible deniability," particularly after Western security agencies uncovered in the spring of 1987 an Iran-backed plan to attack the World Cup soccer matches scheduled to take place in France that summer.

Following the August 7, 1998, attacks, *al-Quds al-Arabi* published a salafi-inspired analysis, and bin Laden's World Islamic Front issued its own communiqué. The issues had expanded once again. By the late summer of 1998 the departure of the American troops and the return of a regime of Islamist truth to the holy land of Arabia was not enough. Western influence must be banished from the Muslim world as a prelude to the expansion of an ecumenic Islamist empire. The communiqué concluded:

> The Muslim Ummah is in a constant state of Jihad, physical, financial and verbal against the terrorist state of America, Israel, Serbia, etc. We can envisage that this is the beginning of much more bloodshed and deaths should the U.S. continue to occupy Muslim land and to oppress Muslims in the Gulf and elsewhere. The Muslims will never rest until their land is liberated from the occupiers and the authority to rule restored to the Muslims from the tyrant, self-appointed, puppet leaders in Muslim countries such as Mubarak of Egypt, Fahd of Arabia, Zirwal of Algeria, Qaddafi of Libya, etc. The struggle will continue against regimes in Muslim countries until al-Khilafah (the Islamic State) is re-established and the law of God dominates the world.[114]

By the fall of 1998, bin Laden had become a "guest" of the Taliban, President Clinton had ordered an ineffective cruise missile attack against targets in Khartoum and Afghanistan, and the latter country had replaced Iran as the sponsoring state of his efforts. Both Iran and Saudi Arabia continued to supply the Taliban and Al Qaeda with generous

114. The communiqué is reprinted in Bodansky, *Bin Laden*, 270 ff.; quotation, ibid., 271.

financial aid, and from Pakistan the Pakistani secret service, the ISI (Inter-Services Intelligence Directorate) continued to assist in the training of Al Qaeda members.

The variety of interpretations that have followed the September 11 terrorist attacks is enormous, ranging from analyses based on rational calculation of the outcomes of asymmetric warfare to moralizing sermons on the ubiquity of evil. In terms of the categories used in this analysis it seems clear that the intention of the attack was to confirm that bin Laden and Al Qaeda were capable of initiating a blow on behalf of God and against Satan.

Like the attacks on the embassies, the attacks on the World Trade Center and the Pentagon involved lengthy planning, a long-term strategy, the use of terrorist "sleeper" cells, and for some, and possibly all, members of the terrorist teams, full awareness of a group suicide, which required a rare degree of commitment and discipline. Moreover, the profile of the September 2001 terrorists was much different than the typical Hamas recruit: they were not young, poor, ill-educated, or psychologically damaged, as so many of their predecessors seemed to be.[115] At the same time as they were technically competent, they lived in a world of signs, portents, and rituals.

Documents left behind by hijackers of three of the four planes on September 11 indicate both the routinization of self-martyrdom and the necessity of going through a precise and demanding ritual. Much of the language used in these documents is crude and doctrinaire. It combines practical precautions for killing (sharpen your knife; make sure no one follows you; put your socks on and make sure to tie your shoelaces tight) with a last-minute pep talk (Your heart should be happy; give a priority to interests of the group; the enemies of Islam were in the thousands but the faithful were victorious) and a promise of paradise in death (open your chest, welcoming death, then you will be in heaven; the houris are calling out to you, "Come over here, companion of Allah"), and some specific rituals to be followed in order to ensure success against "the followers of Satan," which itself is interpreted in ritualistic language of "slaughter," *dhabaha,* rather than the prosaic "killing," *qatala.*[116] Mneimneh pointed out "there is not a word or an

115. Jenkins, "The Organization Men," 7.
116. These documents have been translated in several places. See the *Washington Post,* September 28, 2001, the *National Post* (Toronto), September 29, 2001.

implication" in the entire text "about any wrongs that are being re-dressed" in Palestine, Iraq, or Saudi Arabia.[117] The September attack was, in bin Laden's words, "a martyrdom operation" where the hijackers achieved that status on their own as if it were a private act of worship. But we have seen above that the decision regarding martyrdom is tra-ditionally reached on the basis of widespread community agreement regarding the benefits conferred to the community by extraordinary acts.

Following the attacks of September 11, 2001, bin Laden issued a press release that reiterated the same litany of complaint as the earlier texts. Since World War I and the disintegration of the Ottoman Empire, Mus-lims have been humiliated, their homelands debauched by hypocritical leaders, and so on. It was also clear that the attack was both "propaganda by deed" in the old style and reaffirmation of the symbolic opposition of a salafi to the modern world. This is what made the World Trade Center and the Pentagon such attractive targets. In bin Laden's words, "The Twin Towers were legitimate targets, they were supporting U.S. economic power. These events were great by all measurement. What was destroyed were not only the Towers, but the towers of morale in that country." He went on to justify, in his own mind, the mass murder of civilians: "Yes, we kill their innocents and this is legal religiously and logically. There are two types of terror, good and bad. What we are prac-ticing is good terror. We will not stop killing them and whoever sup-ports them." A few weeks later he confirmed the importance of specta-cle: "Those young men . . . said in deeds, in New York and Washington, speeches that overshadowed all other speeches made everywhere else in the world. The speeches are understood by both Arabs and non-Arabs, even by Chinese."[118]

One of the post-September formulas in his statements is particu-larly rich in symbolism and deserves more detailed analysis. "Hypoc-risy stood behind the leader of global idolatry, behind the Hubal of the age—namely America and its supporters."[119] As noted above, the sym-bolization of the Mongols as idolators and the identification of the United States with the Mongols has become something of a trope. The

117. Makiya and Mneimneh, "Manual for a 'Raid,'" 18–21.
118. *National Post* (Toronto), November 12, 2001, sec. A, p. 9, December 14, 2001, sec. A, p. 4.
119. AP press release, reprinted in the *Calgary Herald,* October 8, 2001, sec. A, p. 1.

invocation of Hubal, however, was new. Hubal was a stone idol that stood in the Kaaba, which had, according to traditional vulgate accounts, been built by Abraham on orders from God as a sanctuary. Between Abraham's day and the time of the Prophet, the Arabs abandoned true religion and worshipped idols, much as the Israelites had done (Exodus 32), Hubal being the most important. By identifying the United States as the Hubal of the age, bin Laden indicated that, like Hubal in the time of the Prophet, it is polluting the Kaaba and the holy land of Arabia, which, according to bin Laden's account, is off limits to infidels. So far the interpretation is no more than a reiteration of familiar themes.

The Hubal story has other implications as well, however. Originally, Muhammad called for the destruction of the idol, but the rulers of Mecca, who benefitted from the commerce that accrued to the city because it housed the idol, objected. Hence arose the first *hijra* to Medina, where the Prophet encountered the "hypocrites," men who accepted only the outward forms of true Islam and, in battle against the pagan Meccans, deserted the Prophet. Notwithstanding their treachery, the Prophet returned to Mecca, defeated the pagans, and destroyed Hubal, and true Islam became a major religion of the world.

By identifying America as the Hubal of the age, therefore, bin Laden was evoking a rich and complex story. Not only is American culture the source of idolatry and its soldiers the polluters of the holy land of Arabia, the Arab and Muslim governments allied with the United States are the Medinese hypocrites of the age and destined to perish as they did in the time of the venerable forefathers.[120] For several years prior to the attacks on the World Trade Center and the Pentagon, it was evident to bin Laden that the final conflict between a single, ecumenic world of apostasy, the world of kufr, and the single ecumenic world of truth, the world of the umma, was about to begin. The entire globe was filled with targets of opportunity: in his imagination, nothing less than the fate of Islam as a whole, and thus the truth of humanity, lay in the balance. It is fair to say bin Laden's narrative has moved a considerable distance from both the Western understanding of commonsense reality and that of most conventional Muslims. For bin Laden, of course, the separation from his pneumopathological vision confirms that Westerners are infidels and ordinary Muslims are apostates. Both, therefore, deserve to die. In this respect, therefore, bin Laden and the Al Qaeda

120. Doran, "Somebody Else's Civil War," 33–37.

terrorists simply gave their own expression to a conventional complex of pneumopathological motives.

The goal of Al Qaeda has the same twilight mode of existence of other second realities. Whether one begins by looking at the "religious" language or the "political" program, the objective seems to be more or less plausible, namely, the reestablishment of a *Khilafa*, a caliphate, from Andalusia to Indonesia, followed by the establishment of a final ecumenic empire.[121] In the words of Roland Jacquard, "Whatever happens to bin Laden, Al Qaeda does not wish to die. The terrorist organization believes that it is entrusted with an eternal mission: to lead the world into the apocalypse by making use of conflicts between religions and civilizations."[122] As with so many other pneumopathological designs for ecumenic tranquillity, the road to peace is constantly interrupted by massive, indeed apocalyptic, conflict. As we noted above, the purpose of the September 2001 attacks was to signal that the way of terrorist killing leads to final tranquillity. Moreover, it is evident enough that much of the "secular" commentary in the Muslim world, particularly in the Middle East, follows the salafist interpretation of international politics: the plight of the Palestinians and the Iraqis, as perpetual victims, explains the entire monstrous Zionist-Crusader conspiracy. One conclusion seems obvious: bin Laden and Al Qaeda are conventional in their motivations, their grievances, and their preference for highly destructive but comparatively low-tech weapons. In one important respect they have, however, achieved a significant innovation. Aum was strictly hierarchical, as are older terrorist organizations such as the PLO. Like Hamas, however, Al Qaeda is a network, which makes a conventional decapitation strategy far less effective than it would be if all that were needed to destroy Al Qaeda were the death of its leader. It is to the last aspect of this terrorist organization that we now turn.

121. Bergen, *Holy War, Inc.*, 21.
122. Jacquard, *In the Name of Osama Bin Laden*, 158–59.

5 Counternetwar

One of the oldest maxims of warfare is the imperative to know your enemy. The premise upon which this analysis of modern terrorism has been undertaken is that our knowledge would be incomplete if the internal, experiential, or spiritual dimension of terrorist activities were ignored. In the previous chapter, we noted that Osama bin Laden and Al Qaeda synthesized a number of trends in modern terrorism, from the transformation of religious apocalyptic language to the routinization of "martyrdom" ops. Syntheses are, in their way, innovations. In one area, namely, organization, Al Qaeda has undoubtedly undertaken a significant innovation: it is organized as a network.

In order to assess the advantages and vulnerabilities of Al Qaeda, it is necessary to outline the formal attributes of a network. This discussion follows the arguments presented in a series of papers and books by analysts associated with the Rand Corporation.[1] Rand was the first organization to be called a think tank, and its first major client, in 1946, was the U.S. Army Air Forces. Much of the more recent work done at Rand is concerned with emergent modes of conflict, including terrorism and the implications of what is now conventionally called the revolution in military affairs (RMA) for the conduct of antiterrorist warfare.[2] The gen-

1. See in particular: Arquilla and Ronfeldt, *The Advent of Netwar;* Arquilla and Ronfeldt, eds., *In Athena's Camp;* Arquilla and Ronfeldt, *Swarming;* Arquilla and Ronfeldt, eds., *Networks and Netwars;* Ronfeldt and Arquilla, "Networks, Netwars, and the Fight for the Future"; Davis and Jenkins, *Deterrence and Influence in Counterterrorism;* Johnson, et al., eds., *New Challenges, New Tools for Defense Decision-Making.* See also Libicki, *The Mesh and the Net;* Berkowitz, *New Face of War.*

2. Not everyone concerned with contemporary strategic and military thinking is of the view that the RMA can make any difference in the way the military conducts operations. See, for example, van Creveld, "In Wake of Terrorism, Modern

eral argument with which we are concerned began with a Rand study on the impact of the "information revolution" on war.[3]

The authors' reflections were motivated in part by the military outcome of the then recently concluded Gulf War, and the enormous information advantage maintained by U.S. forces and those allies with whom they shared intelligence. The outcome of this war and of future wars, they argued, was not primarily a function of capital, labor, and technology, but "of who has the best information about the battlefield." The analogy was akin to one side, the United States, playing chess where they can see the entire board, and the other, the Iraqi, playing *Kriegsspiel,* a derivative game where players can see only their own positions. The chess player will always win even if the *Kriegsspiel* player has two queens.

Historically, technological changes in weapons, communication, transportation, and propulsion have allowed for innovative and advantageous shifts in military organization, doctrine, and strategy. No doubt the building of stealth heavy bombers, tanks, and ships, of electronic intelligence gathering, of digital command-and-control capabilities, and all the other remarkable high-tech equipment in the hands of a modern military organization is impressive. But as van Creveld observed, "behind military hardware there is hardware in general, and behind that there is technology [understood] as a certain kind of know-how, as a way of looking at the world and coping with its problems." In other words, technology is more than advanced hardware and weaponry. More specifically, if technology includes "know-how" and a "certain way of looking at the world," then its most significant feature is not the hardware but how it is organized. This understanding of technology, derived from the work of Jacques Ellul, is directly tied to the information revolution.[4]

The term *information revolution* refers to advances in computerized information and communication equipment—roughly equivalent to building a stealth tank in the previous example—but it also includes

---

Armies Prove to be Dinosaurs of Defense," 57–58. It would seem, however, in light of events five years after van Creveld raised his doubts, that the jury is still out.

3. Arquilla and Ronfeldt, "Cyberwar Is Coming!" 141–65, reprinted in *In Athena's Camp,* 23–60.

4. Van Creveld, *Technology and War,* 1. According to Ellul, technology, *la technique,* mediates human to nonhuman being in such a way that humans continually strive for the one best way of doing things. For a discussion of Ellul's argument, see Cooper, *Action into Nature,* chap. 2.

changes in organization and management theory. This latter aspect—
roughly equivalent to a new "way of looking at the world"—has changed
the way we think about information. Moreover, as we argue below in
more detail, the information revolution has privileged and strengthened
the network as a form of organization over other forms, especially over
hierarchies, which characteristically are heavily weighted in favor of a
top-down information flow. In contrast, "advances in networking technologies now make it possible to think of people, as well as databases and
processors, as resources on a network."[5] From this standpoint, humans
do not give orders to mobilize resources, like a general releasing his
cavalry; generals, like all the other humans in a military organization,
are themselves networked resources.

> The new perspective afforded by the information revolution sustains
> a new understanding. For example, email is not just a speedy version
> of the postal service. It has also enabled people to create "virtual com-
> munities," using instruments such as blogs, which certainly are not
> real communities, though they express some of the attributes of real
> communities. Thus they also constitute a new way of conceptualizing
> the meaning of community or a new way of thinking about commu-
> nity such that virtual and real communities are variants. More gener-
> ally, the information revolution and the organization of it, chiefly by
> way of networks, constitute challenges to other forms of organization.[6]

Networks are conventionally distinguished from clans and tribes, on
the one hand, and from markets and hierarchies on the other. For present purposes the latter distinctions are more important than the former. A hierarchy typically addresses the problems of organizing power,
authority, administration, and governance by establishing a centralized
and coordinated decision-making headquarters. Typically hierarchies
are built around chains of command and animated by rituals and hon-
ors, duties and privileges. To use the classic formula of Max Weber, the
"charisma" of a clan chief becomes routinized as a bureaucratically
rational command-and-control cadre at the top of which is a sovereign
commander-in-chief uttering the words, "I will it." The great early examples of hierarchy in the West are the Church and the army; by the
time of the Treaty of Westphalia (1648) they were superseded, broadly
speaking, by the state.

5. Sproull and Kiesler, *Connecting*, 15.
6. Arquilla and Ronfeldt, "The Advent of Netwar (Revisited)," 286.

The great weakness of hierarchies, as any bureaucrat knows all too well, is that they are unable to process large volumes of complex and ambiguous information. Historically, this weakness appeared initially in failures to control economic transactions, particularly long-distance trade. As a result, state hierarchies were faced with a major problem: they could either attempt to control the new organizational form, the market, or they could limit themselves. From the perspective of organizational theory, the transition from mercantilism to capitalism amounted to the self-limitation by state hierarchies of the reach of their own authority. Those states that managed the transition well were strengthened; those that did not were weakened. The end of the transition was a separation of public and private, of state and market.

The attribute of the market of interest here is not its enormous productivity but the fact that it is competitive and that market actors and players are independent one from another. Personal interests, exchange rates, the search for profits, and the rights of individuals, not the will of the sovereign, constitute the principles of market organization. There is no single animating intelligence or sovereign will but rather, in Hayek's felicitous phrase, "spontaneous order." Where a hierarchy tends toward monopoly institutions—one state-run bank, one state-run airline or trading company—markets tend toward pluralities of institutions: many banks, many airlines, and so on. There are, of course, extended debates regarding the proper limits of the state, but generally speaking "the growth of the market system strengthens the power of the states that adopt that system, even as it ensures that the state alone cannot dictate the course of economic development."[7]

Any organizational form has strengths and limitations. The limitation of the market is not that it produces winners and losers but that it is not adept at quickly reducing the differences between them, which is a common political demand that losers are apt to make. One result may be that they look to state hierarchies to introduce greater equality, which in turn introduces additional and well-known dilemmas and contradictions. Just as organizational forms have strengths and limitations, so too do different forms of organization cooperate and clash. Generally speaking, markets view networks as threats because they disrupt commercial spontaneity; hierarchies view networks as threats because they cannot be controlled by issuing orders. For example, the conflict

7. Arquilla and Ronfeldt, *The Advent of Netwar,* 32.

and cooperation of markets and networks have been documented by economists and management theorists looking at the importance of networks within corporations.[8] As the implications and consequences of the information revolution became apparent, particularly to a new generation, the possibility of nonhierarchic coordination and collaboration among "civil society" organizations or "new social movements" became more obvious as well. Information-age activism, based on associations of nongovernmental organizations (NGOs) focused on postmodern or postmaterialist issues such as the environment, human rights, the plight of aboriginal people, and so on, has been conceptualized by the Rand analysts as "social netwar." Organizations capable of participating in social netwars are not just civil society activists but include such "uncivil" NGOs as drug smugglers and terrorists. Civil or uncivil, networks as networks can be analyzed not only in terms of their common attributes—technology, organizational design, and doctrine— but also in terms of social capital and animating narrative. We will deal with the first three attributes in a general way and then consider the last two in connection with Al Qaeda.

Before doing so, however, it might be useful to distinguish between the term *netwar* and more conventional terms such as *information warfare* or the more modern-sounding *cyberwar*. Both netwar and cyberwar are centrally concerned with information and knowledge as well as with its communication. Cyberwar refers chiefly to command, control, communications and intelligence issues (C3I) and to military action taken to disrupt the information and communications systems of one's adversaries.[9] From C3I to stealth technologies and smart bombs, there is no doubt of American preeminence in cyberwar.[10]

With respect to netwar, however, it is a different story. Whether social or military, netwars involve a mode of conflict where at least one of the protagonists uses the network form of organization, doctrine, strategy, and information-age hardware and know-how. A netwar involving a regular military formation must accommodate the reality that, for example, by no stretch of the imagination is the U.S. military a network: first and foremost it is a hierarchy with many ranks and rituals to ensure it

8. Powell, "Neither Market nor Hierarchy," 295–336.
9. See Arquilla and Ronfeldt, "Cyberwar Is Coming!" 27–32. See also Alberts, Garstka, Hayes, and Signori, *Understanding Information Age Warfare*.
10. See Libicki, "Incorporating Information Technology in Defense Planning," 103–29; Hosek, "The Soldier of the 21st Century," 181–209.

remains both distinct from civil society and internally well articulated. Moreover, just as social netwars refer to a broad spectrum of social conflict, from street demonstrations to drug dealing, so do military netwars refer to a broader spectrum of conflict than regular military operations. These include guerrilla war, terrorism, and other irregular and usually asymmetrical forms of armed conflict. As Arquilla and Ronfeldt put it:

> netwar differs from traditional modes of conflict and crime in which the protagonists prefer to use hierarchical organizations, doctrines, and strategies, as in past efforts to foster large, centralized mass movements along Leninist lines. In short, netwar is about Hamas more than the PLO, Mexico's Zapatistas more than Cuba's Fidelistas, the Christian Identity Movement more than the Ku Klux Klan, the Asian Triads more than the Sicilian Mafia, and Chicago's Gangsta Disciples more than the Al Capone Gang.[11]

The two types of war are not, however, sealed in watertight compartments. We noted above that the information revolution has enhanced the importance of networks. Because cyberwar is centrally concerned with information, even when conducted by a military hierarchy, it stands to reason that the conduct of cyberwar or of information warfare after the information revolution will have important implications for the organization of military operations. Indeed, the integration or partial integration of networked structures into the military hierarchy is one of the dimensions of the revolution in military affairs that has been understudied in existing analyses of the RMA. In theory at least it would seem that modern cyberwar would imply decentralized or networked command and control at the same time as it provides what David Gelernter has dubbed "topsight," an understanding of the big picture that allows for a kind of indirect battlespace management.[12] The management is indirect because topsight does not allow a general to micromanage the battlespace from headquarters; there are no micromanagers. Instead, through the use of information technologies, including humans, knowledge becomes a Clausewitzian capability and platforms and munitions become peripherals, like laser printers for a PC workstation. So, for example, a networked special forces sergeant can instruct an admiral

11. Arquilla and Ronfeldt, eds., *In Athena's Camp*, 277.
12. See Gelernter, *Mirror Worlds*, 52.

commanding a carrier battle group when to launch his attacking planes and where to send them. The low rank in a hierarchy, the sergeant, "outranks" in terms of networked information the high rank in the hierarchy, the admiral. As Libicki put it, "Rather than information being a service to the weapon, the weapon is the dispatch mechanism slaved to the mesh. Units of force would be fire support for information systems." The metaphors of mesh and net are used by Libicki to distinguish between military (mesh) and civilian (net) applications of configurations of information. Specifically, the mesh "points to the holes; as information technology places a finer mesh atop the battlefield, more objects are caught in it." Net "points to the substance of the system; the connectivity of people and their machines suggests new patterns of social conflict and new venues for conflict."[13] In short, a network of terrorists can be opposed by an information mesh, elements of which might include a carrier battle group.

To summarize the general point: the information revolution, which is to say, technology in the double sense of materials and hardware— Libicki's "free silicon"—and of a mode of thinking—the search for the one best way that allows a sergeant to instruct an admiral—has made the efficient operation of both net and mesh—or, in general, networks— possible. Historically, networks (whether net or mesh) have been harder to operate, and thus less efficient, than hierarchies because, on the one hand, they require constant and dense communications in order to exist, but, on the other, this requirement makes it very difficult to come quickly to a decision. As a result of the information revolution, however, sufficient bandwidth and connectivity is available to overcome these problems because, under some conditions, every node can connect with every other. In the words of Manuel Castells, the interconnectedness provided by the information revolution constitutes the "material basis" for a networked civil society—but also of a terrorist network.[14]

Analysts of social networks usually distinguish three distinct types.[15] A chain or line network moves information (or goods or people) along a line of contacts so that end-to-end communication must traverse a

13. Libicki, *The Mesh and the Net*, 51, 3. See also Murdock, "Principles of War on the Network-Centric Battlefield," 86–95, http://carlisle-www.army.mil/usawc/ Parameters/02spring/murdock.htm.

14. Castells, *Rise of Network Society*, 469.

15. See Evan, "An Organization-Set Model of Interorganizational Relations," 181–200.

series of nodes. These may be individuals, groups, or organizations. Second, a network may be organized as a hub-and-spoke system, as in a franchise or a cartel, where nodes at the end of spokes must communicate by the node at the hub. The hub may be central and have access to more information than the nodes at the end of the spokes, but the hub does not command their action. Third, there is an all-channel or full-matrix network, where every node is connected to every other. The third type most closely approximates the principles of the Internet and is best adapted to coordinating open, multiorganizational, and transnational networks quickly.

The chain and hub, or variations such as the spider web, are more secure than all-channel networks but are also slower. Other organizational designs and hybrid forms attempt to create the optimal compromises between speed or efficiency in communications, on the one hand, and security. It is self-evident that security will be a major consideration for networks where stealth and secrecy are important. It is also clear that there may be functional hybrids—a hub and spoke for topsight or even a hierarchy for overall strategic direction and an Internet for tactical operations. Whatever the variations in detail, an all-channel network has the great advantage of speedy collaboration and decentralized decision-making, provided there has been extensive communication prior to making a decision or triggering an action. Thus, extensive and mutual consultation can create near or actual consensus, notwithstanding the physical dispersal of the nodes. The prior consultation can create operational coherence because, in the words of white-supremacist militiaman Louis Beam, "they know what they have to do."[16]

The obvious advantage of a network over a hierarchy in this respect is that it makes a decapitation strike by an adversary much more difficult. For network members there is no need to be online constantly, but when communication is necessary the network members can receive information quickly. The hardware and technologies associated with the information revolution—e-mail, cell phones, faxes, Web sites, all of which may be encrypted,[17] are a great advantage to geographically dispersed

16. Beam issued this remark in his article "Leaderless Resistance" in *Seditionist* no. 2 (February 1992). See his file on the Anti-Defamation League Web site: http://www.adl.org/learn/ext_us/beam.asp?xpicked=2&item=beam#return3. See also Dishman, "Trends in Modern Terrorism," 359.

17. Pleming, "Muslim Extremists Utilize Web Encryption."

nodes. At the same time, however, couriers, carrier pigeons, or the Mongols' pony express, called the "Arrow Riders," could do the job as well. High tech enables a modern network, but low tech is always a possibility.

Given the flexibility of networks, particularly open, all-channel networks, it may seem questionable to speak of a "doctrine" to which network operations adhere. In this context, however, a doctrine is not a rigid set of procedures to be followed under all circumstances but a set of guiding principles and practices that enable members of a network to operate strategically and tactically without a commander issuing orders. Indeed, "leaderlessness," or the principle that any particular leader (or so-called leader) can be replaced easily and quickly by anyone else is a major constituent of netwar doctrine.

A second doctrinal element, "swarming," is a maneuver that involves a convergent attack of several autonomous or semi-autonomous units on a target or targets.[18] Historical examples that illustrate the doctrine of swarming antedate its formulation. The Scythians, the Mongols, the Zulus, the Métis, and the plains Indians of North America were all capable of refining their hunting strategies to swarm their adversaries, appearing suddenly from several directions. The RAF was able to swarm the attacking Luftwaffe during the Battle of Britain from several dispersed airfields, much as the U-boat "wolf packs" could for a time swarm convoys in the Battle of the Atlantic. Moreover, both examples from World War II depended upon controlled information (from radar and Enigma respectively), both blurred the distinction between offense and defense, both were capable of independent action and initiative (fighter pilots and U-boat captains were notoriously un- or even anti-hierarchical), and both depended on rapid dispersal, rather than retreat, combined with readiness for another attacking "pulse."[19]

Elements of swarming can be detected in the battle when the Athenians destroyed the Persian fleet in the narrow waters off Salamis (Herodotus 8.84 ff.); in the destruction of the Spanish Armada in 1558; in the 1968 Tet Offensive in Viet Nam; in the operations of the Chechins against the Russians in 1994–1996; of the Russians against the Nazi Blitzkreig at the battle of Kursk; or of the Somalis against Task Force

18. See Edwards, *Swarming on the Battlefield*, for a detailed account with many historical examples. He used a somewhat more narrow definition of swarming (pp. 2–3).

19. Arquilla and Ronfeldt, *Swarming*, 21.

Ranger in the battle of the Black Sea District in Mogadishu. Swarming is, moreover, the doctrine developed by U.S. Navy strategists governing the optimal use of a new and experimental generation of small, Kevlar and carbon-fiber catamarans, called "Streetfighters," capable of delivering considerable lethality against much larger opponents, especially submarines.[20] Swarming is not necessarily antithetical to discipline.[21] The terrorists in Al Qaeda were unquestionably disciplined; indeed, discipline is necessary for the creation and maintenance of "sleeper" cells that nevertheless "know what to do." At the same time, "bin Laden and his cohorts appear to have developed a swarm-like doctrine that features a campaign of episodic, pulsing attacks by various nodes in the network—at locations sprawled across global time and space where he has advantages for seizing the initiative, stealthily."[22]

When one examines the effects of networks in action, several additional lessons can be drawn. For example, in his analysis of "gangs, hooligans and anarchists," who constitute "the vanguard of netwar in the streets," Sullivan concluded boldly that "networks can prevail over hierarchies in this postmodern battlespace."[23] The imagery of battlespace and of prevailing, however, is somewhat misleading inasmuch as the purpose of netwar is not to deliver the knockout blow, the decisive defeat that seems to be inherent in the ancient Western, as well as modern Clausewitzian, understanding of the purpose of battle. It is true that networks have an advantage against hierarchies in the conduct of netwar. But the question still must be raised as to what the outcome of a successful netwar might be. What is the purpose of netwar, especially when it is a success?

One thing at least seems clear: the Zapatistas had no chance to replace the Mexican government without at the same time abandoning their organization as participants in an international social netwar. Likewise the swarming protestors against the World Trade Organization in the

20. Arquilla and Karasik, "Chechnya," 207–30; Carell, *Scorched Earth;* Bowden, *Black Hawk Down;* Jaffe, "Risk Assessment."

21. Victor Davis Hanson's account of the battle for Rorke's Drift between the Zulus (the swarmers) and the British (the disciplined) may have overemphasized this distinction in his contrast between discipline and bravery. See *Carnage and Culture,* 321 ff.

22. Ronfeldt and Arquilla, "Networks, Netwars, and the Fight for the Future." See also Bonabeau and Meyer, "Swarm Intelligence," 107–14.

23. Sullivan, "Gangs, Hooligans, and Anarchists," 100.

euphonic "Battle of Seattle" could not have replaced the WTO or any of the governments that it comprised, and did not attempt to do so. Jeffrey R. Cooper understates the limitations of netwar protests when he writes: "rather than attacking a neighbour for territorial aggrandizement, non-state opponents might be tempted to inflict pain, and thereby destabilization, on opposing societies."[24] It would be more accurate to say that netwarriors, including terrorists, can *only* inflict pain or destabilize societies. The great strength of networks, at least historically, has been their defensive ability to survive the repressive measures taken by hierarchies. Today, networks can go on the offensive and challenge state hierarchies, but they cannot realistically expect ever to replace them, nor even successfully to challenge a major military hierarchy.

This is not to deny that terrorists and other swarming netwarriors may say that they are out to change the government, the system, or indeed the world. It is also true that terrorists waging netwar tend to use violence less for identifiable state-related purposes than for more generalized ones—not hostage-taking with specific political demands, so much as mass killing to ensure vague but fundamental changes. As Arquilla and Ronfeldt observed several years prior to September 11, 2001, "this reflects a rationality that disdains pursuing a 'proportionate' relationship between ends and means, seeking instead to unhinge a society's perceptions."[25] To use the language introduced in chapter 2, the practice of a persistent disdain for pursuing a proportionate relationship between ends and means is a characteristic of a pneumopathological consciousness. It is important, therefore, to bear in mind the commonsense observation that in international politics networks require hierarchies, and especially states, in order to have something to oppose. All that terrorists and other "uncivil society" networks ever can achieve is to damage, harm, interrupt, and disrupt alternative organizational forms.[26]

Notwithstanding the limitations of the effectiveness of netwar against state hierarchies, networks do possess a number of advantages that have

24. Ronfeldt and Arquilla, "Emergence and Influence of the Zapatista Social Netwar," 171 ff.; Cooper, "Another View of the Revolution," 110.

25. Arquilla and Ronfeldt, "The Advent of Netwar," 284.

26. Often the explicit objectives of terrorist attacks are to degrade markets and damage states, but the action undertaken by the Zapatista network indicates that they can also harm tribes and clans. See Cleaver, "The Zapatista Effect," 621–40; Fox, "Difficult Transition," 151–84.

enabled them to achieve what successes they have enjoyed. First of all, the hardware that provides the material basis for a network—cell phones and wireless Internet access, for example—is not complicated to use.[27] Second, "if the object is pain, not publicity, we may find it difficult to identify the proper target for our response."[28] This is especially true of networked terrorist organizations that are not state-supported, which is to say, NGOs such as Al Qaeda. Third, because networks tend to "pulse" their actions—that is, to combine attack and retreat in a single swarming motion—the tempo of both social and military netwar is often erratic so that it may be unclear when one attack, battle, or campaign begins or ends. Thus, "a network actor may engage in long cycles of quietly watching and waiting, and then swell and swarm rapidly into action,"[29] which also may make it difficult to know *who* the adversary is. Only in retrospect, for example, could Al Qaeda be connected to the U.S. embassy bombings in east Africa, the battle in Mogadishu, the attacks on the USS *Cole* and the French tanker in Yemen, or the series of attacks in Chechnya, Riyadh, Karachi, Casablanca, and Madrid shortly after the destruction of the regime of Saddam Hussein. Likewise afteraction damage assessment of networks is difficult to undertake with accuracy and in a timely fashion.

Edwards's study of several historical examples of swarming identified three factors that influenced the success of the swarmers: elusiveness gained either through mobility or concealment, longer-range firepower or standoff capability, and superior situational awareness.[30] The examples he examined were regular military battles rather than terrorist attacks, for which the importance of standoff capability, at least in the conventional sense of the term, is reduced. On the other hand, with terrorist attacks, a factor excluded by Edwards, namely, a willingness to take casualties, has greater significance. Moreover, "concealment is closely related to superior situational awareness" for the obvious reason that, if an attacker conceals himself he is bound to have greater situational intelligence than his target; or, to reverse the argument, it is difficult to conceal your location, capability, and intent from a target if the target has intelligence superior to the attacker. This is why information, which

27. Zanini and Edwards, "The Networking of Terror in the Information Age," 50.
28. Cooper, "Another View of the Revolution," 110.
29. Arquilla and Ronfeldt, "The Advent of Netwar," 283.
30. Edwards, *Swarming on the Battlefield,* chap. 4.

is central to intelligence assessment, is important, though its importance is hardly confined to netwars, whether social or military. However the balance of intelligence may stand in any particular instance of conflict, a successful "battleswarm" consists in the coordinated convergence, at a moment chosen to have a high impact, of an elusive networked attacker.

We have discussed the technological, organizational, and doctrinal aspects of networks. We have next to consider the importance of social capital and of a persuasive animating narrative.

In the early academic analyses of social networks, the focus was on topics such as friendships among schoolchildren, occupational mobility that depended upon social connections, business partnerships, and other relatively unobtrusive structures that make a social organization work the way it does.[31] Power in a social network was less a personal attribute or an attribute of office than a function of interpersonal relations and of the location where an individual is embedded. What counts is not human capital but social capital, which puts a premium on loyalty and trust.[32] With criminal and terrorist networks, trust is often enhanced by "blood and brotherhood," that is, by kinship, marriage, and shared experiences. At the same time as criminals and terrorists depend on social capital, because of the risks and dangers involved, network loyalty is more fragile than it is in tribes and clans, where it is a mere fact of nature, or in hierarchies, where loyalty and personal commitment are conditions of membership.

One of the methodological weaknesses of the analysts of social networks was that membership was determined by the external mapping of various ties between individuals. This meant that the analyst could include someone in a network even if the individual did not know he or she was part of a network or even that the network existed. Considered as a form of organization, however, and especially a high-risk organization such as a terrorist network, all network members are fully aware that they are members, even though they may not know very many (or perhaps any) other members. The point is not that members might deny their membership; humans can always lie. Rather, membership is, in part, defined by a narrative, by shared stories. A story—any story—gives meaning to experience. Stories told to members of organizations

31. See, for example, Granovetter, "Economic Action and Social Structure," 481–510.
32. Fukuyama, *Trust.*

give meaning to their purposes and interests as well; they sustain a sense of identity, team membership, and belonging; they provide a mission statement that explains how and why "we" will harm and perhaps prevail over "them." In short, stories provide networks with self-consciousness. When members deeply subscribe to the meanings the stories convey, the accumulated social capital of the network is augmented.

All the factors that combine to make networks effective—technology, sophisticated design, a capacity to swarm, social capital, and a compelling narrative—were present and emphasized in the Al Qaeda organization. We will deal briefly first with the external aspects of the Al Qaeda network.[33]

We noted above that the state is a relatively recent and comparatively rare political order, a geographically limited legal structure created by Europeans at the end of a long series of bloody religious wars. Liberty of conscience within European states developed along with the secularization of government; legitimacy of secular laws was derived from the consent of the governed. For large parts of the Islamic world none of these familiar aspects of Western political practice obtain. There are, of course, many third-world tyrannies and regimes where Islamists view democracy as a one-way road to power "on which there is no return, no rejection of the sovereignty of God, as exercised through His chosen representatives,"[34] or, as the more brutal observers have put it: one man, one vote, one time.

In addition, however, Islamic law, for example, is widely viewed as being derived from God in the Koran or from the acts of the Prophet recorded in the Sunna. Because in principle God's law is ecumenic there is, again in principle, no territorial jurisdiction to Islamic law. Accordingly, national states, based on the premise of territorial law, have always been accorded more or less questionable legitimacy in the Muslim world. In terms of Western constitutional practices, as Roger Scruton observed, Islamic unity is pre-political, "the unity of a creed community with a common language sanctified by a holy text."[35] Nor, of course, is there a legal entity, "the Mosque," comparable to the various Western churches. Indeed, absent the caliphate, networks with transnational cooperative

---

33. For further analysis using a somewhat different approach see LCDR Melanie J. Kreckovsky, "Training for Terror: A Case Study of Al-Qaida" (Master's thesis, Monterey Naval Postgraduate School, 2002).

34. Lewis, *Crisis of Islam*, 111–12.

35. Scruton, *The West and the Rest*, 34.

ties constitute "the essence of the Muslim Nation, Islam's most genuine form of sociopolitical identity."[36] Given the limited variety of organizational forms and the somewhat artificial nature of the state in large parts of the Muslim world, the reliance on networks for "sociopolitical identity" is familiar from daily life in the umma. In this same broad context of a cultural resource or presupposition available to Al Qaeda, one might think of the *hijra* of the Prophet, pragmatically rather than symbolically, as an early version of a networked swarm or pulse.

In the weeks following the attack on September 11, 2001, journalists and other investigators relying on open source material tried to assemble a diagram that would explain the relationships of the nineteen hijackers and fifteen others associated with them. One of the most interesting used a proprietary software program called InFlow, developed by Valdis Krebs.[37] It is usually employed to help companies improve internal communications and can represent the strength of the connection between and among individuals in a network. For example, attending a flight school or sharing an apartment with another member of the network counts for more than a telephone call. Krebs used three additional measures: "degrees" of activity, which is the simple number of contacts; "betweenness," which is the position of one member as the mediator in a network between others; and "closeness," which measures direct contact.[38] The software then creates a sociogram or map indicating the major nodes and thus the important members in the network. The three most important were Muhammad Atta, Marwan al-Shehhi, and Nawal Alhazmi. It also shows that, in order to disable the network, more than one-fifth of the nodes have to be removed, which means the attackers of September 11, 2001, created a redundant and robust network. It is also important to note that the networked structure of Al Qaeda facilitates tactical swarming, as evidenced by the east African embassy attacks as well as September 11, 2001.[39]

Nearly all the studies of the September 11 attack emphasize in one way or another the importance of social capital—trust—in the operation of the Al Qaeda network. Hiro, for example, noted that seven of the Saudi terrorists were from the southwestern province of Asir, where

36. Bodansky, *Bin Laden*, 334.

37. See http://www.orgnet.com/.

38. Stewart, *Business 2.0*. See also Muir, "Email Traffic Patterns Can Reveal Ringleaders"; Tyler, Wilkinson, and Huberman, "Email as Spectroscopy."

39. Arquilla and Ronfeldt, "Fight Networks with Networks."

many of the schoolteachers happened to be exiled members of the Egyptian Ikhwan.[40] Corbin drew attention to the fact that the three most important members all resided in Hamburg and attended the Technical University with varying degrees of regularity and enthusiasm. The pattern of their studies is familiar: none studied Western philosophy or the humanities and what religious views they had were learned from various Islamist sources rather than from traditional religious training; in Hamburg, for example, they attended the al-Quds Mosque, a center of Qutbist Islamism.[41] Moreover, Atta and Hazami, like their remote mentor, Qutb, had major difficulties relating to women, especially Western ones.[42] As noted above, many of the lower-level operatives involved in the attacks on the east African embassies or on the USS *Cole* were veterans of the violence in Afghanistan and were known collectively as the Afghan Arabs.[43]

Narrative is important in networks because it explains how essentially acephalous organizations know "what has to be done." With respect to Al Qaeda, the basic doctrine is clear: "How can [a Muslim] possibly accept humiliation and inferiority when he knows that his nation was created to stand at the center of leadership, at the center of hegemony and rule, at the center of ability and sacrifice? How can he possibly accept humiliation and inferiority when he knows that the divine rule is that the entire earth must be subject to the religion of Allah—not to the East, not to the West—to no ideology and to no path except for the path of Allah?"[44] For this reason there can be no bargaining with the infidel enemy: God, not the umma, and certainly not Al Qaeda, is the offended party, just as God, not Stinger missiles, brought victory in Afghanistan against the Soviet Union.[45] Nor can there be imperialism when God has decreed that Islam must be ecumenic.[46] Finally, Al Qaeda will win: because they have overcome "the hatred of fighting and the

40. Hiro, *War without End*, 309.

41. Corbin, *The Base*, 158–59, 137; Ruthven, *A Fury for God*, 112–13; Kepel, *Jihad*, 344; Benjamin and Simon, *Age of Sacred Terror*, 164–66; Vermaat, "Bin Laden's Terror Networks in Europe."

42. Corbin, *The Base*, 143.

43. Benjamin and Simon, *Age of Sacred Terror*, 137–50; Bodansky, *Bin Laden*, 318–19.

44. Abu Gheith, "'Why We Fight America.'"

45. Ruthven, *A Fury for God*, 202–5.

46. See Lewis, *Crisis of Islam*, 55.

love of the present life" that have "captured the hearts" of many Muslims and have resulted in "catastrophes, ... subservience and humiliation";[47] and because they never forget:

> America will eventually pay for its enormities, because Muslims never forget the wrongs they have suffered and they inculcate hatred for their most ancient enemies in their newest converts.... We don't forget our tragedies no matter how much time has passed. Imagine, Mr. President, we still weep over Andalusia and remember what Ferdinand and Isabella did there to our religion, culture and honor! We dream of regaining it. Nor will we forget the destruction of Baghdad, or the fall of Jerusalem at the hands of your Crusader ancestors.... It may be a problem for us, but who will pay the price after a while?[48]

In short, the evidence is clear that Al Qaeda has adopted all the attributes of a network and has been successful in its attacks on two major hierarchies of the late twentieth century, the Soviet Union and the United States.

Notwithstanding the organizational advantages that networks have over hierarchies, even within the limitations of a battlespace designed to disrupt rather than defeat, networks are far from invulnerable. Following the aphorism that it takes a tank to kill a tank, Arquilla and Ronfeldt argue that netwar waged by Al Qaeda can be met only by counternetwar. The great advantage possessed by Al Qaeda is its social cohesion and its consequent ability to plan meticulous and high-casualty swarming attacks. But, they write, "there appears little room for al-Qaida to improve. In contrast, there is much room for the United States and its allies to improve, mostly at the organizational and doctrinal levels."[49] To clarify the issues Ronfeldt and Arquilla introduced the images of Ares and Athena and the contrast between them. Ares, even more than his refined Roman equivalent Mars, was the Greek deification of a wild, warlike spirit, the tempestuous instigator of violence.

In contrast, Athena was first of all a god of citadels, and so of cities, civility, and civilization. Unlike Ares, she was leader in battle, and on one occasion guided the spear of Diomedes into the belly of Ares (*Iliad* 5.856). Moreover, she was the protector of Athens who brought techno-

---

47. Quoted in Benjamin and Simon, *Age of Sacred Terror*, 155.
48. Safar, "An Open Letter to President Bush."
49. Arquilla and Ronfeldt, "Fight Networks with Networks."

logical and communications improvements, such as the war-chariot and the trumpet, to the battlefield. She was the patron of arts and crafts and other highly skilled activities including medicine and weaving—itself an image of networking. Perhaps most important, she was the god of wisdom who sprang fully formed and fully armed from the brow of Zeus, uttering her war cry. On the Athenian Acropolis, the god subordinate to her was Nike, the female god of victory. She is, say Arquilla and Ronfeldt, "the Greek god of war best attuned to the information age. Where warfare is about information, she is the superior deity."[50] Because netwar and counternetwar rely so heavily on information it is important to be "in Athena's camp," to use the title of their study of "conflict in the information age."

This is not to say that "Ares's camp" cannot achieve a brutal, short-term effectiveness. Hama was a village in Syria that was obliterated by artillery on the orders of President Hafez al-Assad in 1982 because its Islamist inhabitants conspired to overthrow Assad's regime.[51] Estimates vary, but between ten thousand and twenty thousand people were killed, and, in the words of Fouad Ajami, "since then, Hama has become a code name for official repression, a promise of the extent to which the regime in Damascus is prepared to go in dealing with those who get in its way."[52] The appeal of "Hama rules," which is the appeal of Ares, is obvious enough, as is the cost. Ignoring for a moment the ethical costs, it is not obvious that such large-scale killing could compel surrender. Van Creveld noted that a "bookkeeping rationality" is required to compel an adversary to surrender. One thing seems clear, from the Algerian war of the 1950s to the Vietnam war of the 1970s, bookkeeping rationality is in short supply among non-Western and non-industrial armies. It is entirely absent from terrorist groups such as Aum Shinrikyo or Al Qaeda: "power can never speak to wrath."[53] More precisely, pneumo-pathologically disordered individuals are incapable of a political conversation involving even their own interests. Besides, avoiding the ethical irrationality of slaughtering noncombatants on such a large scale is central to the way Westerners conduct war.

50. Arquilla and Ronfeldt, "A New Epoch—and Spectrum—of Conflict," 9.
51. Friedman, "Hama Rules."
52. Ruthven, *A Fury for God*, 7; Benjamin and Simon, *Age of Sacred Terror*, 86; Ajami, *Dream Palace of the Arabs*, 189.
53. van Creveld, *Transformation of War*, 143; Ajami, "The Uneasy Imperium," 22–23.

Athena's style of war, then, is a "comprehensive information-oriented approach to battle that may be to the information age what Blitzkreig was to the industrial age."[54] As noted above, technological or hardware superiority alone cannot achieve strategic superiority. At best, only local or tactical victories can be gained by the application of the Hama rules.[55] Thus the "Athenian view" of netwar means targeting the information-rich components of an adversary's order of battle.

Each of the elements of a network—technology, organizational design, social capital, animating narrative, and doctrine—can be disrupted and destroyed by a corresponding counternetwar strategy.[56] In counternarcotics operations, for example, it has become a standard procedure to attack the financial transactions, especially electronic transfers of funds, of traffickers rather than use pesticides on drug crops. The application of this strategy to disrupting the cash flow of Al Qaeda by targeting its many charitable fronts, the underground banking system, or *hawala*, and regular banks that move and launder funds seems obvious enough.[57]

A second counternetwar approach takes advantage of the fact that all electronically mediated information exchanges leave a digital "trace." This feature of information transfer has enabled the FBI, as long ago as 2000, to develop an Internet wiretap program, called "carnivore," to track terrorist e-mail correspondence.[58] Telephone companies routinely log calls, and computers captured from Al Qaeda or from other terrorist organizations are sources of enormous amounts of information.[59] In addition to being used passively to monitor the communications of networks, information technologies can be used actively in counternetwar operations as well. That is, just as adversarial hackers can use the Internet to mount a "cyber-jihad" against Israel, for example, so too can counterterrorist organizations disrupt their opponents.[60] So far as

54. Arquilla and Ronfeldt, "A New Epoch—and Spectrum—of Conflict," 6.

55. Blank, "Preparing for the Next War," 63.

56. The conventional distinction between defensive antiterrorist activity and preemptive or offensive counterterrorist activity applies to netwar conflicts as well.

57. Wechsler, "Strangling the Hydra," 129–43.

58. *Newsweek*, August 21, 2000. There is some question of its effectiveness and there are a large number of privacy issued involved. See, for example, http://www.stopcarnivore.org/.

59. Reeve, *The New Jackals*, 33, 97; Soo Hoo, Goodman, and Greenberg, "Information Technology and the Terrorist Threat," 139.

60. Lemos, "'Hacktivism'"; Kitfield, "Covert Counterattack."

the animating narrative is concerned, we have already mentioned the necessity of correcting the use of terms such as *jihad* with alternatives such as *hiraba*, "unholy war." Behind the immediate issue of narrative, however, is the larger question of the conflict between the Islamist self-understanding and the openly evolving scholarly interpretation of Islamic experience, which we have discussed in passing in chapters 2 and 3. The two modes of discourse—the narrative needed to mobilize a network and the philosophical or scientific search for the truth of existence—are nevertheless linked "because the ultimate prize in a netwar conflict is understanding—not opinion." Accordingly, "the quality of information (not quantity) determines the final outcome."[61] This is a problem to which we return below.

Turning to military operations against terrorist networks such as Al Qaeda, analogous arguments apply. The military theory of counternetwar is straightforward: identify the critical nodes in the network and attack them simultaneously along with the nearest boundaries between the network and the rest of the world.[62] Because terrorist organizations depend on sources of supplies from outside much more than do armies, the first objective must be to cut these sources off and then seek out not the highest leadership cadre but the "middle management." That is, in a netwar, as discussed above, the highest level of leadership exercises "topsight" rather than control. The strategy is akin to that used against organized crime: the mafia don is the last to be arrested because of the benefits arising from monitoring intelligence that the don receives. Moreover, if supply lines and money sources are degraded, one can anticipate an increase in communication between the operational nodes and the higher leadership.[63]

A strategy along these lines was followed by the Israeli government following the 1972 massacre of Olympic athletes in Munich. First, they announced they would kill any member of the Black September terrorist network who was directly or indirectly involved in the Munich attack. This was the first time that any government created dedicated counterterrorist teams and not just antiterrorist police or military units. But

61. Ronfeldt and Arquilla, "Emergence and Influence of the Zapatista Social Netwar," 233.

62. Williams, "Transnational Criminal Networks," 93–94; Arquilla and Ronfeldt, "Afterword (September, 2001)," 364.

63. Arquilla, "Osama Bin Laden, Not Wanted: Dead or Alive."

second, each of the several assassination teams operated independently of the others and, indeed, in ignorance of the existence of the others. One used the conventional operational methods of the Israeli intelligence service, the Mossad, but the others operated with complete anonymity outside all government structures and with but a single contact person in Mossad.[64] The most successful teams were entirely outside the chain of command, including the government. This meant their operations were insulated from political pressures, especially the need to produce results according to a politically prescribed timetable. "The concept," wrote Calahan, "was for the team to combine their specialties into a totally flexible lethal unit," an organization with a soft rank structure (if any) and no rigid operational doctrine. That is, they operated as a network. In this respect the Israeli teams resembled British, American, Australian, and Canadian special forces. The successor program to the post-1972 operation has been called "early retirement" and consists of state-sanctioned assassination carried out by Israeli special forces. Such a strategy is, of course, highly controversial. On the other hand, strict adherence to due process when dealing with terrorists has its drawbacks as well. As Andrew McCarthy, U.S. prosecutor of Ramzi Yousef, who was convicted in the first attack on the World Trade Center, said, prosecution under U.S. law gives defendants evidentiary rights, including "discovery rights," so that "you have to reveal to them things you would prefer they didn't know if their successors are to be stopped from perpetrating further acts of terror."[65]

Methods other than targeted assassination of terrorist network members also exist. In the traditional language of international relations, it is certainly possible for the United States and its allies to exert influence on the states and NGOs that support terrorist operations.[66] In this way, it is possible to increase the risk to what terrorists hold dear, the success of the operation, rather than their own lives. The purpose, however, would be to increase the exposure and thus the risk to individual nodes by increasing the likelihood that they would engage in vulnerable communications. There is some evidence that even in a network dependent

64. See Jonas, *Vengeance*.

65. Calahan, "Countering Terrorism," 10; Graham, "State-sanctioned Assassination," sec. A, p. 12; McCarthy quoted in Corbin, *The Base*, 51. See also Hoffman, "The Case for Torture."

66. See Davis and Jenkins, *Deterrence and Influence in Counterterrorism*.

on social capital, as is Al Qaeda, it is possible to increase and exploit distrust. The possibility has also been raised of engaging in what might be called posthumous destruction of terrorists, a technique once used by General John Pershing.[67] These rather macabre reflections suggest a few final comments on the significance of modern terrorism.

The conclusions to be drawn from the analysis in this chapter and the ones preceding may be stated briefly. First, the immensity of the terrorist attacks of September 11, 2001, was shocking. It can, therefore, easily overwhelm any theoretical or analytical considerations. As Voegelin observed with respect to the political religion of the Nazis, however, it is not enough simply to denounce a particularly foul deed. It is important to understand how a number of distinct elements came together on that day.

First, a long-tested terrorist procedure, airplane hijacking, was combined with a successful and imaginative search for a weapon of mass destruction. It was not what analysts of terrorism had suspected or feared would be the weapon of choice, and there was no evidence that traditional WMDs—chemical, bacteriological, and radiological weapons—are not still sought by terrorists. It seems clear that there are no self-imposed limits to the violence Al Qaeda is prepared to commit, and we may expect the search for other WMDs to continue.

Second, the Al Qaeda organization has developed a complex religious interpretation of its actions that is at once a pneumopathological fantasy and one that has great resonance among many Muslims. In this respect, it is akin to the various race or class doctrines, dogmas, or "ideas" that have undergirded the political religions that have deformed the twentieth-century West. The basic dogma of the Islamists, as enunciated by Abu Gheith quoted above, is that God has entrusted the world to the rule of those who submit to Him, namely, Muslims.

The implications of this doctrine and of its logic are clear. Islamic law, the Sharia, is for Islamists the direct application, enforcement, and execution of the word of God on humanity in the same way that the

---

67. Higgins and Cullison, "Terrorist's Odyssey"; Smythe, *Guerrilla Warrior*, 161–63. Pershing's experiment, burying dead Moro terrorists in the hide of a pig, was not a success. The only people who objected were American humanitarians, and it is unclear whether they objected more to the unnecessary slaughter of pigs or to the notion of posthumous combat.

Communist Party applied the "laws of history" to the Soviet Union or the National Socialists applied the "laws of nature" to the populations they dominated. It follows that no compromise with infidels is possible because infidels are an offense to God. Thus, God's partisans cannot bargain over God's will because that would mean substituting human will for His will; it would mean falling into apostasy and jahiliyya. The compelling "logic of the idea" rather than the oppressive commonsensical implications ensure that Islamism is just another modern ideology. Accordingly, it "can claim none of the sanctity that Islam the religion enjoys." Islamists are remote from their own culture. They pursue a thoroughly modern way of coming to terms with a modernity they also pretend to reject.[68]

The idea or doctrine of Islam that Islamists claim to espouse has never existed. Thus, it must be created, initially in the second reality of the terrorists' imagination. For example, when the ecumene is converted to Islam there will be no occasion for war. It is in this sense, which is imaginary, that Islam is emphatically a religion of peace. Islamists, therefore, like other ideological pneumopaths, are prepared to evoke the future by wrecking the present.

Third, Al Qaeda, unlike most other terrorist organizations, is an extended network, a product of the late Cold War confrontation in Afghanistan. The "Afghan Arabs" were not welcome when they returned home; but their shared military experience was a source of considerable social capital and they could become a new international brigade of salafist, jihadist terrorists. They were cut off from the commonsense world of social reality and lived in a dream world, the product of extensive indoctrination that has produced absolute clarity. For veterans such as the Afghan Arabs, adversity, suffering, or even death is a test, not a deterrent. As was true for the Kharijites, life is an endless jihad, a jihad that goes on until they die or are killed. Their intent on September 11, 2001, was to ambush the West and inaugurate an apocalyptic war in fulfillment of an ideological vision; what they have obtained is Western war: systematic, high tech, rational, calm, and lethal. In other words, pneumopathological conviction has given Al Qaeda its inner strength, and armed struggle will keep it intact until it is degraded or annihilated. As Jenkins said, "The Al Qaeda enterprise itself cannot easily be

68. Pipes, *Militant Islam Reaches America*, 11, 73–75.

deterred. It can be disabled only by permanently disrupting the process that provides it with human and material resources."[69] Indeed, given the networked form of the organization it is more likely to be degraded than annihilated in a decisive confrontation.

The means of so doing are in no way mysterious. First, Al Qaeda can successfully be opposed only by adopting an equally extended scale of operations. This also means that counternetwar strategies have to be used as well as the more familiar military operations that state hierarchies conventionally deploy. Very simply, opposition to terrorist networks will require the extended use of networked special forces, for whom the legendary nineteenth-century adventurer Sir Richard Burton may prove to be the model. That is, the "war on terrorism"—or more precisely, the war on terrorists—is not an Operation Other Than War (OOTW). It is a war that aims not at a decisive victory but at managing and minimizing a threat, at turning terrorism into a nuisance, as Walter Laqueur said.[70]

Second, it is necessary to reconfigure the basic national security architecture. That is, counterterrorism is not a matter of law enforcement, and to imagine that counterterrorist operations could ever be so lands us soon enough in a fool's paradise. It is important, therefore, to be clear about this distinction as well. Law enforcement operations come into play after the fact of a crime. Such operations gather evidence to present before a court, all of which activity takes place within strict and formal legal constraints. In contrast, national security tries to foresee threatening events before they happen and appeals not to law but to reasons of state. Its means are not restricted to gathering evidence and laying it before a court of competent jurisdiction. The methods are sometimes violent and sometimes the tools of police, judge, jury, and executioner are combined in a single action. It would seem that we are likely to have to become accustomed to this more robust and aggressive way of ensuring our own safety.

Within that general context, the first step in coalition networking must be intelligence sharing. Given the secrecy of most intelligence hierarchies even within the same government structure, let alone with foreign nationals and former enemies or rivals, this is a significant chal-

69. Jenkins, *Countering al Qaeda*, 17.
70. Laqueur, *The New Terrorists*, 4; Cronin, "Rethinking Sovereignty," 132.

lenge. It also seems clear that intelligence collection efforts will have to be diverted from traditional military threats to a whole host of organizations that, because of the pneumopathological fantasies of their members, are likely to appear as enigmatic and bizarre to traditional intelligence hierarchies. In any event, bizarre or not, they can quickly become nontraditional, nonmilitary, and nonstate adversaries.

A second step involves narrative and doctrine. It is obvious that there is a wide and deep gulf between the story of Islam and the world as told by Islamist jihadists and salafists and the story told by Western liberal democrats. Absent a persuasive Islamic story that explains to wide audiences in the Muslim world that the terrorist spirituality is perverse, that indicates as clearly as possible that, for example, far from being martyrs, suicidal terrorists are simply murderers and so condemned, not exalted, by Islam, something like the crude and parochial account provided by Huntington's *Clash of Civilizations* or Keegan's contrast between Western "resolve" and Oriental "surprise" is likely to become the new orthodoxy.[71]

Islamist terrorism has a different significance in the Muslim world than it has in the West. To Muslims, Islamism was an attractive pragmatic political strategy because it was otherworldly and the world had not treated Islam well. But radical and violent action simply has played into the hands of the enemies of Islam. That is, the resort to terrorism signifies the failure of Islamism.[72] One must add, however, that the pneumopathological core of Islamism means that it could never succeed. A moderate Islamism, which Kepel detects and argues had an appeal to the new and pious middle classes, is no more conceivable than is a moderate Nazism, which also appealed to the middle classes.[73]

In the West the significance of Islamist terrorism is rather different. If the proof of spiritual merit is murder-suicide, the action of a terrorist suicide bomber is nothing but a futile protest against the same spiritual vacuum that his evil act expresses. Like the killers who could as easily be victims of totalitarian domination, it makes little difference to them whether they live or die.[74] It is with good reason, then, that Scruton called Islamist terrorists a "cult of death." Moreover, it does not take a

71. Huntington, *The Clash of Civilizations*; Keegan, "A Different Kind of War Indeed."
72. Kepel, *Jihad*, 4, 373.
73. See Ruthven, *A Fury for God*, 191.
74. See Arendt, *Origins of Totalitarianism*, 457–59.

crystal ball to understand the likely outcome: "If the peoples of the Middle East continue on their present path, the suicide bomber may become a metaphor for the whole region, and there will be no escape from a downward spiral of hate and spite, rage and self-pity, poverty and oppression, culminating sooner or later in yet another alien domination."[75]

There is, of course, no guarantee that Islamists will ever cease to harvest hate-filled and death-bound recruits. On the other hand, one may expect that the morally compelling narratives against terrorism and the threat it poses not only to Western but more directly to non-Western governments provides plenty of motives to cooperate.

75. Scruton, *The West and the Rest*, 121; Lewis, *What Went Wrong?* 159.

Appendix
History and the Holy Koran

In the course of the analysis of Islamist terrorism, we made a basic analytical distinction that needs to be discussed in more detail. On the one hand, we said, there existed the history of societies and political orders informed by Islam, an account of which we called a history of the Islamic community. We assumed here that the status of the history of this community, its *res gestae,* was as unproblematic as the history of the U.S. mail or of gunpowder. On the other hand we said there existed a paradigmatic Islamic history, which we tentatively described as the account of God and his messengers to humanity. Early in chapter 3 we said further that Islamic history, which we also identified as the "Islamic vulgate," by analogy with the Christian Bible given its official form by Saint Jerome in the fourth century, would be discussed "without prejudice." The intention of this terminology was to maintain the frontier between piety and political science; we assumed here that it was possible to study the Islamic story of God and his messengers to humanity without taking a position with respect to the veracity or the literal truth of Islamic history. But this means that it is possible to be neutral before the actual messages that were delivered concretely on specific occasions. We have seen, notwithstanding the Koranic assurance that there can be no compulsion in matters of religion, that this second assumption, even more than the first one concerning the history of Islam, contains or expresses a major problem.

From time to time, in explicating the significance of Islamic history we have imaginatively adopted the perspective of "the pious Muslim." This was, of course, a simplification because (we further assume) there may be a plurality of perspectives that are compatible with Islamic piety. Simplification or not, for one holding to that position of piety, the plurality of perspectives presents an issue that cannot be so easily discussed nor, implicitly, so easily disposed of or dismissed. To put the matter more simply still: one is either pious or not. For reasons discussed in chapter 2, for a pious Muslim living the reality of Islamic history, a pious Jew or a pious Christian *is* a pious Muslim because, within the experienced reality of Islamic history, Islam is the fulfillment of both Judaism and Christianity, to say nothing of paganism.

On the basis of such an understanding of Islamic history, the adjective in the phrase "Islamic piety" is superfluous. Accordingly, the assumptions we have made, or the attitude we have taken, first, with respect to the distinction between the history of Islam and Islamic history and, second, with respect to the veracity of the latter, may be seen (and for the pious, quite properly) as entirely disingenuous, not to say the expression of an impiety. To begin with, a pious (Muslim) individual, one who we said believed in the Muslim vulgate, would never have made the initial distinction. Furthermore, for a pious (Muslim) individual, the veracity of Islamic history is its meaning, much in the same way as God spoke to Moses from the burning bush. Thus, neutrality with respect to that meaning is rebellion against it, and so rebellion against God's revealed message to Moses.

In short, for a pious individual *the* problem of existence is not understanding the word of God but obeying it. Even within Islam, however, matters are not so simple, as the discussion above of the position of the *faylasuf* indicated. There is an equivalent problem within Western history more generally, a history that, for present purposes, can include the Bible and Greek philosophy as well as Islam.[1] We will first present Leo Strauss's version of this question, then Eric Voegelin's, and finally we indicate how recent scholarship, much of it undertaken outside the Islamic lands, has a bearing on the issues of salafism and Islamism raised in the course of this study.

In 1967, Strauss delivered a lecture, "Jerusalem and Athens: Some Preliminary Reflections," at the City College of New York.[2] According to Strauss, "as far as we Western men are concerned" the genesis of what "Western man" became is "indicated by the names of the two cities

1. For a discussion of historically intelligible units of analysis, such as "Western history," in the discourse of political science, see Cooper, *Eric Voegelin and the Foundations of Modern Political Science,* chap. 8.

2. Reprinted in Strauss, *Studies in Platonic Political Philosophy,* 147–73. The following quotations are from the first few pages.

Jerusalem and Athens." Today, of course, the realities signified by these intelligible analytic terms—the names of the two cities, Athens and Jerusalem—are widely considered to be cultural options. Strauss then questioned the intelligibility of culture and of a cultural understanding of culture, which calls itself a science of culture. His reasoning is straightforward: a science of culture claims to be neutral with respect to the plurality of cultures that actually exist. Accordingly, it fosters a universal tolerance of plurality. But this amounts to an assertion of the rightness of cultural pluralism and so of pluralism as right. That is, the science of culture, far from giving cultures their due, reduces them to elements of something they are not, namely, science. The science of culture does not, therefore, lead to scientific objectivity, as often has been claimed. Indeed, the science of culture, or to be more accurate, a tolerant neutrality with respect to the validity or veracity of the realities expressed by the terms *Athens* and *Jerusalem*, is simply evasive and, *au fond*, unintelligible. The conclusion to be drawn at this point, then, is that there is simply a stand-off between piety and political science.

Strauss did not, however, leave the matter at an impasse. What leads to objectivity, he said on this as on many other occasions, is the attempt to understand the several and various cultures, positions, arguments, philosophies, and so on, as they understood themselves or understand themselves. "Men of ages and climates other than our own did not understand themselves in terms of cultures because they were not concerned with culture in the present-day meaning of the term. What we now call culture is the accidental result of concerns that were not concerns with culture but with other things and above all with the Truth." But this approach, when the object to be understood is the Bible, and so of the biblical exposé of truth—or Truth, as Strauss wrote—presents a major additional problem: it seems to require that the one undertaking the enquiry go beyond the self-understanding of the Bible to say nothing of the Greeks, because it amounts to gaining wisdom, or knowledge of Truth. This consideration leads to a further problem: according to the Bible, "the beginning of wisdom is fear of the Lord; according to the Greek philosophers, the beginning of wisdom is wonder." Can there be two beginnings? But to raise such a question—or any question, for that matter—means that one does not already have the answer, does not already have the knowledge of Truth, or is not wise, however much one may wish to become wise. "We are seekers for wisdom, 'philosophoi,'" said Strauss; but "by saying that we wish to hear first and then to act to decide, we have already decided in favor of Athens against Jerusalem." However, by taking the side of Athens against Jerusalem, one must abandon the attempt to understand Jerusalem on its own or any other terms: for the pious city, the city of righteousness, one must obey and fear the Lord. End of story. To use the imagery of "hearing the word of God," seeking to understand it would already be an act of impiety because (for the pious) God's word demands obedience, not understanding. Indeed, to seek understanding is already to use the imagery of sight, not of hearing: we seek to "*see* what God's word, or any other word, *means*," quite a different enterprise than hearing and obeying.

On the other hand, Strauss pointed out, if one follows through on the side of Athens against Jerusalem one is compelled to treat the Bible as a text suitable for the same kind of "historical-critical study" as the *Nicomachean Ethics* or the Code of Hammurabi. Strauss then proposed an alternative way of reading the Bible and of grasping the tension between Athens and Jerusalem. Unquestionably, Strauss's position on this point is both complex and controversial. Fortunately, it need not concern us. What counts is that Strauss was very much aware of the general problem that concerns us at present.

So was Eric Voegelin. In "The Gospel and Culture," Voegelin discussed this same question along different but complementary lines.[3] Characteristically, Voegelin began with a brief historical reference to the initial absorption of the "life of reason," or the "culture of the time," namely, Hellenistic philosophy, by the community of the gospel. In this way, Voegelin said, the sectarian community was able to become the Christianity of the church. The gospel was acceptable to the culture of the time, furthermore, because it appeared to answer the questions raised by the philosophers.[4] In the *First Apology* of Justin the Martyr, the author claims that the *Logos* of the gospel is the developing *logos* of philosophy. "Hence, Christianity is not an alternative to philosophy, it is philosophy itself in its state of perfection; the history of the Logos comes to its fulfillment through the incarnation of the Word in Christ." Accordingly, the distinction between philosophy and the gospel is the difference between stages in the history of reason.

---

3. Voegelin, "The Gospel and Culture," 172–212. As with the essay of Strauss, the quotations are taken from the opening pages.

4. See also the study of Cochrane, *Christianity and Classical Culture.*

A modern way of posing the same question that has a more direct bearing on the issue under analysis is the controversial 1966 *New Catechism*, published by the Dutch bishops of the Roman Catholic Church. The opening chapter is called "Man the Questioner." It asserts that Christians are human beings with "inquiring minds" and are searching for ways to account for their faith. The motivation of the Dutch bishops is a mirror image of the motivation of Justin: he began as an "inquiring mind" and, following the philosophical schools, was led to the gospel; the bishops, in contrast, had somehow to recover a sense of inquiry because it had been lost and, as is true of many contemporary Christians, they remained in a tranquil state of uninquiring faith. Voegelin adds a "supplement" or a "reminder" that "neither Jesus nor his fellowmen to whom he spoke his word did yet know that they were Christians—the gospel held out its promise not to Christians, but to the poor in the spirit, that is, to minds inquiring, even though on a culturally less sophisticated level than Justin's." The conflict that lay behind the assertion of the Dutch bishops and what expressed itself in the ensuing controversy over the *Dutch Catechism*, as it is generally known, was not between the gospel and philosophy "but rather between the gospel and its unenquiring possession as doctrine."

The conflict, that is to say, is between an inquiring mind and a doctrine that prohibits inquiry. Whatever the pragmatic effectiveness of doctrine as a means of ensuring the credal integrity of a community, the price is invariably the suppression of questions that an inquiring mind is apt to ask. Just as Strauss found a way to deal with the tension between Athens and Jerusalem, so did Voegelin find a way to deal with an inquiring mind in the context of Christianity. To put the issue simply: "the question to which, in Hellenistic-Roman culture, the philosopher could understand the gospel as the answer" concerns "the humanity of man," which "is the same today as it ever has been in the past." The emphasis for both Voegelin and Strauss lies on the questions asked, not the more or less adequate answers received, nor on the equally questionable criteria by means of which the more adequate can be distinguished from the less.

These reflections have a bearing on the issue of Islamist terrorism insofar as Islamists have undertaken the "reducing diets" (to recall the image of Meddeb) of an already astringent regimen. In less colorful language, the issue concerns the relationship of an inquiring mind, which is characteristic of the "humanity of man," and uninquiring obedience to the equally unproblematic word of God, the unproblematic status of which is, to the inquiring mind, evidence only of a dogmatic and closed mind.

The literature on this question in the context of Islam far surpasses anything we can discuss here, and the following sketch is intended chiefly to illustrate a political problem rather than analyze or evaluate the underlying religious, interpretive, or spiritual problem—which, as mentioned above, on philological grounds alone far exceeds my competence.

In 1953, Franz Rosenthal began an article with an understated title, "Some Minor Problems of the Qur'an," in this way: "The basic problem involved in the following discussion is whether we are permitted to doubt the traditional understanding of the Qur'an."[5] In light of the explicit direction given in the Koran (2:1), that "this is the Perfect Book, free from all doubt," the answer, within the context of Islamic history or the Muslim vulgate, is obvious: no doubt at all is permitted because there are no genuine "problems" in the Koran, not minor ones and certainly not major ones. The Koran is not to be doubted because it is meant to be heard and obeyed. Likewise, the title of Warraq's recent book, *What the Koran Really Says*, which reproduced Rosenthal's paper, raises for Islamic history a thoroughly inappropriate but implicit question: what does the Koran really say? We are asked, therefore, to see what God's word means, which is a philosophical inquiry rather than an act of obedience.

This is a radical question, an expression of an inquiring mind, because the appropriate answer to the implicit question is: the Koran records God's eloquence. If one is unsure of what God's eloquence means, master the exegetical tradition and find out. The grave problem with this answer, which is the answer of Rosenthal's "traditional understanding," is that an examination of the tradition will tell you what the exegetes took it to mean, not what God's word means nor even, to follow Strauss's formulation, what it meant to the contemporaries of the Prophet, the pious ancestors, nor to the Prophet himself. To answer that question, which is one that eventually the inquiring mind must consider, brings us to a basic fork in the interpretive road: if one rejects "traditional understanding," which in the Islamic context we may call

5. Reprinted in Warraq [pseud.], ed., *What the Koran Really Says*.

the teachings of the *ulema* (roughly analogous to the teachings and disputes of the pre-Reformation Church), then there is left only independent interpretation, ijtihad, or something like what Strauss called a "historical-critical study."

In the chapters above, we have already considered the conflict between the "traditional understanding" and "independent interpretation" and in this context analyzed the writings of men such as Ibn Taymiyya, Qutb, and bin Laden from the perspective of political science or "historical-critical study." The issue here, however, involves a different and more radical one: it is possible to bring to light the pneumopathological attributes of an Asahara or a bin Laden by analyzing their texts in order to understand them on their own terms. However, it is one thing to try to understand an author as the author understood himself or herself, which we may call the principle of Straussian hermeneutics, but when the author of a text is God, something quite different is involved. A historical-critical study of a text, for example, that Islamic history upholds as "uncreated"[6] in the sense that it is the direct Word of God, is a recipe for conflict, even war. In other words, to examine the text of the Koran as a product of a particular set of historical or cultural or individual experiences is easily seen by those living Islamic history, whether in accord with "traditional understanding" or in terms of some idiosyncratic ijtihad, as an attack on Islam. Mindful of the post-fatwa life of Salman Rushdie, this is why today so many minds inquiring into "problems of the Koran" use pseudonyms. A half century ago Rosenthal could publish in his own name, which speaks to a changed political rather than interpretive climate today.

Today, for Muslims living within Islamic history, matters are made worse when the inquiring minds are also Western and so doubly damned as both infidel and formerly or neo-colonial. For Westerners derailed by dogmatic postcolonial, postmodern sensibilities, things are no better: there can be no serious distinction between scholarship and polemic for postmoderns because there are no inquiring minds. There are only interested minds. Or, as Michel Foucault once put it, there is no knowledge, only power-knowledge. Notwithstanding the unpropitious context

6. For a discussion of the contemporary political relevance of this apparently recondite theological issue, see Ruthven, *A Fury for God*, 39–43; Lewis, *Crisis of Islam*, 8.

for the appearance of a mind inquiring into the text-critical problems of the Koran, or into what the Koran "really says," a good deal of the traditional understanding has been radically revised by the past generation of scholars—inquiring Muslim and non-Muslim minds working in the area of Middle Eastern studies—to give as neutral a designation as possible. Their concerns, to reiterate a point just made, are not with the perverse interpretations of ijtihad nor of the politics of the Ikhwan, though we shall argue that it has political as well as scholarly significance.

Two aspects of the problem concern us. The first deals with recent accounts of the formation of the Islamic community on the basis of what may be termed allegiance to the Islamic vulgate, and second is the textual status of the vulgate documents. The analogous problems in Judaism would consist in the reconciliation of (1) the archeological history of ancient Palestine, which provides a physical record of the gradual historical development of hilltop villagers into a kingdom, which then was conquered and exiled forcibly to Babylon where the "prophets" brought together the theology of the exodus from paganism into monotheism, with (2) the content of this theology, which told the well-known stories of: Yahwe's initial revelation to Moses, the exit from Egypt to Sinai, the episode of the Burning Bush, Yahwe's gift of the Ten Commandments, the wandering in the desert, the conquest of the Promised Land, the Davidic kingdoms, the Babylonian captivity, the revelations of Daniel, and so on.[7]

The Islamic equivalent to the distinction between the history of the tribal villagers of Palestine and their political life, and the theology of the exodus from paganism, has a similar structure: (1) the revelation at Mecca, the creation of the new community in Medina, the early rightly guided caliphs, their conquests, and the creation of the Umayyad Empire, is an equivalent version of (2) the Israelite exodus under different historical circumstances and experiences. Not humiliation, defeat, and exile, but triumphant imperial succession to Rome and Persia furnished the contents of the Muslim story of exodus from paganism to monotheism.

This multidimensional historical/symbolic complex is far more subtle than the Islamic vulgate, which combines the two dimensions into a single story. Voegelin has given the name *historiogenesis* to the creation

7. See Ahituv and Oren, *Origin of Early Israel.*

of the compound story that combines an account of "what happened," the *res gestae*, with a meaning that provides significance to "what happened," in this instance, obedience to the word of God.[8]

We noted in chapter 4 the elaboration of what might be termed a secular vulgate or secular historiogenetic account by Montgomery Watt. Watt provided a conventionally Western and secular account of the origins of the history of Islam. For present purposes it provides a useful starting point and a contrast to both the Muslim vulgate and a remarkable study, published in 1977 by Patricia Crone and Michael Cook, *Hagarism: The Making of the Islamic World.* They argued that Islam began as a messianic movement, "Hagarism," the objective of which was to rule the Holy Land in a peculiar kind of alliance with the Jews. The peculiarity, according to Crone and Cook, was that messianic Israelite redemption was conducted by an army with an Ishmaelite genealogy. "There were," they wrote,

> really only two solutions. On the one hand they [the proto-Muslim "Hagarenes"] could proceed after the manner of the Ethiopian Christians, that is to say by themselves adopting Israelite descent. But in view of the play they had already made of their Ishmaelite ancestry, it is hardly surprising that they should have clung to it throughout their entire doctrinal evolution. On the other hand, if they would not go to the truth, the truth might perhaps be persuaded to come to them. On the foundation of their Ishmaelite genealogy, they had to erect a properly Ishmaelite prophetology. It was a daring move for so religiously parvenu a nation, but it was the only way out.

The tension between Israelite redemption and Ishmaelite genealogy, to say nothing of the transformation of the exodus symbolism from defeat and humiliation to victory and triumph, was extreme. As John Wansbrough remarked in a celebrated review of *Hagarism,* "it seems, indeed, that the problem of identity in Islam is not exclusively a legacy of colonialism; it has been there all the time." Wansbrough himself developed his own systematic analysis of Islamic history about the same time. He explicitly applied to the Koran and the story of the Prophet at Mecca and Medina the techniques of biblical criticism developed over the preceding century and a half by Western scholars. He did so, moreover, on

8. Voegelin, *The Ecumenic Age,* chap. 1.

the commonsensical (at least to an inquiring Western scholar) grounds that if the Christian and Jewish revelations could be discussed using "source-critical" or "historical-critical" methods, so could the Islamic.[9]

In addition to a novel approach to Muslim sacred texts, a kind of "critical history" was applied to the early years of the Umayyad Empire. Between the death of the Prophet in 632 and the establishment of an Arab-ruled Islamic empire by the end of the century, the purely pragmatic necessity of establishing the superiority of Islam over the two competing monotheisms, as well as over Zoroastrianism and "paganism" or paganisms, was obvious.[10] At the same time, the three religious communities strongly outnumbered the ruling Muslims. In addition, the Umayyad rulers were faced with the need to unify a wide range of traditional legal customs in order to reduce the instability of the eighth century that had led to dynastic wars of succession. The point of this effort to create a coherent "theologico-political" synthesis was to create a civil theology or a "minimum dogma" (to use a formula that Voegelin applied to Spinoza's efforts under similar circumstances).

Starting around 800, commentators and scholars invented Islamic history, or what we have called the historiogenetic myth of Islam, on the basis of "trustworthy authorities" who were alleged to have transmitted faithfully the oral reports of the Prophet during the previous five or six generations. Wansbrough argued the Koran was the finalized version of "an extensive corpus of prophetic *logia*" drawn from traditional Judaeo-Christian imagery that gained whatever unity the text has by means of a "limited number of rhetorical conventions." In his second book, Wansbrough argued that Muslim practices underwent a similar kind of transformation so that existing ninth-century practices were said to date from the time of the Prophet. These actions by what he called a "clerical elite," that is, the *ulema*, raised Islam above the other sects—Christian, Jewish, and Zoroastrian—by "neutralizing" Christian Trinitarian doctrine into Muslim unity and attacking Jewish scripture as having been abrogated by successive revelation.[11] These Western analy-

9. See Watt, *Muhammad at Mecca* and *Muhammad at Medina;* Crone and Cook, *Hagarism,* 16; Wansbrough, "Review of *Hagarism,*" 155; Wansbrough, *Quranic Studies;* Wansbrough, *The Sectarian Milieu.* See also Rippin, *The Quran and Its Interpretive Tradition.*

10. See Berkey, *The Formation of Islam,* chap. 2.

11. Wansbrough, *Quranic Studies,* 1, 47; Wansbrough, *The Sectarian Milieu,* 123–27.

ses of the origins of Islam naturally enough provoked considerable controversy both from Muslim traditionalists and from tradition-minded Western Arabists and Orientalists.[12] The controversy has redoubled in light of a parallel line of philological analysis focused on the textual history of Muslim scripture.

Let us begin our summary of this issue with a reprise of some agreed-upon historical data. The earliest texts from the Koran date from 691, fifty-nine years after the death of the Prophet. They are inscribed inside the Dome of the Rock in Jerusalem and vary slightly from the standard Koran. The third caliph, Uthman ibn Affan (644–656) ordered the hitherto oral text to be set down in writing. This "Uthman recension" was to be authoritative and constitutes the first book in Arabic. It is also widely agreed that the political purpose of the Uthman recension was to ensure that, all over the growing Umayyad Empire, Muslims would make reference to the same text and not quarrel, like the Jews and the Christians, over what the scripture said. At the same time, Uthman ordered all "imperfect" copies of the Koran destroyed.

The original Koranic script, called the *rasm*, in which the text established by Uthman was written, is without diacritical marks, written as dots, that are used to distinguish various letters and vowels. The diacritical points were added around the turn of the eighth century on orders of Hajjaj bin Uusuf, governor of Iraq (694–714). The result essentially transformed an orally transmitted text into a written one.

Apart from the inscriptions inside the Dome of the Rock, the earliest text of the Koran was, until recently, the Mail Manuscript in the British Library, which dated from the late seventh century; two other manuscripts, one in the Library of Tashkent, in Uzbekistan, and another in Istanbul at the Topkapi Museum, are from the eighth century. In 1972, a number of manuscripts were discovered in the Grand Mosque of Sanaa, in Yemen, during repairs to the loft between the inner and outer roofs following a major rainstorm. They were turned over to Qadhi Ismail al-Akwa, president of the Yemeni Antiquities Authority. A few years later, al-Akwa showed them to Gerd-Rüdiger Puin, a German Arabist and Islamic paleographer at Saarland University. In 1981, Puin and Hans-

12. See Berg, "Islamic Origins Reconsidered," 3–22, reprinted in Warraq [pseud.], *Quest for the Historical Muhammad,* 489–509. See also Motzki, "The Collection of the Qur'an," 1–34.

Caspar Graf von Bothman, an Islamic art historian and colleague at Saarland, and Albrecht Noth, of the University of Hamburg, obtained support from Germany to preserve, clean, and restore some fifteen thousand sheets and fragments. It turned out that the Sanaa materials were older than the Mail Manuscript.

The Yemeni authorities did not publicize the find or the work done by the Germans. The Germans said very little either and went about their work, which now included making photocopies. In 1997, von Bothman returned to Germany with 35,000 pictures, some of which were clearly palimpsests, manuscripts containing faint earlier texts that had been erased in order to reuse the parchment at a later date. The political reason for their reticence was obvious. As Puin put it, "So many Muslims have this belief that everything between two covers of the *Koran* is just God's unaltered word. They like to quote the textual work that shows that the Bible has a history and did not fall straight out of the sky, but until now the *Koran* has been out of this discussion. The only way to break through this wall is to prove that the *Koran* has a history too. The Sana'a fragments will help us do this."[13]

Another German scholar, the pseudonymous Christoph Luxenberg, has drawn additional implications from the Sanaa discovery and from prior philological work by Günter Lüling.[14] Lüling reopened an argument that had been made in the nineteenth century by Western Orientalists, that a dialect of Aramaic, namely, Syriac, or Syro-Aramaic, had influenced the vocabulary of the Koran. In the Prophet's time, Syriac was the language of written communication in the Middle East. Equally important, the literature written in Syriac was chiefly Christian. Now, the Koran is filled with biblical references, yet the Prophet was an illiterate merchant. Leaving aside the intervention of Gabriel, this means either that Mecca was home to large numbers of Jews and Christians,

---

13. See "A Qur'an Palimpsest from the Sanaa Qur'ans," available at http://home.t-online.de/home/christoph.heger/palimpse.htm (accessed September 9, 2003); see also Lester, "What Is the Koran?"

14. Lüling's original work was privately printed in 1974: *Über den Urkoran: Ansätze zur Rekonstruktion der vorislamisch-christlichen Strophenlieder im Koran.* A second, corrected edition, was published in 1993. It was widely ignored until he published two articles in English, "Preconditions for the Scholarly Study of the Koran and Islam, with Some Autobiographical Remarks" and "A New Paradigm for the Rise of Islam and Its Consequences for a New Paradigm for the History of Israel."

and not just pagan Bedouins, as the Islamic tradition maintains, or the Koran was written some place other than Mecca.[15]

Luxenberg continued his interpretation along the same philological lines as Lüling but drew some even more significant (and controversial) conclusions. Not only was the Koran soaked in Christianity and written in a language that used a large number of Syro-Aramaic words, but the very meaning of the term *Koran* derives from a Syriac word, *qeryana*, which is a technical term in Eastern Christianity that means "lectionary," which is to say, a set of liturgical readings taken from the Bible and read aloud at various ritual occasions during the year.[16] The method used by Luxenberg is complex and can best be judged over the long term by philologically competent scholars. The short-term implications, as the discussion of the dark-eyed houris above has indicated, are politically very important.

More than the fantasies of recruits to "martyrdom operations" are involved in the revisions to the Koran that follow from Luxenberg's argument. For those living within Islamic history, that is, for the pious Muslim, the Koran was not only transmitted from God to the Prophet without human intervention, but it was communicated in perfect Arabic, a unity of form and style and language and content that is itself a representation of the perfection and unity of God.

Luxenberg's argument simply destroys this account entirely. Not only is the Koran a Christian lectionary, the text itself put together at Uthman's command was compiled by people who could not read the language in which parts of it were written, namely, Syro-Aramaic. That is why they misread the passage about the dark-eyed houris as well as several other ones of much greater theological significance.

Even if scholars know that the questions raised by Westerners such as Luxenberg, or by Lüling, Puin, and von Bothman, or by contemporary Muslim scholars have been raised before in the history of Islam, those previous efforts by inquiring minds have long been forgotten. As a result, the current work is bound to be seen widely as yet another attack

15. See Crone, *Meccan Trade and the Rise of Islam*. See also Stille, "Scholars Dare to Look into Origins of Quran," and Stille, "Radical New Views of Islam and Origins of the Koran."

16. Luxenberg, *Die Syro-aramaeische Lesart des Koran*. See also the reviews in the journal of the *Institute for the Secularisation of Islamic Society*, http://www.secularislam.org/books/luxenberg.htm (accessed September 7, 2003); and Phenix and Horn, "Review."

by Western scholarship or by apostate Muslim scholars. As with the controversy over the houris, it should come as no surprise that the Luxenberg thesis was not simply critically examined and analyzed according to the conventions of ordinary scholarship, but the argument has been characterized as a "plot against the Qur'an under the guise of academic study and archive preservation."[17]

Toward the end of her study of the seductive appeals of terrorism, especially of Islamist terrorism, Jessica Stern indicated the challenge to Westerners. Clearly military opposition or a policy change with respect to Israel or Saudi Arabia is not the main issue. Nor is it the simple fact that the cultures and societies and religions of the world provide human beings with many forms of collective identity. "One of our goals," she said, "must be to make the terrorists' purification project seem *less* urgent: to demonstrate the humanity that binds us, rather than allow our adversaries to emphasize and exploit our differences to provide a seemingly clear (but false) identity, at the expense of peace."[18] A concern for the common humanity of all people is possible only for inquiring minds, minds in search of a common humanity. In terms of the historical and the theological issues raised in this appendix, such a person would see in Revelation, whether Jewish, Christian, or Muslim, a symbolic, not a literal truth. The alternative would be to capitulate not to Islam but to fundamentalists who have no need to inquire about anything because their impulses no less than their acts lead to totalitarian domination and the superfluousness of humanity itself.

17. See Geissinger, "Orientalists Plot against the Qur'an." See also Stefan Theil, "Challenging the Qur'an," *Newsweek*, July 28, 2003; Hathout, "Response to 'Challenging the Quran' Article in Newsweek"; Muslim Public Affairs Council, "The Quran and the Challenge to *Newsweek*"; "Muslim Scholar Refutes *Newsweek* Qur'an Article," *Palestine Chronicle*, August 5, 2003, http://www.palestinechronicle.com/article.php?story=20030805183725369.

18. Stern, *Terror in the Name of God*, 280.

Bibliography

Abd al-Fattah, Gam'an. http://www.lailatalqudr.com/stories/p1260503. html. Quoted in Yotam Feldner, "'72 Black Eyed Virgins': A Muslim Debate on the Rewards of Martyrs." Middle East Media Research Institute *Inquiry and Analysis Series* no. 74 (October 30, 2001). http://www.memri.org/bin/opener.cgi?Page=archives&ID= IA7401.

Abd Al-Hadi, Palazzi. http://jerusalempost.com/06092001.html. Quoted in Yotam Feldner, "'72 Black Eyed Virgins': A Muslim Debate on the Rewards of Martyrs." Middle East Media Research Institute *Inquiry and Analysis Series* no. 74 (October 30, 2001). http://www. memri.org/bin/opener.cgi?Page=archives&ID=IA7401.

Abu Gheith, Suleiman. "'Why We Fight America': Al Qa'ida Spokesman Explains September 11 and Declares Intentions to Kill 4 Million Americans with Weapons of Mass Destruction." Middle East Media Research Institute *Special Dispatch Series* no. 388 (June 12, 2002). http://www.memri.org/bin/articles.cgi?Page=archives&Area=sd& ID=SP38802.html.

Abu Zaid, Nasr Hamid. "Divine Attributes of the Qur'an: Some Perspectives." In *Islam and Modernity,* edited by J. Cooper et al. London: Tauris, 1998.

Abu-Rabi, Ibrahim M. *Intellectual Origins of Islamic Resurgence in the Modern Arab World.* Albany: State University of New York Press, 1996.

Abubakar, Muhammad A. "Sayyid Qutb's Interpretation of the Islamic View of Literature." *Islamic Studies* 23 (1984).

Ahituv, Shmuel, and Eliezer B. Oren. *The Origin of Early Israel: Current Debate: Biblical, Historical, and Archaeological Perspectives.* The Irene Levi-Sala Seminar. Beer-Sheva: Ben-Gurion University of the Negev Press, 1998.

Ajami, Fouad. *The Dream Palace of the Arabs: A Generation's Odyssey.* New York: Pantheon, 1998.

———. "The Uneasy Imperium: Pax Americana in the Middle East." In *How Did This Happen? Terrorism and the New War,* edited by James F. Hoge Jr. and Gideon Rose. New York: Public Affairs, 2001.

Akbar, M. J. *The Shade of Swords: Jihad and the Conflict Between Islam and Christianity.* London: Routledge, 2002.

al Rasheed, Wadawi. *A History of Saudi Arabia.* Cambridge: Cambridge University Press, 2002.

Al-Risala. July 7, 2001. Quoted in Yotam Feldner, "'72 Black Eyed Virgins': A Muslim Debate on the Rewards of Martyrs." Middle East Media Research Institute *Inquiry and Analysis Series* no. 74 (October 30, 2001). http://www.memri.org/bin/opener.cgi?Page=archives& ID=IA7401.

Al-Sayad (Beirut). September 13, 1972.

Al-Sharq Al-Awsat. Quoted in Yotam Feldner, "Debating the Religious, Political, and Moral Legitimacy of Suicide Bombings, Part 1: The Debate over Religious Legitimacy." Middle East Media Research Institute *Inquiry and Analysis Series* no. 53 (May 2, 2001). http://www. memri.org/bin/opener.cgi?Page=archives&ID=IA5301.

Alberts, David S., John J. Garstka, Richard E. Hayes, and David S. Signori. *Understanding Information Age Warfare.* Washington, DC: Command and Control Research Program. 2001. http://www.dodccrp.org/.

Annan, Noel, ed. *Report of the Committee on the Future of Broadcasting.* London: HMSO, 1977.

Arendt, Hannah. *Between Past and Future: Eight Exercises in Political Thought.* New York: Viking, 1968.

———. *Essays in Understanding, 1930–1954: Uncollected and Unpublished Works by Hannah Arendt.* New York: Harcourt, Brace and World, 1993.

———. *The Human Condition.* Chicago: University of Chicago Press, 1958.

———. *On Revolution.* New York: Viking, 1965.

———. *On Violence.* New York: Harcourt, Brace and World. 1969.

———. *The Origins of Totalitarianism.* New York: Harcourt, Brace and World, 1966.

Armstrong, Karen. *The Battle for God.* New York: Ballantine, 2000.

———. "War: Is It Inevitable? Islam through History." In *How Did This Happen? Terrorism and the New War,* edited by James F. Hoge Jr. and Gideon Rose. New York: Public Affairs, 2001.

Arquilla, John. "Osama Bin Laden, Not Wanted: Dead or Alive." *Los Angeles Times,* December 30, 2001, op-ed page.

Arquilla, John, and Theodore Karasik. "Chechnya: A Glimpse of Future Conflict?" *Studies in Conflict and Terrorism* 22 (1999): 207–30.

Arquilla, John, and David Ronfeldt. *The Advent of Netwar.* Santa Monica: Rand Corp., 1996. MR-789-OSD.

———. "The Advent of Netwar." In *In Athena's Camp: Preparing for Conflict in the Information Age,* edited by John Arquilla and David Ronfeldt. Santa Monica: Rand Corp., 1997.

———. "The Advent of Netwar (Revisited)." In *Networks and Netwars: The Future of Terror, Crime, and Militancy,* edited by John Arquilla and David Ronfeldt. Santa Monica: Rand Corp., 2001.

———. "Afterword (September, 2001): The Sharpening Fight for the Future." In *Networks and Netwars: The Future of Terror, Crime, and Militancy,* edited by John Arquilla and David Ronfeldt. Santa Monica: Rand Corp., 2001.

———. "Cyberwar Is Coming!" *Comparative Strategy* 12 (1993). Reprinted as RAND RP-223.

———. "Fight Networks with Networks." *Rand Review* 25, no. 3 (2001). http://www.rand.org/publications/randreview/issues/rr.12.01/fullalert.html#networks.

———. "Information, Power, and Grand Strategy: In Athena's Camp— Section 1." In *In Athena's Camp: Preparing for Conflict in the Information Age,* edited by John Arquilla and David Ronfeldt. Santa Monica: Rand Corp., 1997.

———. "Looking Ahead: Preparing for Information-Age Conflict." In *In Athena's Camp: Preparing for Conflict in the Information Age,* edited by John Arquilla and David Ronfeldt. Santa Monica: Rand Corp., 1997.

———. "A New Epoch—and Spectrum—of Conflict." In *In Athena's Camp: Preparing for Conflict in the Information Age,* edited by John Arquilla and David Ronfeldt. Santa Monica: Rand Corp., 1997.

———. "Osama bin Laden and the Advent of Netwar." *New Perspectives Quarterly* 18, no. 4 (2001). http://www.digitalnpq.org/archive/2001_fall/osama.html.

————. *Swarming: The Future of Conflict.* Santa Monica: Rand Corp., 2000.

Arquilla, John, and David Ronfeldt, eds. *In Athena's Camp: Preparing for Conflict in the Information Age.* Santa Monica: Rand Corp., 1997.

————, eds. *Networks and Netwars: The Future of Terror, Crime, and Militancy.* Santa Monica: Rand Corp., 2001.

Arquilla, John, David Ronfeldt, and Michele Zanini. "Networks, Netwar, and Information-Age Terrorism." In *Countering New Terrorism,* by Ian O. Lesser, Bruce Hoffman, John Arquilla, David F. Ronfeldt, Michele Zanini, and Brian Michael Jenkins. Santa Monica: Rand Corp., 1999.

Averroës. "The Decisive Treatise, Determining What the Connection Is between Religion and Philosophy." Translated by George F. Hourani. In *Medieval Political Philosophy,* edited by R. Lerner and M. Mahdi. Ithaca: Cornell University Press, 1963.

Ayubi, Nazih N. *Political Islam: Religion and Politics in the Arab World.* London: Routledge, 1991.

Bacevich, Andrew J. "What It Takes: Our Present Situation Resembles Korea." *National Review,* October 1, 2001. http://www.nationalreview.com/15oct01/bacevich101501.shtml.

Barkun, Michael. "Racist Apocalypse: Millennialism on the Far Right." In *The Year 2000: Essays on the End,* edited by Charles B. Strozier and Michael Flynn. New York: New York University Press, 1997.

————. *Religion and the Racist Right: The Origins of the Christian Identity Movement.* Rev. ed. Chapel Hill: University of North Carolina Press, 1997.

Bashear, Suleiman. "Early Muslim Apocalyptic Materials." *Journal of the Royal Asiatic Society,* 3rd ser., 1 (1991).

Beam, Louis. "Leaderless Resistance." *Seditionist* 2 (February 1992). http://www.adl.org/learn/ext_us/beam.asp?xpicked=2&item=beam#return3.

Bearden, Milton. "Graveyard of Empires: Afghanistan's Treacherous Peaks." In *How Did This Happen? Terrorism and the New War,* edited by James F. Hoge Jr. and Gideon Rose. New York: Public Affairs, 2000.

Bell, Stewart. "Fatwa Would Let Bin Laden Kill Himself." *National Post* (Toronto), November 21, 2001, sec. A, p. 1.

Benjamin, David, and Steven Simon. *The Age of Sacred Terror.* New York: Random House, 2002.

Berg, Herbert. "Islamic Origins Reconsidered: John Wansbrough and the Study of Early Islam." *Method and Theory in the Study of Religion* 9 (1997).

Bergen, Peter L. *Holy War, Inc.: Inside the Secret World of Osama bin Laden.* New York: Free Press, 2001.

Berger, Samuel L., and Mona Sutphen. "Commandeering the Palestinian Cause: Bin Laden's Belated Concern." In *How Did This Happen? Terrorism and the New War,* edited by James F. Hoge Jr. and Gideon Rose. New York: Public Affairs, 2001.

Berkey, Jonathan P. *The Formation of Islam: Religion and Society in the Near East 600–1800.* Cambridge: Cambridge University Press, 2003.

Berkowitz, Bruce. *The New Face of War: How War Will Be Fought in the Twenty-first Century.* New York: Free Press, 2003.

Betts, Richard K. "Intelligence Test: The Limits of Prevention." In *How Did This Happen? Terrorism and the New War,* edited by James F. Hoge Jr. and Gideon Rose. New York: Public Affairs, 2001.

Bin Laden, Osama. "Declaration of War against the Americans Who Occupy the Land of the Two Holy Mosques." 1996. http://www.pbs.org/wgbh/pages/frontline/shows/binladen/who/edicts.html and http://www.msanews.mynet.net/MSANEWS/199610/19961012.3html.

———. "Declaration of the World Islamic Front for Jihad against Jews and the Crusaders." *Al-Quds al Arabi,* February 22, 1998. http://www.fas.org/irp/world/par/docs/980223-fatwa.html.

———. Interview by John Miller. *Frontline,* ABC. October 12, 1998. http://www.pbs.org/wgbh/pages/frontline/shows/binladen/who/interview.html.

Binder, Leonard. *Islamic Liberalism: A Critique of Development Ideologies.* Chicago: University of Chicago Press, 1988.

Black, Antony. *The History of Islamic Political Thought: From the Prophet to the Present.* New York: Routledge, 2001.

Blank, Stephen J. "Preparing for the Next War: Reflections on the Revolution in Military Affairs." In *In Athena's Camp: Preparing for Conflict in the Information Age,* edited by John Arquilla and David Ronfeldt. Santa Monica: Rand Corp., 1997.

Blankinship, Khalid. *The End of the Jihad State.* Albany: State University of New York Press, 1994.

Bodansky, Yossef. *Bin Laden: The Man Who Declared War on America.* New York: Random House, 1999.

Bonabeau, Eric, and Christopher Meyer. "Swarm Intelligence." *Harvard Business Review*, May 2001.

Bouroumand, Ladan, and Roya Boroumand. "Terror, Islam, and Democracy." *Journal of Democracy* 13 (2002).

Bowden, Mark. *Black Hawk Down: A Story of Modern War.* New York: Signet, 2001.

Brackett, D. W. *Holy Terror: Armageddon in Tokyo.* New York: Weatherhill, 1996.

Brockelmann, Carl. *History of the Islamic Peoples.* New York: Routledge, 2000.

Brooke, James. "Newspaper Says McVeigh Described Role in Bombing." *New York Times,* March 1, 1997, sec. A, p. 1.

Buber, Martin. *Moses: The Revelation and the Covenant.* New York: Harper Torch Books, 1946.

Bull, Hedley. *The Anarchical Society: A Study of Order in World Politics.* 3rd ed. New York: Columbia University Press, 1977.

Burke, Edmund. *Letters on Regicide Peace.* Vol. 5, *The Works of the Right Honorable Edmund Burke.* 8 vols. London: Henry G. Bohn, 1854.

Burleigh, Michael. "National Socialism as a Political Religion." *Totalitarian Movements and Political Religions* 1, no. 2 (2000).

Buruma, Ian, and Avisahi Margalit. "Occidentalism." *New York Review of Books* 49, no. 1 (January 17, 2002).

Calahan, Alexander B. "Countering Terrorism: The Israeli Response to the 1972 Munich Olympic Massacre and the Development of Independent Covert Action Teams." Master's thesis, Marine Corps Command and Staff College, April 1995.

Calgary Herald. October 8, 2001, January 21, 2002.

Calvert, John. "The Islamist Syndrome and Cultural Confrontation." *Orbis* 46 (2002).

————. "Sayyid Qutb in America." International Institute for the Study of Islam in the Modern World *Newsletter* 7 (March 2001): 8. http://www.isim.nl/files/newsl_7.pdf.

————. "'The World Is an Undutiful Boy!': Sayd Qutb's American Experience." *Islam and Christian-Muslim Relations* 11, no. 1 (2000).

Cameron, Gavin. "Multi-track Microproliferation: Lessons from Aum Shinrikyo and al-Qaida." *Studies in Conflict and Terrorism* 22, no. 4 (1999).

Campbell, Colin. "The Cult, the Cultic Milieu, and Secularization." *A Sociological Yearbook of Religion in Britain.* London: SCM Press, 1972.

Campbell, Murray. "Taliban Dismisses Shock Over Statues." *Globe and Mail* (Toronto), March 20, 2001, sec. A, p. 9.

Cantwell Smith, Wilfred. *Islam in Modern History.* Princeton: Princeton University Press, 1957.

Carell, Paul. *Scorched Earth: The Russian-German War, 1943–1944.* Boston: Little, Brown, 1966.

Carré, Olivier. "Quelques Mots-clefs de Muhammad Husayn Fadlallah." *Revue Française de Science Politique* 37 (1987).

———. "Bioterrorism and Biocrimes: The Illicit Use of Biological Agents in the Twentieth Century." Center for Counterproliferation Research. 2001. http://www.ndu.edu.ndu/centercounter/full_doc.pdf.

Carus, W. Seth. "The Threat of Bioterrorism." National Defense University, *Strategic Forum* 127 (September 1997). http://www.ndu.edu/inss/strforum/SF127/forum127.html.

Castells, Manuel. *The Information Age: Economy, Society and Culture.* Vol. 1, *The Rise of the Network Society.* Malden, MA: Blackwell, 1996.

Chew, Jenni. "Kill Apocalyptic Terrorists, Says Expert." United Press International, July 2, 2002. http:///www.upi.com/print.cfm?StoryID= 02072002-015107-6051r.

Choueiri, Youssef M. *Islamic Fundamentalism.* Rev. ed. London: Pinter, 1990.

Cleaver, Harry. "The Zapatista Effect: The Internet and the Rise of an Alternative Political Fabric." *Journal of International Affairs* 51, no. 2 (1998).

Clinehens, Neal A. "Aum Shinrikyo and Weapons of Mass Destruction: A Case Study." Research report. 2000. Air Command and Staff College, Air University, Maxwell Air Force Base, AL.

Clutterbuck, Richard. *The Media and Political Violence.* 2nd ed. London: Macmillan, 1986.

Clymer, Adam. "A Day of Terror in the Capital: In the Day's Attacks and Explosions, Official Washington Hears the Echoes of Earlier Ones." *New York Times,* September 12, 2001.

Cochrane, C. N. *Christianity and Classical Culture: A Study of Thought and Action from Augustus to Augustine.* Oxford: Clarendon, 1940.

Cook, David. "The Beginning of Islam as an Apocalyptic Movement." *Journal for Millenial Studies* (Winter 2001). http://www.mille.org/publications/winter2001/cook.html.

———. *Contemporary Muslim Apocalyptic Literature.* Forthcoming.

———. "Moral Apocalyptic in Islam." *Studia Islamica* 86 (1997).

———. "Muslim Apocalyptic and Jihad." *Jerusalem Studies in Arabic and Islam* 20 (1966).

———. *Studies in Classical Muslim Apocalyptic.* Princeton: Darwin Press, 2003.

———. "Taking the Apocalyptic Pulse of Muslims in Israel and Egypt." http://www.mille.org/stew/fall99/cook-fall99.html.

Cook, Michael. "Eschatology, History, and the Dating of Traditions." *Princeton Papers in Near Eastern Studies* 1 (1992).

———. *Muhammad.* Oxford: Oxford University Press, 1983.

Cooper, Barry. *Action into Nature: An Essay on the Meaning of Technology.* Notre Dame: University of Notre Dame Press, 1991.

———. "Constituent Elements in the Genesis of Voegelin's Political Science." *Zeitschrift für Politik* 48, no. 2 (2001).

———. *The End of History.* Toronto: University of Toronto Press, 1984.

———. *Eric Voegelin and the Foundations of Modern Political Science.* Columbia: University of Missouri Press, 1999.

Cooper, Jeffrey R. "Another View of the Revolution in Military Affairs." In *In Athena's Camp: Preparing for Conflict in the Information Age,* edited by John Arquilla and David Ronfeldt. Santa Monica: Rand Corp., 1997.

Corbin, Jane. *The Base: In Search of Al-Qaeda, the Terror Network That Shook the World.* London: Simon and Schuster, 2002.

Crone, Patricia. *Meccan Trade and the Rise of Islam.* Princeton: Princeton University Press, 1987.

Crone, Patricia, and Michael Cook. *Hagarism: The Making of the Islamic World.* Cambridge: Cambridge University Press, 1977.

Cronin, Audrey Kurth. "Rethinking Sovereignty: American Strategy in the Age of Terrorism." *Survival* 44 (2002).

Canadian Security and Intelligence Service. "Chemical, Biological, Radiological and Nuclear (CBRN) Terrorism." 1999. http://www.csis-scrs.gc.ca/eng/miscdocs/2002_e.html.

———. *Doomsday Religious Movements.* Report #2002/03. December 18, 1999. http://www.csis-scrs.gc.ca/eng/miscdocs/200003_e.html.

———. *Public Report 2000.* June 12, 2001. http://www.csis-scrs.gc.ca/eng/publicrp/pub2000_e.html.

Daily Mirror (London). September 7, 1996.

Davis, Paul K., and Brian Michael Jenkins. *Deterrence and Influence in Counterterrorism.* Santa Monica: Rand Corp., 2002.

Day, Jerry. *Voegelin, Schelling, and the Philosophy of Historical Existence.* Columbia: University of Missouri Press, 2003.

de Armond, Paul. "Netwar in the Emerald City: WTO Protest Strategy and Tactics." In *Networks and Netwars: The Future of Terror, Crime, and Militancy,* edited by John Arquilla and David Ronfeldt. Santa Monica: Rand Corp., 2001.

Der Spiegel. Inside 9–11: What Really Happened? New York: St. Martin's, 2002.

Dershowitz, Alan M. *Why Terrorism Works: Understanding the Threat, Responding to the Challenge.* New Haven: Yale University Press, 2002.

Dishman, Chris. "Trends in Modern Terrorism." *Studies in Conflict and Terrorism* 22, no. 4 (1999).

———. "Understanding Perspectives on WMD and Why They Are Important." *Studies in Conflict and Terrorism* 24, no. 4 (2001).

Donner, Fred M. "The Sources of Islamic Conceptions of War." In *Just War and Jihad: Historical and Theoretical Perspectives on War and Peace in Western and Islamic Traditions,* edited by John Kelsay and James Turner Johnson. New York: Greenwood, 1991.

Doran, Michael Scott. "Somebody Else's Civil War: Ideology, Rage, and the Assault on America." In *How Did This Happen? Terrorism and the New War,* edited by James F. Hoge Jr. and Gideon Rose. New York: Public Affairs, 2001.

Durham, Chris. "Trends in Modern Terrorism." *Studies in Conflict and Terrorism* 22 (1999).

Edwards, Sean J. A. *Swarming on the Battlefield: Past, Present, and Future.* Santa Monica: Rand Corp., 2000. MR-1100-OSD.

Egan, Sean P. "From Spikes to Bombs: The Rise of Eco-Terrorism." *Studies in Conflict and Terrorism* 19 (1996).

Ehrlich, Richard S. "For Sale in Afghanistan: U.S.-Supplied Stingers." *Washington Times,* May 21, 1991, sec. A, p. 1.

Eliade, Mircea. *The Forge and the Crucible: The Origins and Structures of Alchemy.* New York: Harper, 1962.

Enayat, Hamid. *Modern Islamic Political Thought.* London: Macmillan, 1982.

Esposito, John L. *Unholy War: Terror in the Name of Islam.* New York: Oxford University Press, 2002.

Euben, Roxanne L. *Enemy in the Mirror: Islamic Fundamentalism and the Limits of Modern Rationalism; A Work in Comparative Political Theory.* Princeton: Princeton University Press, 1999.

Evan, William M. "An Organization-Set Model of Interorganizational Relations." In *Interorganizational Decision Making,* edited by Matthew Tuite, Roger Chisholm, and Michael Radnor. Chicago: Aldine, 1972.

Evans-Wentz, W. Y. *Tibetan Yoga and Secret Doctrines: Or Seven Books of Wisdom of the Great Path, According to the Late Lama Kazi Dawa-Samdup's English Rendering.* 2nd. ed. Oxford: Oxford University Press, 1958.

Falkenrath, Richard A., Robert D. Newman, and Bradley A. Thayer. *America's Achilles' Heel: Nuclear, Biological, and Chemical Terrorism and Covert Attack.* Cambridge: MIT Press, 1988.

Fanon, Frantz. *The Wretched of the Earth.* Preface by Jean-Paul Sartre. Translated by Constance Farrington. New York: Grove Press, 1963.

Federation of American Scientists. http://www.fas.org/irp/world/para/docs/980223-fatwa.htm.

Feldner, Yotam. "Debating the Religious, Political, and Moral Legitimacy of Suicide Bombings, Part II: The Debate over Political and Moral Legitimacy." Middle East Media Research Institute *Inquiry and Analysis Series* no. 54 (May 3, 2001). http://www.memri.org/bin/opener.cgi?Page=archives&ID=IA5401.

———. "Debating the Religious, Political, and Moral Legitimacy of Suicide Bombings, Part III." Middle East Media Research Institute *Inquiry and Analysis Series* no. 65 (July 26, 2001). http://www.memri.org/bin/opener.cgi?Page=archives&ID=IA6501.

———. "Debating the Religious, Political, and Moral Legitimacy of Suicide Bombings, Part IV." Middle East Media Research Institute *Inquiry and Analysis Series* no. 66 (July 27, 2001). http://www.memri.org/bin/opener.cgi?Page=archives&ID=IA6601.

———. "Suicide, Martyrdom, Terrorist Attacks, or Homicide: A Debate in the Arab Media." Middle East Media Research Institute *Special Dispatch Series* no. 378 (May 12, 2002). http://www.memri.org/bin/opener.cgi?Page=archives&ID=SP37802.

Firestone, Reuven. *Jihad: The Origins of Holy War in Islam.* Oxford: Oxford University Press, 1999.

Fowden, Garth. *Empire to Commonwealth: Consequences of Monotheism in Late Antiquity.* Princeton: Princeton University Press, 1993.

Fox, Jonathan. "The Difficult Transition from Clientelism to Citizenship: Lessons from Mexico." *World Politics* 46, no. 2 (1994).

Foxell, Joseph W., Jr. "Current Trends in Agroterrorism (Antilivestock, Anticrop, and Antisoil Bioagricultural Terrorism) and Their Potential Impact on Food Security." *Studies in Conflict and Terrorism* 24 (2001).

Frankel, Glen. "Sale of Explosive to Libya Detailed." *Washington Post*, March 23, 1990, sec. A, p. 1.

Friedman, Thomas L. "Hama Rules." *New York Times*, September 21, 2001, sec. A, p. 4.

Fukuyama, Francis. *Trust: The Social Virtues and the Creation of Prosperity.* New York: Free Press, 1995.

Gause, F. Gregory, III. "The Kingdom in the Middle: Saudi Arabia's Double Game." In *How Did This Happen? Terrorism and the New War,* edited by James F. Hoge Jr. and Gideon Rose. New York: Public Affairs, 2001.

Gelernter, David. *Mirror Worlds, or The Day Software Puts the Universe in a Shoebox . . . : How It Will Happen and What It Will Mean.* New York: Oxford University Press, 1991.

Gerlach, Luther P. "The Structure of Social Movements: Environmental Activism and Its Opponents." In *Networks and Netwars: The Future of Terror, Crime, and Militancy,* edited by John Arquilla and David Ronfeldt. Santa Monica: Rand Corp., 2001.

Ghiglieri, Michael. *The Dark Side of Man: Tracing the Origins of Male Violence.* Cambridge, MA: Perseus Books, 1999.

Gibbs, Jack P. "Conceptualization of Terrorism." *American Sociological Review* 54 (1989).

Geissinger, Aisha. "Orientalists Plot against the Qur'an under the Guise of Academic Study and Archive Preservation." *Muslimedia,* May 16–31, 1999. www.muslimedia.com/archives/features99/orientalist.htm.

Gold, Dore. *Hatred's Kingdom: How Saudi Arabia Supports the New Global Terrorism.* Washington, DC: Regnery, 2003.

Goldhizer, Ignaz. *Muslim Studies.* Edited by S. M. Stern. Translated by C. R. Barker and S. M. Stern. Chicago: Aldine, 1967.

Goodall, Jane. *Through a Window: My Thirty Years with the Chimpanzees of Gombe.* Boston: Houghton Mifflin, 1990.

Graham, Patrick. "State-sanctioned Assassination." *National Post* (Toronto), August 18, 2001, sec. A, p. 12.

Granovetter, Mark S. "Economic Action and Social Structure: The Problem of Embeddedness." *American Journal of Sociology* 91 (1985).

Gurr, Nadine, and Benjamin Cole. *The New Face of Terrorism: Threats from Weapons of Mass Destruction.* London: Tauris, 2000.

Gwartney, James, and Robert Lawson. *Economic Freedom of the World: Annual Report.* Vancouver: Fraser Institute, 2003.

Haddad, Yvonne Yazbeck. "The Qur'anic Justification for the Islamic Revolution: The View of Sayyid Qutb." *The Middle East Journal* 37, no. 1 (1983).

———. "Sayyid Qutb: Ideologue of Islamic Revival." In *Voices of Resurgent Islam,* edited by John Esposito. New York: Oxford University Press (1983).

Hahout, Maher. *Final Call.* September 4, 2001. Quoted in Yotam Feldner, "'72 Black Eyed Virgins': A Muslim Debate on the Rewards of Martyrs." Middle East Media Research Institute *Inquiry and Analysis Series* no. 74 (October 30, 2001). http://www.memri.org/bin/opener.cgi?Page=archives&ID=IA7401.

Haim, Sylvia G. "Sayyid Qutb." *Asian and African Studies* 16 (1982).

Hanson, Victor Davis. *Carnage and Culture: Landmark Battles in the Rise of Western Power.* New York: Anchor, 2002.

Harmon, Christopher C. *Terrorism Today.* London: Cass. 2000.

Hashimi, Sohail. "The Terrorists' Zealotry Is Political, Not Religious." *Washington Post,* September 30, 2001, sec. B, p. 1.

Hassan, Nasra. "An Arsenal of Believers." *New Yorker,* November 19, 2001. http://www.newyorker.com/fact/content/?011119fa_FACT1.

Hathout, Maher. "Response to 'Challenging the Quran' Article in *Newsweek.*" *iViews,* August 4, 2003. http://www.iviews.com/articles/Articles.asp?ref=IV0308-2054.

Hawting, G. R. *The Idea of Idolatry and the Emergence of Islam: From Polemic to History.* Cambridge: Cambridge University Press, 1999.

Hellhom, David, ed. *Apocalypticism in the Mediterranean World.* Tübingen: Paul Siebech, 1989.

Hesson, Elizabeth C. *Twentieth-Century Odyssey: A Study of Heimito von Doderer's Die Dämonen.* Columbia: Camden House, 1982.

Higgins, Andrew, and Alan Cullison. "Terrorist's Odyssey: Saga of Dr. Zawahiri." *Wall Street Journal,* July 2, 2002, sec. A, p. 1.

Highfield, Roger. "Explosion Could Have Wrecked City Center." *Daily Telegraph* (London), August 13, 1993, p. 1.

Hiro, Dilip. *War without End: The Rise of Islamist Terrorism and Global Response.* London: Routledge, 2002.

Hitti, P. K. *History of the Arabs.* New York: St. Martin's, 1963.

Hodgson, Marshall G. S. *The Order of Assassins.* The Hague: Mouton, 1955.

———. *The Venture of Islam: Conscience and History in a World Civilization.* 3 vols. Chicago: University of Chicago Press, 1974.

Hoffman, Bruce. "The Case for Torture." *National Post* (Toronto), January 26, 2002, sec. B, p. 2.

———. "Holy Terror: The Implications of Terrorism Motivated by a Religious Imperative." *Studies in Conflict and Terrorism* 18 (1995).

———. *Inside Terrorism.* New York: Columbia University Press, 1998.

———. "Rethinking Terrorism and Counterterrorism since 9/11." *Studies in Conflict and Terrorism* 25 (2002).

———. "Re-Thinking Terrorism in Light of a War on Terrorism." Testimony before the House Subcommittee on Terrorism and Homeland Security, September 26, 2001. http://www.rand.org/publications/CT/CT182/.

———. *Terrorism and Weapons of Mass Destruction: An Analysis of Trends and Motivations.* Santa Monica: Rand Corp., 1999. P-8039.

———. "Terrorism and Weapons of Mass Destruction: Some Preliminary Hypotheses." *Nonproliferation Review* 4, no. 3 (1997).

Hoffman, Valerie. "Muslim Fundamentalists: Psychosocial Profiles." In *Fundamentalisms Comprehended,* edited by Martin E. Marty and R. Scott Appleby. Chicago: University of Chicago Press, 1995.

Hoge, James F., Jr., and Gideon Rose. *How Did This Happen? Terrorism and the New War.* New York: Public Affairs, 2001.

Holtom, D. C. *Modern Japan and Shinto Nationalism.* Chicago: University of Chicago Press, 1943.

Homer-Dixon, Thomas. "On the Threshold: Environmental Changes as Causes of Acute Conflict." *International Security* 16 (1991).

Hosek, James R. "The Soldier of the Twenty-first Century." In *New Challenges, New Tools for Defense Decision-Making,* edited by Stuart Johnson et al. Santa Monica: Rand Corp., 2003.

Hourani, Albert. *Arabic Thought in the Liberal Age, 1798–1939.* 1970. Reprint, London: Oxford University Press, 1983.

Hoyland, Robert. *Seeing Islam as Others Saw It: A Survey and Evaluation of Christian, Jewish, and Zoroastrian Writings on Early Islam.*

Vol. 13, *Studies in Late Antiquity and Early Islam.* Princeton: Darwin Press, 1997.

Huizinga, Jan. *Homo Ludens: A Study of the Play Element in Culture.* Boston: Beacon Press, 1955.

Huntington, Samuel. *The Clash of Civilizations and the Remaking of World Order.* New York: Simon and Schuster, 1996.

Ibrahim, Saad Eddin. "Anatomy of Egypt's Militant Islamic Groups: Methodological Note and Preliminary Findings." *International Journal of Middle East Studies* 12 (1980).

Ibrahim, Saad Eddin, and Nicholas S. Hopkins, eds. *Arab Society: Social Science Perspectives.* Cairo: American University of Beirut Press, 1985.

Ignatieff, Michael. *Virtual War: Kosovo and Beyond.* Toronto: Viking, 2000.

Institute for National Strategic Studies. "Globalization Study." National Defense University, Washington, DC, 2000.

Iriye, Akira. *Power and Culture: The Japanese-American War, 1941–1945.* Cambridge: Harvard University Press, 1981.

Jaffe, Greg. "Risk Assessment: Plans for a Small Ship Pose Big Questions for the U.S. Navy." *Wall Street Journal,* July 11, 2001, sec. A, p. 1.

Jansen, J. J. *The Neglected Duty: The Creed of Sadat's Assassins and Islamic Resurgence in the Middle East.* New York: Macmillan, 1986.

Jacquard, Roland. *In the Name of Osama bin Laden: Global Terrorism and the bin Laden Brotherhood.* Translated by George Holock. Durham: Duke University Press, 2002.

Jenkins, Michael. *Countering al Qaeda: An Appreciation of the Situation and Suggestions for Strategy.* Santa Monica: Rand Corp., 2002.

———. "International Terrorism: A New Mode of Conflict." In *International Terrorism and World Security,* edited by David Carlton and Carlo Schaerf. London: Croom Helm, 1975.

———. *The Likelihood of Nuclear Terrorism.* Santa Monica: Rand Corp., 1985. P-7119.

———. "The Organization Men: Anatomy of a Terrorist Attack." In *How Did This Happen? Terrorism and the New War,* edited by James F. Hoge Jr. and Gideon Rose. New York: Public Affairs, 2001.

———. *Will Terrorists Go Nuclear?* Santa Monica: Rand Corp., 1975. P-5541.

———. "Will Terrorists Go Nuclear?" *Orbis* 29, no. 3 (1985).

Johnson, Stuart et al., eds. *New Challenges, New Tools for Defense Decision-Making.* Santa Monica: Rand Corp., 2003.

Jonas, George. *Vengeance.* New York: Simon and Schuster, 1984.

Juergensmeyer, Mark. *Terror in the Mind of God: The Global Rise of Religious Violence.* Berkeley: University of California Press, 2000.

———. "The Worldwide Rise of Religious Nationalism." *Journal of International Affairs* 50 (1996).

Kagan, Frederick W. "The Korean Parallel: Is it June, 1950 All Over Again?" *New York Weekly Standard,* October 2, 2001.

Kaplan, David E. "Aum Shinrikyo, (1995)." In *Toxic Terror: Assessing Terrorist Use of Chemical and Biological Weapons,* edited by Jonathan B. Tucker. Cambridge: MIT Press, 2000.

Kaplan, David E., and Andrew Marshall. *The Cult at the End of the World: The Terrifying Story of the Aum Doomsday Cult, from the Subways of Tokyo to the Nuclear Arsenals of Russia.* New York: Crown, 1996.

Katzman, Kenneth. *Terrorism: Near Eastern Groups and State Sponsors.* Washington, DC: Congressional Research Service, Library of Congress, 2001.

Kauppi, Mark V. "Terrorism and National Security." *National Security Studies Quarterly* 4 (1998).

Keddie, N. R. *Sayyid Jamal ad-Din "Al-Afghani:" A Political Biography.* Berkeley: University of California Press, 1972.

Keeley, Lawrence H. *War before Civilization: The Myth of the Peaceful Savage.* New York: Oxford University Press, 1996.

Keegan, John. "A Different Kind of War Indeed." *National Post* (Toronto), October 8, 2001, sec. A, p. 10.

———. *A History of Warfare.* New York: Random House, 1994.

Kelley, Jack. *USA Today,* June 26 2001. Quoted in Yotam Feldner, "'72 Black Eyed Virgins': A Muslim Debate on the Rewards of Martyrs." Middle East Media Research Institute *Inquiry and Analysis Series* no. 74 (October 30, 2001). http://www.memri.org/bin/opener.cgi?Page=archives&ID=IA7401.

Kelsay, John. *Islam and War: The Gulf War and Beyond: A Study in Comparative Ethics.* Westminster: John Knox Press, 1993.

Kepel, Gilles. *Jihad: The Trail of Political Islam.* Translated by Anthony F. Roberts. Cambridge: The Belknap Press of Harvard University Press, 2002.

————. *Muslim Extremism in Egypt: The Prophet and the Pharaoh.* Berkeley: University of California Press, 1984.

Kerr, Malcolm H. *Islamic Reform: The Political and Legal Theories of Muhammad Abduh and Rashid Rita.* Berkeley: University of California Press, 1966.

Khadduri, Majid. *War and Peace in the Law of Islam.* Baltimore: Johns Hopkins University Press, 1955.

Khaled, Leila. *My People Shall Live: The Autobiography of a Revolutionary.* London: Hodder and Stoughton, 1973.

Kidder, R. "The Terrorist Mentality." *Christian Science Monitor,* May 15, 1986, sec. A, p. 14.

Kingdom, H. "Who Were the Zealots?" *New Testament Studies* 17 (1970).

Kitfield, James. "Covert Counterattack," *National Journal,* September 16, 2000.

Kocieniewski, David, and Raymond Bonner. "For Terrorists, the Menace of Silence." *New York Times,* August 25, 1996, sec. A, p. 17.

Kolnai, Aurel. *The War against the West.* New York: Viking. 1938.

Koppel, Ted. "Terrorism and the Media: A Discussion." In "Lost in the Terrorist Theatre," edited by Jeanne J. Kirkpatrick et al. *Harper's Magazine,* October 1984.

Koren, Judith, and Yehuda D. Nevo. "Methodological Approaches to Islamic Studies." *Der Islam* 68 (1991).

Kramer, Martin. "The Moral Logic of Hizballah." In *Origins of Terrorism: Psychologies, Ideologies, Theologies, States of Mind,* edited by Walter Reich. Cambridge: Cambridge University Press, 1990.

Krebs, Valdis. *InFlow.* 2003. http://www.orgnet.com/.

Kreckovsky, LCDR Melanie J. "Training for Terror: A Case Study of Al-Qaida." Master's thesis, Monterey Naval Postgraduate School, 2002.

Lacey, Marc. "Attacks Were Up Last Year, U.S. Terrorism Report Says." *New York Times,* May 1, 2002, sec. A, p. 1.

Landes, Richard. "What Happens when Jesus Doesn't Come: Jewish and Christian Relations in Apocalyptic Time." *Terrorism and Political Violence* 14 (2002).

Laoust, Henri. *Essai sur les Doctrines Sociales et Politiques d'Ibn Taimiya.* Cairo: Institut français d'archéologie orientale, 1939.

Lapidus, Ira M. "The Separation of State and Religion in the Development of Early Islamic Society." *International Journal of Middle Eastern Studies* 6 (1975).

Laqueur, Walter. "Left, Right, and Beyond: The Changing Face of Terror." In *How Did This Happen? Terrorism and the New War,* edited by James F. Hoge Jr. and Gideon Rose. New York: Public Affairs, 2001.

———. *The New Terrorists: Fanaticism and the Arms of Mass Destruction.* New York: Oxford University Press, 1999.

———. "Postmodern Terrorism." *Foreign Affairs* 75, no. 5 (1996).

Lawrence, T. E. *The Seven Pillars of Wisdom.* London: Penguin, 1977.

Leaman, Oliver. *An Introduction to Medieval Islamic Philosophy.* Cambridge: Cambridge University Press, 1985.

Lemos, Robert. "'Hacktivism': Mideast Cyberwar Heats Up." *ZDNet News,* November 5, 2000. http://zdnet.com.com/2100-11-525308.html.

Lester, Toby. "What Is the Koran?" *Atlantic Monthly,* January 1999. http://www.theatlantic.com/issues/99jan/koran.htm.

Lewis, Bernard. *The Assassins: A Radical Sect in Islam.* London: Weidenfeld and Nicholson, 1967.

———. *The Crisis of Islam: Holy War and Unholy Terror.* New York: Modern Library, 2003.

———. *The Emergence of Modern Turkey.* 2nd ed. Oxford: Oxford University Press, 1968.

———. "License to Kill: Usama bin Laden's Declaration of Jihad." *Foreign Affairs* 77 (1998).

———. *What Went Wrong? Western Impact and Middle Eastern Response.* New York: Oxford University Press, 2002.

Lewis, W. R. *The British Empire in the Middle East, 1945–1951.* Oxford: Oxford University Press, 1984.

Libicki, Martin C. "Incorporating Information Technology in Defense Planning." In *New Challenges, New Tools for Defense Decision-Making,* edited by Stuart Johnson et al. Santa Monica: Rand Corp., 2003.

———. *The Mesh and the Net: Speculations on Armed Conflict in a Time of Free Silicon.* McNair Paper no. 28. Washington, DC: National Defense University, 1994.

———. "The Small and the Many." In *In Athena's Camp: Preparing for Conflict in the Information Age,* edited by John Arquilla and David Ronfeldt. Santa Monica: Rand Corp., 1997

Lieven, Anatol. "The Cold War Is Finally Over: The True Significance of the Attacks." In *How Did This Happen? Terrorism and the New War,* edited by James F. Hoge Jr. and Gideon Rose. New York: Public Affairs, 2001.

Lifton, Robert Jay. *Destroying the World to Save It: Aum Shinrikyo, Apocalyptic Violence and the New Global Terrorism.* New York: Metropolitan Books, 1999.

Lindblom, Charles. *Politics and Markets: The World's Political-Economic Systems.* New York: Basic Books, 1977.

Lonergan, Bernard. *Insight: A Study of Human Understanding.* New York: Philosophical Library, 1957.

Luft, David S. *Robert Musil and the Crisis of European Culture, 1880–1942.* Berkeley: University of California Press, 1980.

Lüling, Günter. "A New Paradigm for the Rise of Islam and Its Consequences for a New Paradigm for the History of Israel." *Journal of Higher Criticism* 7 (2000).

———. "Preconditions for the Scholarly Study of the Koran and Islam, with Some Autobiographical Remarks." *Journal of Higher Criticism* 3 (1966).

———. *Über den Urkoran: Ansätze zur Rekonstruktion der vorislamisch-christlichen Strophenlieder im Koran.* 2nd ed. Erlangen: Verlagsbuchhandlung H. Lüling, 1993.

Luxenberg, Christoph. *Die Syro-aramaeische Lesart des Koran: Ein Beitrag zur Entschlüsselung der Qur'ansprache.* Berlin: Das Arabische Buch, 2000.

Madelung, Wilfred. "Apocalyptic Prophecies in Hims during the Umayyad Age." *Journal of Semitic Studies* 41 (1986).

———. *The Succession to Muhammad: A Study of the Early Caliphate.* Cambridge: Cambridge University Press, 1997.

Makiya, Kanan, and Hassan Mneimneh. "Manual for a 'Raid.'" *New York Review of Books,* January 17, 2002.

Malamat. A. "The Struggle against the Philistines." In *A History of the Jewish People,* edited by H. H. Ben-Sasson. Cambridge: Harvard University Press, 1976.

Margalit, Avisahi. "The Suicide Bombers." *New York Review of Books,* January 16, 2003. http://www.nybooks.com/articles/15979.

McGuire, Maria. *To Take Arms.* London: Macmillan, 1973.

Medd, Roger, and Frank Goldstein. "International Terrorism on the Eve of a New Millennium." *Studies in Conflict and Terrorism* 20 (1997).

Meddeb, Abdelwahab. *The Malady of Islam.* Translated by Pierre Joris and Ann Reid. New York: Basic Books, 2003.

Menon, Rajan. "The Restless Region: The Brittle States of Central and

South Asia." In *How Did This Happen? Terrorism and the New War*, edited by James F. Hoge Jr. and Gideon Rose. New York: Public Affairs, 2001.

Metraux, Daniel A. *Aum Shinrikyo's Impact on Japanese Society*. Lewiston: Edwin Mellen, 2000.

Mitchell, Richard P. *The Society of Muslim Brothers*. Oxford: Oxford University Press, 1969.

Mohaddessin, Mohammad. Interview. By Daniel Pipes and Patrick Clawson, with Alireza Jafarzadeh, interpreter. Washington, D.C., March 3, 1995. In *Middle East Quarterly* 2, no. 3 (September 1995). http://www.meforum.org/article/267.

Monaghan, Rachel. "Single-Issue Terrorism: A Neglected Phenomenon?" *Studies in Conflict and Terrorism* 23 (2000).

More, Thomas. *Utopia*. Edited by Edward Surtz and J. H. Hexter. Vol. 4 of *The Yale Edition of the Complete Works of St. Thomas More*. New Haven: Yale University Press, 1965.

Mottadeh, Roy. "Islam and the Opposition to Terrorism." *New York Times*, September 30, 2001, sec. B, p. 2.

Motzki, Harald. "The Collection of the Qur'an: A Reconsideration of Western Views in Light of Recent Methodological Developments." *Der Islam* 78 (2001).

Moussalli, Ahmad S. *Radical Islamic Fundamentalism: The Ideological and Political Discourse of Sayyid Qutb*. Beirut: American University of Beirut Press, 1992.

———. "Sayyid Qutb's View of Knowledge." *American Journal of Islamic Social Sciences* 7 (1990).

Muir, Hazel. "Email Traffic Patterns Can Reveal Ringleaders." *Newscientist.com* (March 27, 2003). http://www.newscientist.com/news/news.jsp?id=s99993550.

Mullins, Mark R. "Aum Shinrikyo as an Apocalyptic Movement." In *Millennium, Messiahs and Mayhem: Contemporary Apocalyptic Movements*, edited by Thomas Robbins and Susan J. Palmer. New York: Routledge, 1997.

Murad, Abdal-Hakim. "Bin Laden's Violence Is a Heresy against Islam." *Islam for Today*. http://www.islamfortoday.com/murad04.htm.

Murdock, Paul. "Principles of War on the Network-Centric Battlefield." http://carlisle-www.army.mil/usawc/Parameters/02spring/murdock.htm.

Musil, Robert. *Der Mann ohne Eigenschaften.* Edited by Adolf Frisé. Hamburg: Rowohlt, 1960.

Muslim Public Affairs Council. "The Quran and the Challenge to *Newsweek.*" August 5, 2003. http://www.mpac.org/home_article_display. aspx?ITEM=592.

Naipaul, V. S. *India: A Wounded Civilization.* New York: Knopf, 1977.

National Post (Toronto). September 29, November 12, December 14, 2001.

Navarro, Peter and Aron Spencer. "September 11, 2001: Assessing the Costs of Terrorism." *Milken Institute Review* (4th quarter, 2001).

Nevo, Yehuda D., and Judith Koren. "Towards a Prehistory of Islam." *Jerusalem Studies in Arabic and Islam* 17 (1994).

Niebuhr, H. Richard. *The Meaning of Revelation.* New York: Macmillan, 1962.

Newsweek. January 11, 1999, August 21, 2000.

Nicholson, R. A. *A Literary History of the Arabs.* Cambridge: Cambridge University Press, 1969.

Nietzsche, F. "Human, All Too Human." In *The Portable Nietzsche,* edited by W. Kaufmann. New York: Viking, 1954.

Observer. October 28, 2001.

Palmer, Andrew, Sebastian Brock, and Robert Hoyland, eds. *The Seventh Century in West-Syrian Chronicles,* Vol. 15 of *Translated Texts for Historians.* Liverpool: Liverpool University Press, 1993.

Parachini, John. "Combatting Terrorism: Assessing Threats, Risk Management, and Establishing Priorities." In *Toxic Terror: Assessing Terrorist Use of Chemical and Biological Weapons,* edited by Jonathan B. Tucker. Cambridge: MIT Press, 2000.

Payne, Philip. *Robert Musil's 'The Man Without Qualities': A Critical Study.* Cambridge: Cambridge University Press, 1988.

Pedahzur, Ami, William Eubank, and Leonard Weinberg. "The War on Terrorism and the Decline of Terrorist Group Formation: A Research Note." *Terrorism and Political Violence* 14 (2002).

Peters, Rudolph. *Islam and Colonialism: The Doctrine of Jihad in Modern History.* The Hague: Mouton, 1979.

Pfirrmann, Gerhardt. "Religiöser Charakter und Organisation der Thagbrüderschaften." Ph.D. diss., University of Tübingen, 1970.

Phenix, Robert R., Jr., and Corneilia B. Horn. Review. In *Hugoye: Journal of Syriac Studies* 6 (2003). http://syrcom.cua.edu/Hugoye/vol6No1/ HV6N1PR/PhenixHorn.html.

Pipes, Daniel. *Militant Islam Reaches America.* New York: Norton, 2002.

Pleming, Sue. "Muslim Extremists Utilize Web Encryption." Reuters. February 6, 2001. Reported in National Center for Policy Analysis, *Policy Digest,* September 13, 2001.

Pollack, Kenneth. *The Threatening Storm: The Case for Invading Iraq.* New York: Random House, 2002.

Postman, Neil. *Amusing Ourselves to Death.* Toronto: Penguin, 1985.

Powell, Walter W. "Neither Market nor Hierarchy: Network Forms of Organization." *Research in Organizational Behavior: An Annual Series of Analytical Essays and Critical Reviews* 12 (1990). Edited by Barry M. Straw and L. L. Cummings.

Qutb, Sayyid. *Milestones.* Damascus: Holy Koran Publishing, 1978.

Rahman, Fazlur. *Islam.* 2nd ed. Chicago: University of Chicago Press, 1979.

Ranstorp, Magnus. "Terrorism in the Name of Religion." *Journal of International Affairs* 50 (1996).

Rapoport, David C. "Fear and Trembling: Terrorism in Three Religious Traditions." *American Political Science Review* 78 (1984).

———. "Messianic Sanctions for Terror." *Comparative Politics* 20 (1987–1988).

———. "Sacred Terror: A Contemporary Example from Islam." In *Origins of Terrorism: Psychologies, Ideologies, Theologies, States of Mind,* edited by Walter Reich. Cambridge: Cambridge University Press, 1990.

———. "Terrorism and Weapons of the Apocalypse." *National Security Studies Quarterly* 5 (1999).

Rauf, Muhammad Abdul. "Hadith Literature: The Development of the Science of Hadith." In *Arabic Literature to the End of the Umayyad Period,* edited by A. F. L. Beeston et al. Cambridge: Cambridge University Press, 1983.

Reader, Ian. "Imagined Persecution: Aum Shinrikyo, Millennialism, and the Legitimation of Violence." In *Millennialism, Persecutions, and Violence,* edited by Catherine Wessinger. Syracuse: Syracuse University Press, 2000.

———. *A Poisonous Cocktail? Aum Shinrikyo's Path to Violence.* Copenhagen: Nordic Institute of Asian Studies, 1996.

———. *Religious Violence in Contemporary Japan: The Case of Aum Shinrikyo.* Nordic Institute of Asian Studies monograph series no. 82. Richmond: Curzon Press, 2000.

———. "Spectres and Shadows: Aum Shinrikyo and the Road to Megiddo." *Terrorism and Political Violence* 14 (2002).

Reeve, Simon. *The New Jackals: Ramzi Yousef, Osama bin Laden, and the Future of Terrorism.* Boston: Northeastern University Press, 1999.

Rhoads, Christopher. "Long-Term Economic Effects of Sept.11 May Be More Costly." *Wall Street Journal,* June 7, 2002.

Rippin, Andrew. *Muslims: Their Religious Beliefs and Practices.* 2nd ed. London: Routledge, 2001.

———. *The Quran and Its Interpretive Tradition.* Burlington: Ashgate, 2001.

Roberts, Brad. *Hype or Reality: The "New Terrorism" and Mass Casualty Attacks.* Alexandria: Free Hand Press, 2000.

Ronfeldt, David. *Beware the Hubris-Nemesis Complex: A Concept for Leadership Analysis.* Santa Monica: Rand Corp., 1994. MR-461.

Ronfeldt, David, and John Arquilla. "Emergence and Influence of the Zapatista Social Netwar." In *Networks and Netwars: The Future of Terror, Crime, and Militancy,* edited by John Arquilla and David Ronfeldt. Santa Monica: Rand Corp., 2001.

———. "Networks, Netwars, and the Fight for the Future." *First Monday* 6, no. 10 (October 2001). http://www.firstmonday.org/issue6_10/ronfeldt/index.html.

———. "What's Next for Networks and Netwars?" In *Networks and Netwars: The Future of Terror, Crime, and Militancy,* edited by John Arquilla and David Ronfeldt. Santa Monica: Rand Corp., 2001

Rosenau, William. "Aum Shinrikyo's Biological Weapons Program: Why Did It Fail?" *Studies in Conflict and Terrorism* 24, no. 4 (2001).

Rosenthal, Erwin J. *Political Thought in Medieval Islam: An Introductory Outline.* Cambridge: Cambridge University Press, 1958.

Rosenthal, Franz. "On Suicide in Islam." *Journal of the American Oriental Society* 66 (1946).

Rubin, Barnett R. "Arab Islamists in Afghanistan." In *Political Islam: Revolution, Radicalism, or Reform,* edited by John L. Esposito. Boulder: Lynne Rienner, 1997.

Rumi, Jalal al-Din. *Tales from the Masnavi.* Translated and edited by A. J. Arberry. Richmond: Curzon Press, 1993.

Ruthven, Malise. *A Fury for God: The Islamist Attack on America.* London: Granta, 2002.

Sacks, Jonathan. *The Dignity of Difference: How to Avoid the Clash of Civilizations.* London: Continuum, 2002.

Sadeq, Adel. "Chairman of the Arab Psychiatrists Association Offers Diagnoses: Bush Is Stupid; Perpetrating a Suicide/Martyrdom Attack Is Life's Most Beautiful Moment; We'll Throw Israel into the Sea." Middle East Media Research Institute *Special Dispatch Series* no. 373 (April 30, 2002). http://www.memri.org/bin/opener.cgi?Page=archives&ID=SP37302.

Safar, Ibn Abd al-Rahman al-Hawali. "An Open Letter to President Bush." October 15, 2001. http://www.as-sahwah.com/viewarticle.php?articleID-704.

Sale, Murray. "Nerve Gas and the Four Noble Truths." *New Yorker,* April 1, 1996.

Schacht, Joseph. *The Origins of Muhammedan Jurisprudence.* Rev. ed. Oxford: Oxford University Press, 1953.

Schbley, Ayla H. "Religious Terrorists: What They Aren't Going to Tell Us." *Terrorism* 13, no. 3 (1990).

Schwartz, Stephen. *The Two Faces of Islam: The House of Sa'ud From Tradition to Terror.* New York: Doubleday, 2002.

Scruton, Roger. *The West and the Rest: Globalization and the Terrorist Threat.* Wilmington, Del.: ISI Books, 2002.

Shepard, William. *Sayyid Qutb and Islamic Activism: A Translation and Critical Analysis of Social Justice in Islam.* Leiden: Brill, 1996.

Simon, Steven, and Daniel Benjamin. "Real or Imagined Threats?" *Survival* 42 (2000).

Sivan, Emmanuel. *Radical Islam: Medieval Theology and Modern Politics.* New Haven: Yale University Press, 1990.

Smith, Wilfred Cantwell. *Islam in Modern History.* Princeton: Princeton University Press, 1957.

Smithson, Amy E., and Leslie-Ann Levy. *Ataxia: The Chemical and Biological Terrorism Threat and the U.S. Response.* Washington, DC: Stimson Center Report no. 35, 2000.

Smythe, Donald. *Guerrilla Warrior: The Early life of John J. Pershing.* New York: Scribner's, 1973.

Soo Hoo, Kevin, Seymour Goodman, and Lawrence Greenberg. "Information Technology and the Terrorist Threat." *Survival* 39, no. 3 (1997).

Sprinzak, Ehud. "From Messianic Pioneering to Vigilante Terrorism: The Case of the Gush Emunim." *Journal of Strategic Studies* 10 (1987).

Sproull, Lee, and Sara Kiesler. *Connecting: New Ways of Working in the Networked Organization.* Cambridge: MIT Press, 1991.

Stafford, David. *From Anarchism to Reformism: A Study of the Political Activities of Paul Brousse within the First International and the French Socialist Movement, 1870–90.* Toronto: University of Toronto Press, 1971.

Stern, Jessica. *Terror in the Name of God: Why Religious Militants Kill.* New York: HarperCollins, 2003.

———. "Terrorist Motivations and Unconventional Weapons." In *Planning the Unthinkable: How New Powers Will Use Nuclear, Biological, and Chemical Weapons,* edited by Peter R. Lavoy, Scott D. Sagan, and James J. Wirtz. Ithaca: Cornell University Press, 2000.

———. *The Ultimate Terrorists.* Cambridge: Harvard University Press, 1999.

———. "Will Terrorists Turn to Poison?" *Orbis* 37 (1993).

Stewart, Thomas A. *Business 2.0.* 2001. http://crab.rutgers.edu/~goertzel/netwar.htm.

Stille, Alexander. "Radical New Views of Islam and the Origins of the Koran." *Silk Road Communications.* 2002. http://www.silkrc.com/XCultures/Islam/koran.htm.

———. "Scholars Dare to Look into Origins of Quran." *New York Times,* March 2, 2002.

Strauss, Leo. *Studies in Platonic Political Philosophy.* Edited with an introduction by Thomas L. Pangle. Chicago: University of Chicago Press, 1983.

Sullivan, John P. "Gangs, Hooligans, and Anarchists: The Vanguard of Netwar in the Streets." In *Networks and Netwars: The Future of Terror, Crime and Militancy,* edited by John Arquilla and David Ronfeldt. Santa Monica: Rand Corp., 2001.

Tadmor, H. "The United Monarchy." In *A History of the Jewish People,* edited by H. H. Ben-Sasson. Cambridge: Harvard University Press, 1976.

Taheri, Amir. *Holy Terror: Inside the World of Islamic Terrorism.* London: Sphere Books, 1987.

Tantawi, Muhammed Sayyed. "Leading Egyptian Government Cleric Calls for 'Martyrdom Attacks that Strike Horror into the Hearts of the Enemies of Allah.'" Middle East Media Research Institute *Special Dispatch Series* no. 363 (April 7, 2002). http://www.memri.org/bin/opener.cgi?Page=archives&ID=SP36302.

Thiel, Stefan. "Challenging the Qur'an," *Newsweek* 28 (July 28, 2003). http://www.stacks.msnbc.com/news/940974.asp.

Thomas, Timothy L. "Al Qaeda and the Internet: The Danger of 'Cyber-planning.'" *Parameters* (Spring 2003): 112–23. http://carlisle-www.army.mil/usawc/Parameters/issues.htm.

Tibetan Book of the Dead. Edited by W. Y. Evans-Wentz. Oxford: Oxford University Press, 1927.

Time. December 23, 1998, January 11, 1999.

Trinh, Sylvaine, and John R. Hall. "The Violent Path of Aum Shinrikyo." In Hall et al., *Apocalypse Observed: Religious Movements and Violence in North America, Europe, and Japan.* London: Routledge, 2000.

Tucker, Jonathan B. *Toxic Terror: Assessing Terrorist Use of Chemical and Biological Weapons.* Cambridge: MIT Press, 2000.

Tyler, Josh, Dennis Wilkinson, and Bernardo A. Huberman. "Email as Spectroscopy: Automated Discovery of Community Structure within Organizations." 2003. http://joshtyler.com/.

United Nations Conference on Trade and Development. *World Investment Report, 2002.* http://ro.unctad.org/Templates/WebFlyer.asp?intItemID=2399&lang=1.

United Nations Development Program. *Arab Human Development Report, 2002.* http://www.undp.org/rbas/ahdr/english2002/html.

U.S. Congress. Senate. Committee on Government Affairs, Permanent Subcommittee on Investigations. *Global Proliferation and Weapons of Mass Destruction.* Washington, DC: Government Printing Office, 1996.

U.S. State Department. *Patterns of Global Terrorism, 1995.* Washington, DC: U.S. Department of State Publication 10321, 1996.

———. *Patterns of Global Terrorism, 2001.* Washington, DC: Government Printing Office, 2002.

van Creveld, Martin. "In Wake of Terrorism, Modern Armies Prove to be Dinosaurs of Defense." *New Perspectives Quarterly* 13, no. 4 (Fall 1996).

———. *The Rise and Decline of the State.* Cambridge: Cambridge University Press, 1999.

———. *The Sword and the Olive: A Critical History of the Israeli Defense Force.* New York: Public Affairs, 1998.

———. *Technology and War: From 2000 BC to the Present.* New York: Free Press, 1989.

———. *The Transformation of War.* New York: Free Press, 1991.

Vermaat, Emerson. "Bin Laden's Terror Networks in Europe." Mackenzie Institute Occasional Paper. May 26, 2002. http://www.mackenzieinstitute.com/commentary.html.

Voegelin, Eric. *Crisis and the Apocalypse of Man*. Edited by David Walsh. Vol. VIII, *History of Political Ideas*. Vol. 26 of *The Collected Works of Eric Voegelin*. Columbia: University of Missouri Press, 1999.

———. "The Eclipse of Reality." In *What Is History? and Other Late Unpublished Writings*, edited by Thomas A. Hollweck and Paul Caringella. Vol. 28 of *The Collected Works of Eric Voegelin*. 1990. Available, Columbia: University of Missouri Press, 1999.

———. *The Ecumenic Age*. Edited by Michael Franz. Vol. IV, *Order and History*. Vol. 17 of *The Collected Works of Eric Voegelin*. Columbia: University of Missouri Press, 2000.

———. "The Gospel and Culture." In *Published Essays: 1966–1985*, edited by Ellis Sandoz. Vol. 12 of *The Collected Works of Eric Voegelin*. 1990. Available, Columbia: University of Missouri Press, 1999.

———. *Hellenism, Rome, and Early Christianity*. Edited by Athanasios Moulakis. Vol. I, *History of Political Ideas*. Vol. 19 of *The Collected Works of Eric Voegelin*. Columbia: University of Missouri Press, 1997.

———. *Hitler and the Germans*. Translated and edited by Detlev Clemens and Brendan Purcell. Vol. 31 of *The Collected Works of Eric Voegelin*. Columbia: University of Missouri Press, 1999.

———. *Israel and Revelation*. Edited by Maurice P. Hogan. Vol. I, *Order and History*. Vol. 14 of *The Collected Works of Eric Voegelin*. Columbia: University of Missouri Press, 2001.

———. *The Middle Ages to Aquinas*. Edited by Peter von Sivers. Vol. II, *History of Political Ideas*. Vol. 20 of *The Collected Works of Eric Voegelin*. Columbia: University of Missouri Press, 1997.

———. *Modernity without Restraint: The Political Religions; The New Science of Politics; and Science, Politics and Gnosticism*. Edited by Manfred Henningsen. Vol. 5 of *The Collected Works of Eric Voegelin*. Columbia: University of Missouri Press, 2000.

———. "The Mongol Orders of Submission to European Powers, 1245–1255." In *Published Essays, 1940–1952*, edited by Ellis Sandoz. Vol. 10 of *The Collected Works of Eric Voegelin*. Columbia: University of Missouri Press, 2000.

———. "The People of God." In *Renaissance and Reformation*, edited by David L. Morse and William M. Thompson. Vol. IV, *History of Political Ideas*. Vol. 22 of *The Collected Works of Eric Voegelin*. Columbia: University of Missouri Press, 1998.

———. *Published Essays, 1953–1965.* Edited by Ellis Sandoz. Vol. 11 of *The Collected Works of Eric Voegelin.* Columbia: University of Missouri Press, 2000.

———. *Review of Politics* 15 (1953).

von Clausewitz, Carl. *On War.* Edited and translated by Michael Howard and Peter Paret. Princeton: Princeton University Press, 1984.

von Doderer, Heimito. *Die Dämonen: Roman; Nach der Chronik des Sektionsrates Geyrenhoff.* Translated by Richard and Clara Winston. Munich: Biederstein, 1957.

———. *Die Merowinger, Oder die Totale Familie.* Munich: Biederstein, 1962.

———. *Die Wiederkehr des Drachen: Aufsätze/Traktate/Reden.* Edited by Wendellin Schmidt-Dengler. Munich: Biederstein, 1970.

———. *The Demons.* New York: Knopf, 1961.

von Drehle, David. "World War, Cold War Won: Now the Gray War." *Washington Post,* September 12, 2001.

Waltz, Susan. "Islamist Appeal in Tunisia." *Middle East Journal* 40 (1986).

Wansbrough, John. *Quranic Studies: Sources and Methods of Scriptural Interpretation.* Oxford: Oxford University Press, 1977.

———. "Review of Hagarism." *Bulletin of the School of Oriental and African Studies* 41 (1978).

———. *The Sectarian Milieu: Content and Composition of Islamic Salvation History.* Oxford: Oxford University Press, 1978.

Warraq, Ibn [pseud]. *What the Koran Really Says: Language, Text, and Commentary.* Amherst: Prometheus, 2003.

Washington Post. September 28, 2001.

Watanabe, Manabu. "Religion and Violence in Japan Today: A Chronological and Doctrinal Analysis of Aum Shinrikyo." *Terrorism and Political Violence* 10, no. 4 (1988).

Watt, W. Montgomery. *Muhammad at Mecca.* Oxford: Clarendon, 1953.

———. *Muhammad at Medina.* Oxford: Clarendon, 1956.

Weber, Max. "The Social Psychology of the World Religions." In *From Max Weber: Essays in Sociology,* edited by H. H. Gerth and C. Wright Mills. New York: Oxford University Press, 1946.

Wechsler, William F. "Strangling the Hydra: Targeting al Qaeda's Finances." In *How Did This Happen? Terrorism and the New War,* edited by James F. Hoge Jr. and Gideon Rose. New York: Public Affairs, 2001.

Wensinck, A. J. *A Handbook of Early Muhammadan Thought*. Leiden: Brill, 1971.

Wessinger, Catherine. *How the Millennium Comes Violently: From Jonestown to Heaven's Gate*. New York: Seven Bridges Press, 2000.

Whittlow, Mark. *The Making of Byzantium, 600–1025*. Berkeley: University of California Press, 1996.

Whitsel, Brad. "Ideological Mutation and Millennial Belief in the American Neo-Nazi Movement." *Studies in Conflict and Terrorism* 24, no. 2 (2001).

Whitsel, Bradley C. "Catastrophic New Age Groups and Public Order." *Studies in Conflict and Terrorism* 23 (2000).

Williams, Phil. "Transnational Criminal Networks." In *Networks and Netwars: The Future of Terror, Crime, and Militancy*, edited by John Arquilla and David Ronfeldt. Santa Monica: Rand Corp., 2001.

Wolfe, Alan. "The Home Front: America Responds to the New War." In *How Did This Happen? Terrorism and the New War*, edited by James F. Hoge Jr. and Gideon Rose. New York: Public Affairs, 2001.

Wright, Robert. "Muslims and Modernity." 2001. http://state.msn.com/.

———. *Sacred Rage*. New York: Simon and Schuster, 1986.

Zaharia, Fareed. "The Return of History: What September 11 Hath Wrought." In *How Did This Happen? Terrorism and the New War*, edited by James F. Hoge Jr. and Gideon Rose. New York: Public Affairs, 2001.

Zanini, Michele, and Sean J. A. Edwards. "The Networking of Terror in the Information Age." In *Networks and Netwars: The Future of Terror, Crime, and Militancy*, edited by John Arquilla and David Ronfeldt. Santa Monica: Rand Corp., 2001.

Zeidan, David. "The Islamic Fundamentalist View of Life as a Perennial Battle." *Middle East Review of International Affairs* 5 (2001). http://meria.idc.ac.il/journal/2001/issue4/jv5n4a2.htm.

Note: The works listed above were used in the preparation of this book. Joseph Croitoru's *Der Märtyrer als Waffe: Die historischen Wurzeln des Selbstmordattentats* (Munich: Hanser, 2003) appeared after the manuscript was completed. It also contains an extensive bibliography on the question of suicide and terrorism.

Index